teach®
yourself

the middle east
since 1945
stewart ross

For over 60 years, more than
50 million people have learnt over
750 subjects the **teach yourself**
way, with impressive results.

be where you want to be
with **teach yourself**

Acknowledgements

The author would like to express his sincere thanks to Dr Ghazwan S. Boutros for his most useful help and advice during the writing of the second edition of this book.

For UK order enquiries: please contact Bookpoint Ltd, 130 Milton Park, Abingdon, Oxon, OX14 4SB. Telephone: +44 (0) 1235 827720. Fax: +44 (0) 1235 400454. Lines are open 09.00–17.00, Monday to Saturday, with a 24-hour message answering service. Details about our titles and how to order are available at www.teachyourself.co.uk

For USA order enquiries: please contact McGraw-Hill Customer Services, PO Box 545, Blacklick, OH 43004-0545, USA. Telephone: 1-800-722-4726. Fax: 1-614-755-5645.

For Canada order enquiries: please contact McGraw-Hill Ryerson Ltd, 300 Water St, Whitby, Ontario L1N 9B6, Canada. Telephone: 905 430 5000. Fax: 905 430 5020.

Long renowned as the authoritative source for self-guided learning – with more than 50 million copies sold worldwide – the **teach yourself** series includes over 500 titles in the fields of languages, crafts, hobbies, business, computing and education.

British Library Cataloguing in Publication Data: a catalogue record for this title is available from the British Library.

Library of Congress Catalog Card Number: on file.

First published in UK 2004 by Hodder Education, 338 Euston Road, London, NW1 3BH.

First published in US 2004 by The McGraw-Hill Companies, Inc.

This edition published 2006.

The **teach yourself** name is a registered trade mark of Hodder Headline.

Typeset by Transet Limited, Coventry, England.
Printed in Great Britain for Hodder Education, a division of Hodder Headline, 338 Euston Road, London, NW1 3BH, by Cox & Wyman Ltd, Reading, Berkshire.

The publisher has used its best endeavours to ensure that the URLs for external websites referred to in this book are correct and active at the time of going to press. However, the publisher and the author have no responsibility for the websites and can make no guarantee that a site will remain live or that the content will remain relevant, decent or appropriate.

Hodder Headline's policy is to use papers that are natural, renewable and recyclable products and made from wood grown in sustainable forests. The logging and manufacturing processes are expected to conform to the environmental regulations of the country of origin.

Impression number   10 9 8 7 6 5 4 3
Year   2010 2009 2008 2007

contents

01

the crossroads of the world

This chapter will cover:
- definitions of the Middle East
- the region's physical geography
- its diverse racial and social mix
- the religions of the Middle East.

What is the Middle East?

Mick Jackson's award-winning film for television *Threads* (BBC, 1984), exploring the effects of nuclear war on Western civilization, was criticized in some circles as overly fanciful. One of the film's principal assumptions, however, was never challenged: the Third World War would be sparked by events in the Middle East. Jackson's assertion is as alarmingly valid today as two decades ago.

Why?

The roots of conflict and instability in the Middle East twist deep into the soil of history, far beyond the compass of this book, to Biblical times. One may even speculate whether they lie deeper still, in the prehistoric millennia when the great continents were formed. For the Middle East is the only region on earth where three continents meet. Here, in a gigantic crossroads between Europe, Asia and Africa, peoples from East, West, North and South have come together over the centuries to trade, exchange views, worship – and make war.

Before going further, we need to be clear about our terms. Defining the 'Middle East' is fraught with difficulty because, at the simplest level, 'east' and 'west' are relative to one's vantage point: speaking literally, India is Egypt's 'middle east', and so on. The US State department and some United Nations bodies, sticking to an older, more logical and geographically precise stance than most, prefer 'Near East' for the region lying between the Mediterranean Sea and the Indian Ocean. But this does not avoid another problem.

As many scholars have pointed out, to English speakers 'the East' remains a value-laden expression. Australians, inhabitants of the East but European-American in culture, are traditionally made honorary Westerners. 'Middle East' is a European phrase whose current usage comes from the Second World War command structure of the British Army. It is far from ideal to persevere with a label which, to some minds, still carries imperialist overtones. There is, however, no widely accepted alternative.

Finally, commentators rarely agree on a precise geographical definition of the Middle East. This book takes in Lebanon, Palestine/Israel and Egypt along the eastern seaboard of the Mediterranean, Syria and Jordan further inland, Iraq and Iran bordering the Persian Gulf, and the Arabian peninsular states of Saudi Arabia, Yemen, Oman, Dubai, the United Arab Emirates

(UAE) and Kuwait. A broader approach might embrace Greece, all the Arab states of North Africa, the Sudan, Afghanistan, Cyprus and Turkey. Our narrower definition excludes – with one exception – all states that play in the Union European Football Association (UEFA) Champion's League football competition or who participate in the Eurovision Song Contest. The exception is Israel. But as we will see, Israel is accustomed to being the odd one out in Middle Eastern affairs.

The geography of the Middle East

Seaways

Seen from space, the Middle East is largely a patchwork of browns and yellows within blue borders. This simplified view reveals basic truths about the region's troubled history. The prevalent dun colour of the land reminds us that much of it is barren and inhospitable, making the few fertile areas – the splashes of green amid the swathes of beige – all the more valuable and sought after. A great deal of Middle Eastern turmoil since the ending of the Second World War has been about who controls this favoured terrain.

The blue areas are, of course, the sea. Here again simple geography teaches a vital lesson. The multiplicity and complexity of the region's seaways emphasize their importance to world trade. In 1945 it was perhaps even more important than today. The reason was the Suez Canal, the 163 km (101 mile) link between the Mediterranean and the Red Sea constructed with great difficulty almost 150 years ago by the remarkable French engineer Ferdinand de Lesseps. Although now too small for the largest ships, in 1945 it offered virtually all vessels a fuel- and time-saving short cut on the journey between Europe and Asia. It was in the interest of all nations with ambitions of world influence to see that such a vital waterway, described by the British Prime Minister Anthony Eden as 'Britain's windpipe', remained safe and open to all.

At the northern end of the Suez Canal lies the Mediterranean, the sea that joins the Middle East to Europe, the Atlantic and the Americas. This alone gives it key strategic importance. At the close of the Second World War this importance was paramount because the eastern Mediterranean, via the Dardanelles and the Black Sea, was the Soviet Union's only southerly link with the world's oceans.

Leaving the Suez Canal at its southern end, the great majority of ships sail down the Gulf of Suez, through the steamy Red Sea and into the Indian Ocean. From here they have access to any number of destinations in the eastern hemisphere. One or two, however, may take an altogether different course, turning north-east after leaving the Suez gulf and entering the narrower Gulf of Aqaba through the Strait of Tiran. At its northern end lie two towns, Aqaba and Eilat. In 1945 this was also the meeting point of three frontiers, making it a likely trouble spot.

Another such unstable area was encountered by ships that chose to bear to port (left) after passing the British base at Aden and followed the Arabian coastline until a seaway appeared in the north-west. This is the Arabian (or Persian, depending on one's politics or education) Gulf, a strip of sea dividing Arabia from Iran and giving the states along its shores access to the wider world. Today, as they have done for nigh on a century, tanker after tanker passes through its narrow neck at the Straits of Hormuz laden with oil for the world's automobiles, trucks, industries and homes.

For its seaways alone, in 1945 the Middle East was a region of supreme strategic importance.

Rivers and lakes

The Middle East is arid. Rainfall is generally slight and erratic; in the inland desert areas it rarely exceeds 80 mm (5 inches) a year. The entire Arabian peninsular contains only one river that flows all the year round. Throughout the region life-sustaining water is found mostly underground, emerging on the surface only in oases or through bore holes. The exceptions – and they are mighty exceptions – are three river systems. These are the Nile in North Africa, the River Jordan (including the Sea of Galilee) running parallel to the eastern shore of the Mediterranean, and the Tigris-Euphrates. This last rises in Turkey and flows through Syria and Iraq to the head of the Persian Gulf.

Many millennia ago these broad rivers were the umbilical cords of our human civilization. Beside their waters first appeared the most significant of all human achievements: farming, cities, law, the wheel and writing – the rest, one might say, has been mere footnotes. Be that as it may, the cords were cut long ago and the footnotes are now our major concern.

figure 1 the Near East

The magnificent heritage of the river civilizations of Mesopotamia and ancient Egypt serves as an important reminder to those raised in other cultures never to underestimate or take for granted the peoples of this fertile crescent. They may not be at the forefront of today's technology, but they are acutely aware that they were planting crops and erecting awe-inspiring palaces when the rest of the world was eking out a living by scavenging and hunting. Furthermore, as we shall see (pages 10–14), these people gave the world the three great religious faiths whose tenets underpin much of the morality of the modern world. It is a heritage of which the region is justly proud, and it does not take kindly to outsiders telling them – or even directing them – how to manage their own affairs.

Politically speaking, a river is either a uniting force or a boundary. In the case of the Nile and the Tigris-Euphrates it is the former, the very lifeblood and *raison d'être* of both Egypt and Iraq. Now, as in 1945, the Jordan is somewhat different. It had not always been so. Like the Nile, in Biblical times the Jordan had been a unifying artery through a dry land. Dreamers hope that one day it will serve the same purpose again.

The Jordan is also geographically unlike the region's other two great waterways in that it does not reach the open sea. Indeed, it is unique as furthest below sea level (400 m/1,300 feet at its southern end) of any river in the world. It rises on the slopes of Mount Hermon on the borders of Syria and Lebanon, flows into the Sea of Galilee, where it pauses for a while before meandering south through a huge rift valley to perish, along with any fish that venture that far, in the salty graveyard of the Dead Sea. The Hebrew author who located Sodom and Gomorrah, the biblical cities of infertile sin, on the shores of this lifeless expanse was not without a grim sense of humour.

Towns and cities

In 1945, the people of the Middle East lived where they had always done – where there was water. This meant essentially three types of settlement. First there were the coastal towns and cities that made money from trade (Port Said and Alexandria in Egypt, for example), fishing (Gaza in Palestine) and, in a few cases, pilgrimage (Jedda in Saudi Arabia). Many were small, somewhat run down and hampered by poor transport links inland. An interesting exception was the historic Palestinian port of Jaffa, at one time or another governed by ancient Egyptians, the Israelites, the Assyrians, Alexander the Great, the

Turks and Richard the Lionheart. In the early twentieth century its history took another twist when Jewish immigrants founded a new suburb which they called the 'Hill of Spring', or Tel Aviv. Swelled by successive waves of Jewish immigrants, by 1945 Tel Aviv-Jaffa was Palestine's largest and most important city.

The second group of settlements was the cities of the rivers. The greatest were Cairo and Baghdad, thriving and exciting metropolises by any standards, with all the advantages and disadvantages of city life. Perhaps we should also add Damascus to this list since it draws its water from the River Barada before the stream disappears again into the desert. The Syrian capital is probably the world's oldest continuously inhabited settlement.

The river cities of Iran included several in the west athwart waters that flowed into the Persian Gulf, and three ancient capitals. These were Shiraz, famous for its wine, gardens and poets, Isfahan, the city of azure mosques, and Tehran, where the 'Big Three' of Stalin, Roosevelt and Churchill gathered in the latter stages of the Second World War to hammer out a post-war division of the spoils.

The third group of settlements was the oases. Into this category came some of the great cities of the early twenty-first century, particularly the Saudi capital of Riyadh and the Jordanian capital of Aman (the 'royal David's city' of the Christmas carol). In 1945 both were pale shadows of what they were to become. Riyadh, in particular, was little more than a straggle of mudbrick houses, mosques and tatty, ramshackle palaces set about a confluence of stony wadis (dry river beds that run only occasionally). Far more important were the Muslim holy cities of Mecca and Medina, both a fair distance from the Red Sea and some height above sea level.

Peoples and societies

Arab nationalism

The Middle East is widely associated with the word 'Arab'. This, unfortunately, adds little to our understanding of the region. Before the emergence of Islam almost 1,400 years ago, an Arab was someone, almost certainly a nomad, who lived on the Arabian peninsular. Around them dwelt such varied Semitic peoples as Syrians, Persians, Egyptians, Jews, Babylonians and so forth, all speaking their own languages. With Islam the situation became more complex because Arabic, the language of the Arabian peninsular and now the Koran, became the formal language of much of the Middle East. This has left us with only one reasonably coherent definition of an Arab: someone who speaks the Arabic language.

In the second half of the nineteenth century, nationalism burned bright across Europe. As well as forging the German and Italian nations, it rattled the British in Ireland and helped create a host of small but fiercely patriotic states in the Balkans. The reverberations were felt in the Middle East, too, where from the 1860s onwards, Arab intellectuals began to talk of an Arab nation. The romantic concept rested on three legs – two historical, one linguistic. The first was the shared past of the people who had spread Islam; the second the common heritage of an empire (the Caliphate) that at its height had been larger than that of the Romans; and the third a common language. The Arab 'awakening' found its first voices in literary and scientific societies. One of its earliest focal points was the Syrian Protestant College of Beirut, later to become the American University of that city. As we shall see in the next chapter, during the First World War, Arab nationalism moved into the political sphere when Arabs helped the Allies dismantle the empire of the Ottoman Turks which had previously encompassed all Arab lands.

By the 1920s Arab nationalism was going nowhere. It was increasingly in competition with the individual nationalisms of the Egyptians, Iraqis, Syrians, Jordanians, Lebanese, Saudis and others. Politicians and poets of the time – like the Iraqi dictator Saddam Hussein in more recent years – liked to talk of Pan-Arabism, a coming together of all Arabic-speaking peoples, but no individual or group emerged as a focal point around which they might coalesce. The concept was still there in 1945, but it was no nearer realization than it had been at the beginning of the century.

Diversity

Anyone who has travelled across the Middle East will be instantly aware why Arab nationalism has made so little headway. The majority of people might understand the same holy Koranic language, but the local variations used in everyday life by Arabic speakers are as numerous today as they were 50 years ago. Even something simple like the numbers one to ten sound very different in the mouths of, say, Lebanese, Saudis and

Egyptians. It is not just a matter of accent, either. Common words and phrases also vary widely. Not only that, but each speaker normally insists that their dialect is closest to the Koranic original. Consequently, to adapt a phrase often used about the Americans and the British, the Arabs are a people divided by a common language.

Shared ethnic ancestry is not an essential component of nationalism, but it might help. Here again Arab nationalism ran into problems. Although the majority of the peoples of the Middle East were originally Semitic, over the millennia any vestige of racial exclusivity – an unpleasant concept at the best of times – had totally disappeared. This is backed up by a glance at the figurative art of the ancient Egyptians: their land was evidently populated by a broad racial mix thousands of years ago.

The situation at the close of the Second World War was further complicated by the existence of numerous Middle Eastern groups who did not regard themselves as Arab. The largest in number were the Farsi-speaking Iranians, heirs to a very different culture from much of the rest of the region. Even within Iran itself there was a host of separate tribes, languages and dialects. Iraq, with its sizeable population of Kurds, was similarly diverse. In 1914, Baghdad had the largest concentration of Jews in the entire Middle East. Other cultural and linguistic minorities scattered across the region included Armenians, Turks, Nubians and Greeks. Claiming the right to establish a separate state of its own, by far the most troublesome minority were the Jews of Palestine.

Diversity was as much social as racial and linguistic. In many parts of the region structures of society that had lasted for centuries were still largely intact. With some exceptions, at the basic level it took the form of the traditional family headed by the father-husband. This patriarchal pattern was repeated in the tribe, clan, or extended family, giving society a semi-feudal structure of small, highly independent units. One feature of this fragmented and very personal arrangement was that local loyalty was usually stronger than loyalty to the state or its government. Indeed, as we shall see in Chapter 2, in several areas the concept of the nation state was only just beginning to take hold. Even in the twenty-first century it was still competing with more traditional allegiances. For example, the Iraqi regime of Saddam Hussein relied heavily on members of his clan, the Bejat, and their tribal allies around the town of Tikrit.

The division between town and countryside – house dwellers and tent dwellers – had long been another pronounced feature of the region. During the twentieth century it tended to accentuate as the gap between lifestyles changed. Western influences – cars, dress, social customs, liberal education and a different attitude towards women – were increasingly noticeable in the big cities, the ports of the Mediterranean seaboard and areas where a few families were growing rich on the income provided by oil. In such places public pronouncements on the traditional lifestyle were often divided, swinging between singing its praises when challenged by the West, to mocking it as primitive and backward in the company of urban compatriots. Since at least the end of the First World War, in some Arab-speaking lands the term 'Bedu' – a traditional nomadic tribesman – was being used as a term of abuse.

Nowhere was the divide in the Arab world clearer than between Egypt and the rest of the Arabic-speaking areas. Subject to prolonged Western influence for well over a century, and with a population larger than those of Arabia, Syria, Lebanon, Palestine and Transjordan (see page 30) combined, flourishing industry, an established bureaucracy and a sophisticated banking system, Egypt was an anathema among its traditional-minded neighbours. It would have taken a minor miracle to persuade it to combine with them into anything resembling an Arab nation state.

Religion

No picture of the Middle East in 1945, or at any time, is complete without reference to religion. The region is, after all, the birthplace of Judaism, Christianity and Islam (in chronological order of inception). The spiritual heart of all three remains in the lands where they originated. It is, of course, too simplistic to say that the turmoil that has wracked the area in recent years is purely or even largely religious in origin – no more were the medieval Crusades, those ultimately unsuccessful attempts by Western Christians to conquer and hold the Muslim-controlled holy places of the Bible. Nevertheless, as well as inspiring and supporting believers, religion invariably spiced the rhetoric of Middle Eastern conflict. We cannot go any further, therefore, until the complex vocabulary and background of the three faiths involved are understood.

Judaism

Judaism, the religion of the Jews, was the only one of the three major Middle Eastern religions linked to a specific people. (Islam was tied to a language, Arabic, but not to a race.) At its heart lay the belief that the one God – creator of the universe and the embodiment of divine love and divine justice – had chosen the Jews to be the vehicle of His way: 'For you are a people consecrated to the Lord your God: of all the peoples on earth the Lord your God chose you to be His treasured people' (*Book of Deuteronomy*). The Jews' very personal God had made a pact (covenant) with them: in return for being His chosen people they were to obey His pattern and structure of life set out in His teaching (the Torah). As long as they did this, one day all other people would recognize God's ways and follow them too. Then the whole earth would bear witness to the love, peace and justice of God.

Another part of God's covenant involved giving His people a specific land. This was Israel. With its sacred capital of Jerusalem, at its largest (known as 'Greater Israel' in the twentieth century) it had once stretched beyond the east bank of the River Jordan. However, for a series of complex reasons, by late Roman times very few Jews actually lived in the promised land. They had been dispersed (the Diaspora) and lived in small, mostly urban communities around Europe and, to a lesser extent, the Middle East. A few went back to Israel – the Holy Land – on pilgrimage, and a tiny number still lived there. For the great majority, however, the idea of returning to Israel was not a practical concept but a religious one. Going back to the promised land was equated with the establishment of perfect peace and harmony on earth.

At least that is how it was seen until the nineteenth century.

Christian Europe had rarely treated the Jews well or even fairly. As a distinctive minority, they were an obvious target for racial hatred, a tendency reinforced by the Roman Catholic Church when it condemned them as the people who had killed Jesus Christ. Even more unjustly, in the nineteenth century an unholy alliance of the political right, the Roman Catholics, and the Orthodox Church blamed them for conspiring to bring about the excesses of the French Revolution.

At different times during the century, Russia, France, Syria, Hungary and several other states witnessed outbreaks of cruel anti-Semitism. The nineteenth century was also the age of nationalism. Understandably, therefore, a number of Jews began to link the ancient concept of a return to the promised land (Israel) with modern nationalism. In other words, if the Germans, Italians, Serbs, and so forth could have their own state, why not the Jews? The name adopted by the new movement was 'Zionism'. It derived from 'Zion', a poetic name for Israel.

Zionism was never a single, clear-cut movement. There were some for whom it represented a religious ideal, while others saw it as a political expedient to provide the Jews with a safe haven. Whatever the motives, since the obvious place for the establishment of a Jewish homeland was where it had been in Biblical times, by 1945 the turmoil that Zionism was causing in Palestine was beginning to impact upon the entire region (see Chapter 3).

Christianity

The Jewish faith spoke of a redeemer who would reconcile humankind to God. Christians believed that in Jesus Christ they had found this redeemer. Born in Bethlehem to humble parents, Jesus had been crucified outside Jerusalem by the Romans (with the connivance of the Jewish authorities), and had then supposedly come back to life for a while. According to accounts written shortly afterwards – the New Testament of the Bible – he had also proclaimed himself to be the long-expected redeemer: none other than the Son of God. He was reported to have performed miracles that bore out his supernatural powers.

Eventually adopted by the Roman Empire, Christianity spread far more widely than Judaism had ever done. Although it accepted aspects of its Jewish ancestry, such as God's Ten Commandments (laws) for living a righteous life, it was a much less specific, more metaphysical faith than Judaism. According to the New Testament, unlike Judaism and, later, Islam, Jesus did not set down a practical code for holy living, nor did he exclude any people or race from becoming Christian. His two basic tenets were to love God and love your neighbour as yourself. God Himself was perceived less as a human-type being and more of an embodiment of love.

A faith based upon such abstract foundations was open to widely differing interpretations. These manifested themselves in dramatic schisms within the 'Church', as the body of Christians was known. Very simply, those following the leadership of the

Pope in Rome separated from the Orthodox Church centred on Constantinople (Istanbul). Then the Orthodox Church split between Greek and Russian varieties, and the Roman Church into Catholics and Protestants. There were also all kinds of lesser divisions, such as the Coptic Christians of Abyssinia (Ethiopia) and the Maronites of Syria, not to mention the myriad of divisions within Protestantism.

One thing all these various Christian Churches had in common was a shared history with the Jews and a veneration for the places in Palestine where Jesus had lived, taught and died. In spite of this, Christians amounted to less than five per cent of the population of the Middle East in 1945.

Islam

Islam, which means literally 'surrender' (to God or 'Allah'), was the historical successor to Judaism and Christianity. Inheriting aspects of both, it accepted the Biblical figures of Noah, Moses and Jesus as true prophets. It reserved the position of last and greatest prophet for Mohammed, a seventh-century inhabitant of the Arabian town of Medina who, Muslims believe, received God's word. As it was delivered to him via the Angel Gabriel, Mohammed had it written down in the Koran. Hence the basic Muslim profession of faith: 'There is no god but God; Mohammed is the prophet of God.'

The Koran, backed up by early traditions set out in the Hadith, forms the basis of the Muslim faith. Indeed, compared with Christianity, it was rather more than a faith: it was also a set of specified religious practices and, more widely, a whole way of life. These closely linked Islam to politics and gave rise to the concept of the Islamic state. Before the twentieth century, the idea of an Islamic country having a non-sectarian government was an anathema. This way of thinking was revived in the later twentieth century when states such as Iran attempted to return to a unified Islamic government, law and culture.

Islam's strengths were many and real. Its blunt simplicity gave believers certainty and self-confidence: they had accepted the right way and so were destined for a heaven redolent with physical as well as spiritual delights. The unwavering rituals of prayer five times a day, the annual fast and the once-in-a-lifetime pilgrimage to Mecca settled the lives of believers within a secure and reassuring framework. The faith's emphasis on community – the essential equality of all believers and the need for the wealthy and fortunate to support those less well positioned than themselves – helped give the faith a mass following.

From the beginning, Islam displayed undertones of violence that distressed adherents of more pacific beliefs and philosophies. Much of the faith's early expansion was carried out by a Holy War ('jihad') that established a Muslim empire, or Caliphate, stretching from India to Spain. The conquered were presented with the unenviable choice between conversion to Islam or taxation (Jews and Christians), or death (pagans). From time to time since then, more extreme Muslim groups have resurrected the concept of jihad to justify armed resistance to perceived oppression.

The contest for the position of caliph – head of the Muslim political-religious state – was sometimes accompanied by astonishing cruelty. The first caliph of the Abbasid dynasty, for instance, broadcast his ruthlessness by taking the name as-Saffah or 'Blood-shedder'. Violence also manifested itself in brutal punishments handed down in some fundamentalist societies. Nevertheless, it may be argued that these, like the veiling of women, were based on tribal custom and not Islam.

Despite the precise nature of many of its teachings, Islam, like other faiths, has had its fair share of schism and split. The largest and most enduring began as a dispute over the leadership of the movement and went on to acquire distinctly separate theological positions. The majority, comprising mostly Arab Muslims, were the Sunni. The minority, based originally in Iran (Persia), were the Shia. Other sects include the Isma'ili, the Ahmadiyah and, perhaps, the Druze, although there is some dispute whether the latter are really Muslims at all.

Unfortunately for the peace of the Middle East, the Muslims, just like the Jews and Christians, regard Jerusalem as a holy city. It was the direction in which Muslims originally faced when praying and, according to tradition, was the place from which Mohammed once physically ascended into heaven (see page 41). In short, a place well worth fighting for.

Summary

This is the colourful stage on which our tragic drama is set. In some ways, the Middle East in 1945 was little different from what it had been 500 years previously. It was still a largely barren region where water sources and fertile land were jealously guarded. Despite the widespread and uniting prevalence of the Arabic language and the Muslim faith, there remained startling differences between city and desert, interior and coast, Africa and Asia, rich and poor. In other words, it was as mysterious, proud, fragmented, diverse and unquestionably important as ever.

Nevertheless, the previous 50 years had seen crucial changes. First, the developed world's thirst for oil was making the region, where the largest deposits of the liquid gold were to be found, among the most strategically vital on earth. Second, at the end of the First World War the Middle East's dominant power, the Turkish Ottoman Empire, had collapsed. In its place had sprung up an unstable patchwork of uneasily independent states and territories governed by imperial European powers. Finally, the traditional settlement pattern was threatened by a determined attempt to establish in the region the entirely new state of Israel.

The story of these developments, completing the picture of the Middle East in 1945, is the subject of the next chapter.

02

states and mandates: Middle Eastern politics to the end of the Second World War

This chapter will cover:
- the collapse of the Ottoman Empire
- Allied plans for the Middle East made during the First World War
- the emergence of new independent states by 1945
- the continuation of British and French power in the region.

Ottoman collapse

At the beginning of the twentieth century, the governments of the Great Powers of Europe showed no special interest in the Middle East, and that of the United States even less. As long as shipping passed through its waters uninterrupted, pilgrims made their way unmolested to its holy places, and a growing volume of oil flowed from its wells in the Gulf, they were by and large content. The prevailing masters – the relatively easy-going Ottoman and Persian Empires – were permitted to run their own shows without undue interference. For what was on offer, the cost and political danger of large-scale intervention was simply not worth it.

The Turkish Ottoman Empire, with its ancient capital of Constantinople (Istanbul), had dominated the Middle East for 400 years. For about half this period – at least since the emergence of Russia as a major power – Ottoman power had commonly been regarded as 'in decline'. However, unlike the British Empire, which suffered a political heart attack and passed away almost overnight, its Turkish counterpart lingered on with surprising resilience. It was still breathing in 1900, although it had lost almost all its possessions in Europe. Elsewhere, Western imperial powers had helped themselves to bits they wanted: the Russians in the Caucasus, the French in Algeria and Tunisia, and the British in Cyprus, Egypt and some grubby coaling stations and sandy ports around the fringe of the Arabian peninsular. Finally, after a fresh wave of depredations shortly before the First World War, the Ottomans were left with the rump of an empire that embraced, roughly speaking, the modern states of Turkey, Iraq, Saudi Arabia, Syria, Lebanon, Jordan, and Israel-Palestine.

The eventual demise of the Ottoman Empire was brought about by its decision to join the First World War on the side of the Central Powers (Germany, Austria-Hungary and Bulgaria). Turkish armies, fighting throughout the Middle East, tied down many Allied troops and inflicted notable reverses upon them in Mesopotamia (modern Iraq), on the Gallipoli peninsular, and in the Caucasus. In the end, though, single successes did not add up to an overall victory, and on 30 October 1918 the demoralized and near-bankrupt Ottomans signed an armistice.

figure 2 the Middle East in the First World War

Three agreements

For some while the Allies had been discussing what to do with Ottoman possessions when the First World War ended. Before Russia succumbed to a Communist revolution, the British and French had even suggested that it might like to take Istanbul and control of the Dardanelles as part of the spoils of a victorious war. It is anyone's guess whether they meant to honour such generous terms. Of several other wartime agreements concerning Ottoman possessions, at least three were equally contentious.

The MacMahon-Hussein correspondence

The first may be found amid the lengthy correspondence between Sir Henry MacMahon, the British Consul-General in Egypt, and Hussein, the Grand Sharif or Emir (in reality a sort of hereditary governor) of Mecca. MacMahon headed one of the 20 or so British government departments with a finger in the Middle Eastern pie. Hussein was a clever if enigmatic figure. As head of the respected Hashemites, a tribe (blood-related 'clan' might be more accurate) descended from the Prophet Mohammed, and guardian of the Muslim holy cities of Mecca and Medina, he had as good a claim as anyone to speak for the Islamic Arab 'nation'. Since the emir's allegiance to the Ottomans was shaky, MacMahon took it upon himself to persuade him, by correspondence, to come over to the Allied side.

From a British point of view, the correspondence course was a great success. The Arabs, led by Hussein's son Faisal and assisted and perhaps even inspired by the able and eccentric self-publicist T. E. Lawrence 'of Arabia', rose up in the Hejaz (western Arabia) and drove north to link up with British forces in Palestine. This was all very gallant and dramatic, but what precisely had these dashing, robe-clad Arab irregulars been fighting for?

The Arabs believed MacMahon had offered independence to all Arab lands excepting certain 'portions of Syria lying to the west of the districts of Damascus' (Sir Henry MacMahon, 24 October 1914). Apart from the fact that the British government – whatever their man in Cairo said – had little intention of surrendering control over so vast a region to unknown forces, the wording of the agreement itself is unclear. Part of the problem lies in the translation between English, a fairly specific language, and the more poetic Arabic. Unjustly and probably in a fit of frustrated pique, one European specialist wrote a few years later that each word of Arabic had five meanings: the original one, the opposite, a literary meaning unconnected to the first two, something to do with a camel, and something obscene. The nature of the 'districts of Damascus' and the precise 'portions' of territory have been hotly disputed. Did the latter, for instance, include Palestine? And if they did, what were the boundaries of that inexact area?

The Sykes-Picot Agreement

From a practical point of view, the MacMahon-Hussein agreement was rendered largely irrelevant by a secret understanding negotiated by the vigorous British diplomat Sir Mark Sykes and his French counterpart François Georges-Picot. In simple terms, to keep the Russians out of the region, the Sykes-Picot Agreement divided the Middle East into five parts. Britain and France were each to have an area they controlled directly and another that lay within their 'sphere of influence'. The huge British sphere contained a rather vague 'Independent Arab State'. The fifth area was the 'international sphere' of Palestine.

The Balfour Declaration

The third Middle Eastern agreement was more of a one-sided announcement. On 2 November 1917, the intellectual British Foreign Secretary, Arthur James Balfour, declared that, 'His Majesty's Government viewed with favour the establishment in Palestine of a national home for the Jewish people'. Although many reasons have been suggested for Britain's willingness at this point to back the idea of a Jewish homeland in the Middle East, none of them is entirely convincing. In the end, though, the motive was irrelevant. What did matter was that the world's foremost imperial power had given its blessing to the idea of a homeland in the Middle East for a specific racial group. Moreover, they had done so without consulting either those already living there or someone – perhaps the Emir Hussein? – who might speak on their behalf.

These three examples of imperial diplomacy proved crucial to the way the Middle East would develop after the dissolution of the Turkish Empire. The next step, therefore, is to examine how this wartime chicanery impacted upon the region in the post-Ottoman era.

The Arabian peninsular

Saudi Arabia

The British might have backed the Grand Sharif Hussein of Mecca as the principal power in the region of Arabia, but at least one of his neighbours believed the choice to be wrong. This was the virile and intelligent Abdulaziz Al Saud, a shortened version of a name which, in full, reads like an exercise in Old Testament genealogy. In the early twentieth century, Abdulaziz had captured the oasis town of Riyadh and established it as the capital of his desert state.

This vigorous princedom combined Bedouin toughness with the puritan fanaticism of a fundamentalist Islamic sect known as the Wahabites. Nominally loyal to the Ottomans before the First World War, during the conflict Abdulaziz received British subsidies. Afterwards the man the West knew as simply Al Saud ('The Saud') allowed his aggressive followers to expand his domain in several directions, most notably into Hussein's territory of the Hejaz. For a time Abdulaziz ruled as King of the Hejaz and Sultan of the Najd (Arabia's barren interior) before establishing himself as the absolute and independent King of Saudi Arabia (1932).

The new state's status rose sharply during the Second World War, when its vast oil reserves began to be exploited energetically by Aramco (the Arabian American Oil Company). Foreign workers appeared, as did more welcome foreign money. To a people whose way of life had in many respects altered little since the days of the Prophet himself, it was often confusing, sometimes alarming.

Yemen

In Roman times, because of its comparatively fertile climate and superb position as a commercial entrepôt, Yemen was known as 'Arabia Felix' – ('Fortunate Arabia'). Sadly, like a woman exploited for her beauty, Yemen's natural bounty brought it an unfortunate history. In the nineteenth century it was divided between the Ottoman-held north and the British-held south. With the collapse of Ottoman power, North Yemen became independent while the South remained British.

The North's government passed into the hands of a somewhat ferocious imam (a type of holy politician that is a common feature of Islam) by the name of Yahya Ibn Mohammed. After squabbling with his British and Saudi neighbours, by the end of the Second World War Imam Yahya's very personal rule was attracting substantial internal dissatisfaction.

A string of protectorates

Oman, Yemen's equally well-positioned neighbour along the south-eastern coast of Arabia, had once been the most powerful state on the peninsular. By 1945, such glory was a faded dream. The fractured state was the private possession of the reactionary Sultan Said Bin Taimur, whose authority rested on British protection.

Equally dependent upon Britain at this time was the cluster of sheikhdoms known today as the United Arab Emirates (UAE). Then styled the Trucial States, this loose tribal association had accepted British protection in the nineteenth century in return for agreeing to forego war, piracy and slavery. Like its neighbour Oman, its oil reserves had yet to be exploited. Once this began to happen, it transformed itself into the UAE, with Abu Dhabi as its capital (1971).

Qatar, Bahrain and Kuwait were the last three beads on the string of British protectorates decorating the north-east coast of the Arabian peninsular. Having long since signed agreements similar to those pertaining in Oman and the Trucial States, in 1945 all three were still under the protection of the British crown. Only Kuwait had begun widely to exploit its oilfields. Significantly, this had led Iraq, its powerful northern neighbour, to dig up old and somewhat fanciful claims to ownership of tiny Kuwait. While Britain retained a presence in the region, such claims remained purely rhetorical. At the end of the century, however, long after Britain's withdrawal, Iraq's Saddam Hussein would try again, this time backing rhetoric with steel (see Chapter 11).

Iran

Excepting Turkey, which lies outside the scope of this book, Iran is the Middle East's only major non-Arab state. Its official language, Farsi (or Persian), is Indo-European. The country's adherence to Shia Islam also contrasts with the largely Sunni Islam of most Arabs, and it is justly proud of the glorious and independent heritage of its Persian past, reaching back to Classical times and beyond. Not surprisingly, tension between

Arab and Iranian has always played a significant part in the history of the Middle East.

Like the Mediterranean Arab states, Persia (the name by which it was known at the time) received serious interest from the European imperial powers from the late eighteenth century onwards. The chief would-be predators were Russia, contemplating expansion from the north, and Britain, hopeful of securing the south for its oil and because of its strategic importance in relation to India.

The first generous foreign oil concessions were granted to British firms (the forerunners of British Petroleum – BP) in 1901. Six years later, Britain and Russia, paying scant heed to Persian wishes, settled their differences by each taking a sizeable chunk of the country as their sphere of influence. Before and during the First World War, Persia was beset by famine, inflation and extreme political instability exacerbated by foreign intervention. The chaos continued after the war until Reza Khan, an army officer of ambition and ability, seized control of first the army, then the government and, finally in 1925, the throne.

Styling himself Reza Shah Pahlavi, the new shah changed the name of the country to Iran (derived from Aryan, originally meaning 'noble') and set about trying to modernize it and free it from foreign influence. This left him hated by conservatives at home and mistrusted abroad. Pro-Nazi sympathies alienated him still further and, when an Anglo-Soviet force invaded during the Second World War to keep open the route from the Gulf to the Soviet border, he abdicated and fled the country.

The new shah, Reza's son Mohammed Reza, was eager for support against Soviet-backed separatist movements in the north, and sided with the Americans. However, religious conservatives, hostile to all foreigners, remained very influential. The ending of the Second World War found the 26-year-old Shah Mohammed Reza, like his father, balancing precariously between past and present, tradition and modernization, Islam and secularism. It was an unenviable position he shared with several other of the region's governors.

Egypt

Of all the lands of the Middle East, it is perhaps Egypt, with its awe-inspiring pyramids and sphinx, that is the most alluring. Yet for centuries, the wider world's knowledge of this increasingly peripheral feature of the Ottoman sphere was minimal. All this changed at the end of the eighteenth century when Napoleon I invaded the country in an attempt to disrupt British communications with India. The French emperor was accompanied by scholars, scientists and soldiers whose impact made Egypt probably the most Western-orientated state in the Middle East.

After Napoleon's defeat, Egypt's fortunes waxed and waned under a succession of rulers owing nominal allegiance to Constantinople. The opening of the Suez Canal (see page 3), together with bankruptcy and political instability, ensured that Western scrutiny of the country remained tight. Finally, in 1882, a British force occupied Cairo to guard their country's interests. Although announced as a temporary measure, the occupation lasted 40 years in theory, and in reality a lot longer.

Until the outbreak of the First World War the government of Egypt took the form of a triple bluff. As the country was still within the Ottoman Empire, ultimate authority theoretically rested with the Sultan in Constantinople. For years, however, Egypt had paid little heed to its Turkish overlords. The country was run in the name of its 'khedive' (vice-sultan), his ministers and the advisory Assembly of Delegates. In practice, real power rested with neither the Ottomans nor the Egyptians but with a succession of British consuls. With a poetic touch of oriental romanticism, the system was known as the 'veiled protectorate'.

The veil was rudely ripped off when Britain went to war with the Ottomans in 1914. It gave Egypt a sultan of its own, then promptly took away his authority by declaring the country a full protectorate under a high commissioner. (One of these, Sir Henry MacMahon, we have already met – see page 19). Military rule kept the country relatively quiet during the war. But immediately it ended, Egyptian nationalists, furious that independence was being offered to the 'unbreeched barbarians' of the Hejaz but denied to themselves, demanded immediate British withdrawal. When the British hesitated, a wave of strikes brought the country to a standstill. Protesters flooded the streets and violence against the occupiers and those associated with them mounted rapidly. The situation was not helped by an imperial official declaring that an Englishman could extinguish an Egyptian flare-up merely by spitting on it.

The British had little option but to accept Egypt's independence, although they reserved various powers to themselves pending a full treaty. They demanded control of 'imperial communications'

– i.e. the Suez Canal – a guiding hand in foreign policy, security for foreign interests and minorities, and sole control over the Sudan, a land they and the Egyptians had conquered at the end of the previous century. Such a formidable list illustrates clearly that the newly independent Egypt remained very much within the British sphere of influence.

The country's constitution – a form of constitutional monarchy based, surprisingly, on that of Belgium – proved as insubstantial as its independence. The ball of power bounced elusively between three walls: the king (Fuad I, followed in 1936 by his son Farouk), the nationalist Wafd Party, and the British. Amid the chaos, two key developments emerged. One was a militant Islamic, anti-Western movement, the Muslim Brotherhood (1928). The second was a spirit of fellowship with other Arabs, particularly those also perceived to be suffering at the hands of imperialist Europeans. Nowhere was such suffering deemed to be more painful than in the troubled land of Palestine.

In 1936, Britain finally got the treaty it demanded of the Egyptian government, maintaining a strong British presence in the country. This swelled considerably during the Second World War, when the Egyptians gave reluctant support to the Allies in their struggle against fascism. The ending of the war found Egypt in a radical mood. Anti-British feelings were on the increase, fanned by nationalists demanding that the 1936 treaty be revised and all British forces withdrawn. The militant Muslim Brotherhood was now a mass movement.

During the war, Egypt had played a key role in forming the Arab League with Iraq, Lebanon, Saudi Arabia, Syria, Transjordan and North Yemen. Its aim was to promote Arab unity and co-operation, and present a united front on common political issues. Foremost among these were events in Palestine.

Iraq

One of the principal reasons for the instability of the Middle East in recent times has been the painful process of defining and creating nation states in a region to which the concept was largely alien. Iraq is a classic example. Like Palestine, Saudi Arabia and other Middle Eastern countries of modern origin, at the beginning of the twentieth century a state named Iraq did not exist. Roughly speaking, the region that now carries the name comprised three Mesopotamian provinces of the Ottoman

Empire based around the cities of Mosul in the north, Baghdad in the east-centre and Basra in the south. As Mesopotamia, the region boasted a rich and glorious history and Baghdad could justifiably claim to have once been one of the great cities of the world. Now, however, having been fought over by Ottomans and Persians (and at one time governed from Shiraz), all that remained of former splendours were shattered stones and proud stories.

It was the British who brought Mesopotamia out of the shadows. Having already established diplomatic and commercial links, during the First World War they invaded it from the head of the Gulf. After initial setbacks, imperial forces took Baghdad and by the time of the armistice were in occupation of all three Mesopotamian provinces. Back in Britain, civil servants and politicians scratched their heads and wondered what to do with their new acquisition.

Their hand was forced by events. As we saw earlier (page 19), the Arabs felt betrayed by the Allied failure to honour agreements made with Hussein, the Hashemite Grand Sharif of Mecca, to grant them independence after the defeat of the Ottomans. One of Hussein's sons, Faisal, a close friend of T.E. Lawrence, had made a name for himself as leader of the wartime Arab revolt. Immediately after the war, he had been chosen as king of an independent Syria that was to include the region of Palestine (see page 28). The Mesopotamian Arabs, not to be outdone and determined to create an independent state of their own, chose Faisal's brother Abdullah as their king. Within two years of the end of the war, the greater part of Mesopotamia was in armed revolt against the British, who were perceived as denying them nationhood.

The French inadvertently offered a solution to the problem by driving Faisal from Syria. The British then invited him to London and, in a stroke of extraordinary imperial hauteur, offered him the throne of Mesopotamia. The condition was that he shared control with Britain, which had no intention of letting go of an area that looked as if it might contain significant oilfields. Faisal agreed to a binding treaty with Britain, his bemused people accepted him in a plebiscite and, on 23 August 1921, he was crowned king of the newly created country of Iraq. Meanwhile, the British had found alternative employment for his brother Abdullah (see page 30).

The Anglo-Iraqi attempt to produce a workable constitution for Iraq in the 1920s makes an interesting comparison with the

American-Iraqi effort of the present century. Unlike the US-inspired republicanism of 2005, the former opted for a democratic scheme loosely based on the British constitutional monarchy. Not surprisingly, since the concepts of nation and democracy are slow-growing plants, its history was somewhat chequered. By the time of its collapse in 1958, Iraqis had been subjected to the rule of no less than 50 cabinets.

A common wish for full independence from Britain united the bulk of Iraqi politicians. However, once this goal had been achieved in the 1930s, any vestige of stability melted away. The many ethnic, religious, social and political differences within the manufactured state were almost impossible to reconcile. The massacre of Christian Assyrians by Iraqi troops shortly after independence is a striking example of the sort of lawless behaviour that threatened to become endemic. Faisal, an alien and politically inexperienced king imposed by a colonial power, was unable to control the situation. King Ghazi, his equally inexperienced son, made matters worse by involving the military in politics. His early death in a sports car crash brought his infant son Faisal II to the throne, with his uncle Abdullah acting as regent.

By the outbreak of the Second World War, the army was the principal force in Iraqi politics. Following the fall of France, a group of commanding officers decided that the cause of Arab nationalism might be better served by an alliance with the Axis powers rather than with the beleaguered Britain. This provoked a swift and successful British invasion, the removal of the army from politics and a declaration of war on the side of the Allies. When the fighting ended in 1945, the fledgling state of Iraq found itself in a familiar position: under the sway of the British and unsure how best to tackle an uncertain future.

Syria, Lebanon and Transjordan

Syria

At the end of the nineteenth century, Syria was another famous Middle Eastern region whose illustrious past contrasted unhappily with an unsure present. Long since absorbed into the Ottoman Empire, it was a vast, fuzzy-frontiered area that included all of modern Syria, Lebanon, Jordan and Israel-Palestine. Like Egypt, for many years it had been subjected to the direct influence of Europeans (and, unusually, Americans, whose missionaries had established a Christian college in Beirut.) In this case, however, it was the French and not the British who had been the major players. They had built the country's railways and on one occasion had even sent in an expeditionary force to quell fighting between a Druze-Muslim alliance and the Maronites. In the cities, Western influence was clearly visible in the dress and lifestyle of the wealthier classes, not to mention in the splendid Franco-Arab cuisine.

The First World War split Syrians three ways. The majority, for whom Islam was of paramount importance, tended to support the old empire as a bastion of their faith. Minorities, especially the Jews and Christians, looked favourably on the Allies. The third group were the Arab nationalists. Inspired by words of Sharif Hussein and the actions of his son Faisal, they too looked to the Allies for salvation.

Modern Syria came into being after the war. The British remained in Palestine, the French in Lebanon, and as we have seen Faisal was declared king of a smaller but independent Syria. The French would have none of this, and the League of Nations – then little more than an Anglo-French club – agreed that Syria should become a French mandate on terms similar to those of the British presence in Palestine.

In many ways Syria prospered under the French. Indeed, it is unlikely that so diverse a country could have held together without the dominating hand of a colonial power. Nevertheless, it became increasingly clear that the French had little intention of handing over power to the Syrians, at least not in the immediate future. By the late 1930s, Syria had a constitution, an elected government and its first president, but in the face of a resolute French 'non' the entire apparatus of independence remained addled.

The deadlock was broken by the Second World War. The French Vichy regime, which had made a pact with the Nazis after the defeat of France in 1940, maintained its hold over Syria and allowed it to be used as a German air base. This drew an Allied invasion, spearheaded by the British who witnessed the unhappy spectacle of Frenchmen (Vichy supporters) fighting Frenchmen (the Free French led by General Charles de Gaulle). Prompted by Britain, the Free French agreed to Syria's independence and another president, Shukri al-Kuwatli, was elected in 1943.

It was not until 1946 that the French finally left Syria – again with British prompting – allowing the country onto the world stage as an independent founder member of the Arab League and the United Nations.

Lebanon

Lebanon was unusual among the states of the Middle East. First, separated from the hinterland by the spine of Mount Lebanon, this beautiful and balmy land tended to look west more than most other Arab states. Its links with the rest of the Mediterranean were reinforced by a commercial tradition that went back to the time of the pharaohs. For much of its recent history its core was the prosperous silk trade.

Lebanon's second unusual feature was the make-up of its population. Some 50 per cent of Lebanese were Christian: Maronites, Orthodox Roman Catholics and Protestants. The first two traditionally received French support, the third had strong links with the USA. The other half of the population comprised both Sunni and Shia Muslims, Druze (a secret, exclusive and sometimes British-backed monotheist sect generally recognized as closer to Islam than anything else – see page 14) and Jews.

Such diversity, spiced with centuries of mistrust that had burst into fighting from time to time, was not an ideal recipe for harmonious living. It was hardly surprising, therefore, when in the late twentieth century trouble flared to the south of Lebanon, it spread north over the border with hideous consequences (see Chapter 7). The situation was encapsulated in a traditional Arab joke: God laughed when He created the Sudan and wasn't thinking when He created Arabia; so what were You doing, asked the bemused Lebanese, when You created our beautiful land of cedar trees, blue seas and cool breezes? Ah, God smiled, just wait until you see who I've given you as neighbours.

Lebanese history between the World Wars followed a pattern similar to Syria's. Occupied by the Allies in 1918, it was made a French mandate. Arab nationalists resented the way Syria had been carved up and among certain sections of the Lebanese population pro-Syrian sentiments remained strong. Such feelings persisted after 1945 and are important to an understanding of events in more recent times.

Under a generally beneficent French supervision the tradition of a balanced government emerged. The post of president traditionally went to a Maronite, that of prime minister to a Sunni Muslim, with the speaker of the chamber of deputies being a Shia. As in neighbouring Syria, the French – pre-war, Vichy and Free – were reluctant to hand over full authority to the locals. They were eventually forced to do so by British pressure at the end of the Second World War. The new, fully independent Lebanese Republic emerged as a member of the Arab League and United Nations in 1946.

Transjordan

Sharif Hussein of Mecca, it will be remembered, had two prominent sons. One, Faisal, had led the Arab revolt and had been installed by the British as King of Iraq. The second, Abdullah, had used British money and arms to tie down the large Turkish garrison in Medina during the Arab revolt. When the war ended he had diverted his forces to more personal aims, attempting to get the better of Ibn Saud. After an ignominious defeat which had obliged the portly prince to flee across the desert in his nightshirt, he led what was left of his forces to attack the French in Syria.

The route from the Hejaz to Damascus took Abdullah, his 2,000 followers and their six machine guns across the British mandate of Palestine. This sprawling territory extended from the Mediterranean, across the River Jordan and expanses of barren desert, to an uncertain border with the territory of Ibn Saud. While Abdullah was resting in the village of Aman and casting about for local Bedouin support (never too difficult to obtain when there was prospect of booty), the Liberal British colonial secretary, Winston Churchill, was holding a conference in Cairo on the future of the Middle East.

The last thing Churchill wanted was Abdullah stirring up trouble with the French. To divert him, the British cut their Palestinian mandate into two. It was an extraordinary piece of state-making. The British retained the more fertile and more politically sensitive area to the west of the River Jordan, keeping for it the name Palestine. The rest – an impoverished and rocky desert with no towns, no rivers and scarcely any inhabitants (a total of about 200,000 was estimated, most of them Bedouin nomads) – they handed to Abdullah as the Emirate of Transjordan. The new emir seemed pleased enough with his windfall which, in area, amounted to almost three-quarters of British Palestine.

figure 3 the Central Middle East after the Second World War

A treaty gave Transjordan a nominal independence, leaving financial, military and foreign affairs in British hands. Funded and protected by his British benefactors, who also provided him with one of the best fighting forces in the region (the Arab Legion), Abdullah survived to win full independence for his country after the Second World War. In 1949, he changed its name to the one it still bears today: the Hashemite Kingdom of Jordan.

By then, however, the outlook of the entire region had changed dramatically. To find out how and why, we now need to focus on the remaining quarter of Britain's Middle Eastern mandate: Palestine.

03 the promised land

This chapter will cover:
- Palestine before the First World War
- British attempts to govern their Palestinian mandate between the Wars
- the effect of the Second World War and the Holocaust on the Palestinian situation
- increasing violence within Palestine leading to the declaration of the state of Israel in 1948.

Palestine

Palestine enjoyed its last few years of Ottoman rule. Recent reforms had made the region more prosperous and stable. Pilgrims, including the Emperor of Germany, came in ever increasing numbers to its holy places and major powers considered it sufficiently important to set up consulates in Jerusalem as well as in the regional capital, Damascus.

Palestine was also attracting Europeans as both temporary residents and permanent immigrants. Among the latter were small numbers of Jews fleeing poverty, prejudice and persecution in Eastern Europe. These usually poor and dispirited people were at first no more than a trickle. Over time, though, their number rose to a steady stream that carried with it long years of fear, mistrust, hatred and, eventually, the horror and suffering of war.

This chapter traces that story. It starts with the rise of Zionism and Arab-Jewish animosity to 1918, then covers the inter-war years when an increasingly divided Palestine was in British hands. The third part deals with the effect of the Second World War on the situation, leading to civil war and the foundation of the state of Israel.

Zion

'Our country'

As we saw in Chapter 1, there had always been Jews living in Palestine. Indeed, one estimate says that at the start of the nineteenth century, the majority of the population of Jerusalem were Jews. As might be expected, there were sporadic outbreaks of racial and religious friction, but by and large Jews and Arabs and their Turkish master rubbed along reasonably amicably.

Zionism changed the situation irrevocably. Following violent attacks on Jewish communities in Russia, in 1882 a group of Jewish exiles met in Constantinople. They named themselves the 'Lovers of Zion' and called for 'a home in our country. It was given to us by the mercy of God; it is ours as registered in the archives of history.' The 'our country' they spoke of was Palestine.

The Jewish state

The next important step in the Zionist movement came some ten years later. An Austrian Jew named Theodore Herzl, journalist and playwright, was asked by his newspaper to cover an anti-Semitic (anti-Jewish) scandal in France. His reporting convinced him that there was a 'Jewish problem' that could be solved only by the creation of a Jewish nation state. He set out his ideas in a highly influential little book, *The Jewish State* (1896). Interestingly, he did not specifically plump for Palestine as the place where this state might be established. A sparsely populated area of Argentina was one option – how different might the history of the last half-century have been had the suggestion caught on!

The year after Herzl's publication saw the first meeting, in Basle, Switzerland, of the World Zionist Organization. Here the mood was far more positively pro-Palestine and a mission was sent out to explore the ground. Its reply encapsulates with poetic precision what would become the tragedy of Palestine: 'The bride is beautiful but she is married to another man'. In other words, the region was well-suited to settlement but was already inhabited.

Undaunted, Jewish leaders set about furthering their programme of raising national awareness, winning international support and encouraging immigration into Palestine. In his quest for backing by a major power, Herzl first tried Constantinople. This was the obvious choice since Palestine still lay within the Ottoman Empire. The Sultan was unwilling to welcome more Jewish immigrants into a region where they were already attracting criticism as unwanted outsiders.

Herzl then turned to Britain, still the world's wealthiest and most influential nation and certainly the leading imperial power. Here he received a more favourable reception (as well as a suggestion that part of East Africa might make a less controversial national home for the Jews than Palestine). Although Britain did not formally agree to back Zionism, foundations were laid for a relationship that became official with the Balfour Declaration (see page 20).

Supremacy and immigration

An intellectual link had also been established between Zionism and imperialism. The principal motive for Britain's acquisition of an empire was commercial. It was justified on less materialistic grounds: Europeans were more politically, technologically and perhaps even morally advanced than the peoples they governed so it was their duty – 'the white man's burden' – to civilize them.

After the First World War the British colonial secretary, Winston Churchill, an enthusiastic supporter of empire, spelled out the link between Zionism and British imperialism when he declared that a 'National Home' for the Jews in Palestine would be, 'good for the world, good for the Jews and good for the British Empire'. Zionists supported such sentiments by arguing that an influx of European Jews, bearing European culture and values, could only benefit the region. They were sure that Palestinian Arabs, perhaps hostile at first, would soon be won over when they saw the economic and political advantages that Jewish immigration brought.

The lower esteem in which many Jews held the Arabs is reflected in the extraordinary Zionist slogan: 'A land without people for a people without land'. No one disputed the second half of the catchphrase, but to dismiss the 535,000 Muslims (mostly Arabs) and 70,000 Christians living in Palestine in 1914 as non-existent was extraordinarily dangerous arrogance.

Prominent members of the European and American Jewish community helped establish banks and funds to assist Jewish immigration into Palestine. The most prominent individual benefactor was the French philanthropist Baron Edmond de Rothschild. Precise figures are impossible to come by, but perhaps 35,000 Jews entered Palestine in the 30 years before the outbreak of the First World War. By the same date, Jews may have owned two per cent of Palestinian land.

The proportion of Palestinian land held by the Jews in relation to their numbers was greatly less than that held by Arabs. Furthermore, the number of Jews entering Palestine was as nothing compared with the estimated 2 million who went to live in the United States over the same period. Here they formed an economic and political community whose influence would impact powerfully on the Middle East in the latter half of the century.

Seeds of conflict

The arrival of perhaps 1,000 Jewish immigrants per annum in a region where their co-religionists had lived in comparative harmony with their neighbours for centuries need not in itself have caused problems. Difficulties arose not over numbers but attitudes.

Many Jewish immigrants had absorbed Zionist propaganda about their supremacy to the local people and about the land being theirs by moral (and even religious) right. Moreover, the new arrivals were often separatist. The original Palestinian Jews had been city dwellers, integrating within the communities of Gaza, Hebron, Jaffa, Jerusalem and elsewhere. As we saw with the foundation of Tel Aviv (see page 7), the immigrants planted exclusive colonies within Palestine, 47 of them by the end of the First World War.

The perceived threat of Zionism to the Arab way of life produced an understandable reaction. Palestinian Arabs, at least the educated section of their community, began to think in terms of a Palestinian nation. They went as representatives of Palestine to the Turkish Parliament in Constantinople and several exclusively Palestinian Arabic newspapers gave voice to the new nationalism.

Arab leaders took political action, too. They petitioned Constantinople to halt Jewish immigration, and when this failed they set up anti-Zionist societies in Palestine, Beirut and Constantinople. Finally, starting as early as 1886, Arabs occasionally took matters into their own hands and attacked the unwanted intruders. Although these outbreaks were small scale, they began a cycle of violence that endures to this day.

The British mandate

As we saw in Chapter 2, during the First World War Britain had raised both Arab and Jewish hopes. The correspondence between Sir Henry MacMahon and Emir Hussein of Mecca had left the latter with the impression that the bulk of the Ottoman district of Syria would become an independent state. The Balfour Declaration of the following year, masterminded by the Russian-born Anglo-Jewish academic Chaim Weizmann, had offered formal British support for a Jewish homeland in Palestine. Given the mounting tension between Arabs and Jews in Palestine before the war broke out, these apparently contradictory agreements could do nothing but increase inter-communal strains.

The post-war settlement

Since it would play such a major role in the Middle East from the Second World War onwards, it is worth noting here the American position regarding the Balfour Declaration and the future of the provinces of the former Ottoman Empire. Briefly, President Wilson's position was that the Arab peoples should have 'absolutely unmolested opportunity of autonomous development'. At the same time, he supported the idea of a national home for the Jews in Palestine.

Recognizing the possible contradictions in his policy, Wilson then appointed the King-Crane Commission to examine the situation in Palestine. It reported that the extreme Zionist position – all Palestine (including lands east of the River Jordan) ought to become a Jewish state – was both wrong and impossible to achieve. The answer lay in some sort of compromise. Since a Jewish homeland within or adjacent to an Arab state would need to be organized and refereed by a third party, Wilson came round to accepting the status quo. Britain, having seized Palestine during the war, continued in possession of what became known as a League of Nations mandate.

Before this came about, the Palestinian Arabs saw their hopes of independence finally dashed. Emir Faisal, briefly King of Syria, had included Palestine within his kingdom. When he was obliged to swap Syria for Iraq, the British kept control of Palestine while the French moved into what remained of Syria. Shortly afterwards the British separated off the eastern part of Palestine, beyond the River Jordan, as an emirate for Faisal's brother Abdullah. Palestinian Arabs were to refer to 1920, the year when all this happened, as 'the year of catastrophe'.

The Allies, largely ignoring the wishes of the people whose future they were determining, agreed the details above at a conference in San Remo. The mandate status of Palestine was later confirmed by the League of Nations. It meant that Britain's position there was strictly temporary – its task was to administer the territory while preparing it for democratic independence. However, the mandate also included the principles of the Balfour Declaration – the establishment of a Jewish national home in Palestine – and a Jewish Agency was to be set up to assist the British in this task. The only part of the settlement that angered some extreme Zionists was the total exclusion of Abdullah's Transjordanian fief from the homeland territory.

Britain's headache

The Arabs rejected the idea of a British mandate from the start. As far as they were concerned, its only positive feature was the recognition of Palestine as a separate political entity. The rest they abhorred. What right had foreigners either to divide their land or force them to accept a state within a state? What they wanted, quite reasonably, was a fully democratic Palestine that embraced all peoples living there. Some moderate Arab leaders suggested a compromise whereby the US would replace Britain as the supervising power. Since the mandate was responsible to the League of Nations, a body that the US Congress had rejected, the idea was a non-starter.

The intensity of Britain's headache becomes clear when we understand why the Palestinian Jews rejected a single democratic Palestine. Not only would it mean abandoning the concept of the Jewish homeland, but it would also make them a small and disliked minority (perhaps ten per cent) in a predominately Arab-Muslim state. In such a situation, they feared, their rights and perhaps even their livelihoods would be imperilled.

British administrators carried out the logistical side of their mandated duties with laudable efficiency. Their efforts to improve life in Palestine attracted some 50,000 Arab immigrants as well as many more Jews. They modernized transport by expanding the rail network and building roads; they built schools and sewage treatment plants, laid water pipelines and increased the provision of electricity. All the while, though, their task was made harder and harder by the background of inter-communal violence.

As far as the second part of Britain's mandated duties was concerned – preparing Palestine for democratic self-government while also honouring the Balfour Declaration – most far-seeing administrators soon realized it was impossible. Caught between two irreconcilable communities, they came to see the mandate as a sort of curse. Consequently, since no time limit had been set on it, observers began to wonder whether they would ever leave.

Such rumours were reinforced by activity at the eccentric Sodom and Gomorrah Golfing Society, where the élite of the occupying power, under armed escort, perspired around a brown and barren course beside the Dead Sea. The trophy for which they competed was a statue of Lot's wife. The original had been carved with biblical correctness from a block of salt. When it wore away, the club committee replaced it with a more lasting version in durable marble. The symbolism was clear: the British were there for the duration.

1920s

It is estimated that the Jewish population of Palestine doubled in the ten years after the First World War. Immigrants did not arrive in a steady flow. After an initial rush, the British, worried by the Arab reaction, imposed limits. At the same time, Jewish land purchases continued apace. These were sometimes made from absentee Arab landlords. On a number of occasions such acquisitions led to Arab peasants being turned off land they and their ancestors had farmed for years. Tensions ran understandably high and the British declaration that it was not their intention to turn Palestine into a Jewish state cut little ice with disaffected Arabs. Moreover, the appointment of Sir Herbert Samuel, a Jew, as Britain's first all-powerful High Commissioner for Palestine hardly displayed tactful even-handedness.

There were serious outbreaks of Arab-Zionist fighting immediately after the First World War. These reflected the uncertainty of the political situation, Arab disappointment at the rejection of their demand for independence, and their fear over what they saw as the potentially overwhelming tide of Jewish immigration. Conciliatory statements by the British and a fall in Jewish immigration (there was actually a net emigration in 1927) helped the situation remain calm until 1929.

As ever, the Arabs were not helped by divisions within their ranks. Their nominal leader was Amin al-Husseini, Grand Mufti (expert on Muslim religious law) of Jerusalem. His authority was weakened by traditional rivalry with the an-Nashasibi family and by the fact that his positions as mufti and president of the Supreme Muslim Council were both British appointments. Opposition to Zionism was divided between several organizations, such as the Husseini-led Arab Executive and the Nashasibi-led National Defence Party. When ancient town-country, tribal and religious divisions are added to the mix, the failure of the Palestinian Arabs to present a united front is understandable.

The Jews were less divided. During the 1920s they generally co-operated with the British, setting up the apparatus of a distinctively Jewish state: elected assembly, trade unions, schools, industrial enterprises and so forth. They even had their own defence organization, the Haganah. Nevertheless, rifts were starting to appear within the Zionist ranks. The majority followed the more moderate ('Labour') leaders of the World Zionist Organization, Chaim Weizmann in London and David Ben Gurion in Palestine. They sought a socialist Jewish state in Palestine separate from a Palestinian Arab one. The Haganah would be needed to defend this state, but force was not an integral part of it.

Opposition to this Labour view came from Ze'ev Jobotinsky and his World Union of Zionist Revisionists. These hard-liners attracted considerable support during the late 1920s and set up a militant security force of their own, the Irgun. They followed what came to be termed the 'iron wall' policy, based on four principles. First, the Jews were the standard-bearers of a superior Western civilization into the Middle East. Second, Zion had to comprise all Palestine on both banks of the Jordan ('Greater Israel'). Third, the Arabs would never voluntarily accept this. Fourth, the only answer, therefore, was force: Zionists had to carve out their state and secure it behind an iron wall. Only then, when the Arabs knew they could never win, would they accept the presence of the Jewish state in the Middle East. When present-day observers wonder why peace between Arab and Israeli is so elusive, they have only to consider the iron wall views of the Revisionists to grasp at least part of the answer.

1930s

The uneasy post-war peace collapsed in 1929. The trouble was sparked off, oddly enough, by furniture. Jews believed that the 'Wailing Wall' in old Jerusalem represented the only tangible relic of the ancient kingdom of Israel. At this place of prayer and sometimes painful remembrance (hence 'wailing') Jews had met for centuries, bringing with them chairs and other items of furniture to make their observances more comfortable. Unfortunately, the same piece of architecture was also charged with deep significance for Muslims.

The wall and its environs, the third most sacred site in the Islamic world, were owned by Muslims. Broadly interpreting the words of the Koran, tradition held that the Prophet Mohammed had one night ascended to heaven from an outcrop near the wall now graced by the Dome of the Rock. It was also believed that Mohammed's holy horse had been tethered to the wall itself. Not only that, but immediately above the wall stood the al-Aqsa mosque. In short, in Muslim eyes it was not the sort of place where folding garden chairs were wholly appropriate.

Inter-community tension over co-usage of the sacred site was fired up by the taunting of extremists on either side. On 23 August, the Muslim community went on the rampage and indulged in a full-scale orgy of murder, rape and pillage in which 133 Jews and 116 Arabs were killed, the great majority of the latter by the British security forces as they struggled to restore order. Whatever slight hope there had been of Jew and Arab living together in a single harmonious Palestine was now gone.

During the rest of the 1930s, the situation deteriorated further as the British floundered from one expedient to the next. After the August Massacre, for example, they ordered a reduction in Jewish immigration only to reverse the decision under Zionist pressure. Similarly, when Jewish refugees from Nazi Germany began flooding into Palestine (30,000 in 1933 rising to 61,000 in 1935), the British again cut immigration before increasing it once more. The result was simply confusion and resentment. By the time of the Second World War there were some 300 Zionist colonies in Palestine. The 467,000 Jews, who owned about 15 per cent of the land, made up almost one-third of the population.

The Arab response was a national revolt. Husseini called a general strike, taxes were not paid, local government broke down, and violence in all its forms increased. This time it was directed at both Jews and the British. The former fought back with the services of the Haganah and the terrorist-like Irgun. The latter declared martial law and increased the Palestine garrison to over 20,000 troops. One British officer went as far as to prepare Special Night Squads of Jews to attack Arab villages. Within four years perhaps 5,000 Arabs had been killed and 15,000 wounded.

The Arab revolt forced the British to accept the inevitable: they would not be able to prepare Palestine for independence as a single democratic state. The Peel Commission Report (1937) recommended that Palestine be partitioned into Jewish and Arab states, with Jerusalem and neighbouring Holy Places remaining under British control. Interestingly, a somewhat similar partition plan had been agreed by Chaim Weizmann and King Faisal 20 years earlier. It had been dropped after rejection by other Arab leaders; acceptance would have avoided an immense amount of blood and tears.

Although Labour Zionists cautiously welcomed the Peel proposal, Husseini and his advisors rejected it outright. Confused, the British government then put forward another idea: a Jewish homeland within an Arab state, and strict limits on Jewish immigration. This compromise was turned down by both sides. The Arabs were way beyond trusting the British, and it was now the turn of the Jews to feel betrayed.

By the outbreak of the Second World War, Palestine was in turmoil. Intolerance and incompetence had changed a complex two-sided struggle between Jews and Arabs into an impossible three-sided one in which Arabs, Jews and the British were all at loggerheads. If there was a way out of this slough, it was certainly not well signposted.

The state of Israel

Palestine in wartime

The outbreak of war in 1939 had a considerable impact on the Palestinian situation. Moderate Arabs and Jews agreed to support Britain and its allies in their struggle against fascism, and inter-community conflict died down considerably. As many as 27,000 Jews and 25,000 Arabs (particularly the famous Arab Legion) fought with the British Army. With huge funds pouring into the mandate to support the 250,000 Allied troops based there, the economy flourished. The Jewish sector did particularly well, developing its industry to meet Allied war needs.

There were exceptions on both sides to this comparative harmony. The Grand Mufti drew down much disapprobation upon his head by making his way to Germany and entering into negotiations with the Nazis. His reputation tarnished, after the war he chose to settle in Egypt rather than Palestine. On the other side, Revisionist Zionists of the Irgun and the Stern Gang, a group of hard-line Zionist terrorists, carried out a series of attacks on British personnel and positions. Their most notorious achievement was the assassination of a British minister in Cairo.

Two things irked the more fervent Zionists. One was the proposed partition of their promised land, the other was Britain's attempt to curry favour with the Arabs by limiting further Jewish immigration. The British, as we have seen, had extensive interests around the Persian Gulf (see page 22). An uninterrupted oil supply from these protectorates and Saudi Arabia was essential for the war effort. Although large numbers of immigrants continued to arrive in Palestine (perhaps 40,000 in 1940), there were several high-profile tragedies involving boatloads of helpless refugees.

Another effect of the war was to draw the United States deeply into Middle Eastern politics for the first time. Like Britain, the US needed Arab oil and poured money into Saudi Arabia to keep it stable and on side. The pro-Arab stance of President F. D. Roosevelt ran contrary to the pro-Zionist feeling of the country at large. Following a visit of Ben Gurion to the US, the Biltmore Programme of support for the Zionist project gained widespread backing, even from Congress and presidential election candidates.

By the end of the war, as the full extent of the horrifying Nazi slaughter of some 6 million European Jews became known, the tide of support for Zionism ran even stronger. Both President Truman and his Congress urged Britain to take a more relaxed line over Zionist immigration.

Meanwhile, the Palestine question was having positive effects within the Arab world. In 1945, Egypt organized an Arab League that comprised itself, Syria, Saudi Arabia, Transjordan, Iraq, Lebanon, and Yemen. The League's primary purpose was to foster unity and co-operation among Arab peoples. To begin with its activities were largely cultural, social and economic. Political activity was limited by the fact that only Egypt and Yemen were truly independent. Saudi Arabia and Jordan were reliant upon Western funds, while Syria, Lebanon and Iraq were still under occupation. Nevertheless, the League established a Higher Committee to lobby against Zionism. Given the massive worldwide sympathy for the Jewish people after the Holocaust, the League had to measure its efforts with tact and care.

End of the mandate

Post-war Britain, exhausted, impoverished and much weakened, clung to its Palestinian mandate. Its personnel were still subject to terrorist attacks by Zionist extremists, most notably when the King David Hotel in Jerusalem was bombed, killing 91 people. Immigration, much of it technically illegal, continued to swell the Jewish population. The British Labour government wished to shed its burden of responsibility and get out of Palestine as swiftly as possible, while maintaining sufficient bases there to protect the Suez Canal. At the end of 1945, therefore, it invited the US to form a joint committee to look into the situation in Palestine.

The committee's proposals, emerging as the Morrison-Grady Plan, were rejected by both Zionists and Arabs. Further plans, proposals, schemes and so on were thrown up and then rejected until Britain surrendered and handed over the entire Palestinian business to the newly formed United Nations (UN). A UN Special Committee on Palestine (UNSCOP) came up with a suggestion not unlike that put forward by the Peel Commission: separate Jewish and Arab states, united in an economic union, with Jerusalem and its environs under international control. 'Israel' was accepted as the name of the Jewish state-to-be. The UNSCOP proposal was accepted by the UN General Assembly at the end of 1947, with Britain and all Muslim countries voting against. After some uncertainty, Britain declared that its Palestinian mandate would end on 14 May 1948.

The boundaries of the two UN-arranged states were contorted to incorporate the wishes of both Jews and Arabs. Such mathematical frontiers were hopelessly unrealistic and, as soon as they were known, fighting broke out as each side strove to alter and extend them. In other words, the UN's intervention had polarized the position in Palestine rather than placated it.

The Zionist campaign was predominantly masterminded by the Jewish Agency, headed by Ben Gurion, which controlled the disciplined and relatively experienced Haganah forces numbering at least 40,000. The Irgun and Stern Gang terrorist groups worked more or less together with the official forces. The Palestinians were less warlike and certainly less well organized. Their own force of about 3,000 men, led by a Husseini relative of the Mufti, was poorly equipped. Many of its guerrilla attacks were on fellow Palestinians who had sold land to Zionists. The Arab League's contribution, an 'Arab Liberation Army' of 3,000 disorganized volunteers, contributed little. At one stage it refused to help the hard-pressed Husseini and even co-operated with the Haganah. Better motivated were 2,000 Muslim Brotherhood volunteers from Egypt.

Unfortunately for the Palestinians, few, if any, Arab states were really interested in helping them. Certainly three neighbouring countries – Egypt, Transjordan and Syria – all saw the chaos on their borders as an opportunity for territorial expansion of their own. So behind the scenes, while the world was shocked by hot-blooded killings such as the massacre of 254 Arab villagers in Deir Yassin by the Stern Gang and the brutal ambush of a medical convoy by Palestinians, politicians were making a more cold-blooded appraisal of the situation.

Most startling were secret meetings between Abdullah, now the self-styled King of Transjordan, and a Ukrainian-born, US-educated Zionist politician named Golda Meir. Abdullah, having picked up his own kingdom through a stroke of British hard-nosed political chicanery, was nothing if not a realist. He shared with the more fervent Zionists the view that territory was what you could get, not what you ought to have. Consequently, he had no problem reaching an agreement with the equally realistic Mrs Meir. In the event of full-scale war between Israel and the Palestinians, he should take over Palestinian territory on the West Bank of the Jordan and leave the Israelis to grab what they could of the rest.

As the date for the expiry of the British mandate drew closer, the fighting intensified. The all too familiar pattern of terrorist attack, reprisal, counter-reprisal, and so on was by now commonplace. While it is impossible to say precisely who was primarily responsible for the escalation, there are indications that Zionist extremists were more to blame than most. By May 1948, Zionist forces had fought their way into the ports of Haifa and Jaffa, broken the siege of Jerusalem and defeated the Arab Liberation Army.

The Arab League now warned that if the Zionists made a unilateral declaration of independence, regular Arab forces would immediately attack the newly-formed Israel. In secret, however, most Arab leaders feared that war would simply be an excuse for Transjordan to expand to the west. To make this more difficult, King Abdullah was given nominal command of the Arab League forces. He produced no co-ordinated plan of attack.

Nevertheless, the Zionists were alarmed that Arab pressure might force King Abdullah to break his pact with them. Golda Meir put herself in considerable personal danger and, disguised as an Arab woman, sneaked across the Jordan for another secret meeting with Abdullah. Clearly troubled, the wily monarch explained that it might not be possible to honour his previous agreement. He could not afford to fall out with fellow Arabs. After all, they had chosen him as their commander in chief …

Meir returned safely to Zionist territory where her news was received with no surprise. Two days before the end of the British overlordship, the Zionist Provisional State Council met to decide the future. The Americans were strongly urging caution. Ben Gurion successfully advised his colleagues to reject their advice. The time had come, he declared, for the Jews to form what they had long dreamed of – the state of Israel.

Israeli independence was declared on 14 May 1948, the day the last British High Commissioner left Palestine. The boundaries of the new country were not defined. Both Israelis and Arabs knew that they would be decided by the rifle, not the pen. The following day troops from Egypt, Transjordan, Syria, Lebanon, and Iraq invaded Israel.

04

Gamal Abdul Nasser

This chapter will cover:
- the First Arab-Israeli War
- the effects of this war on Middle East stability
- the rise of President Nasser in Egypt
- the causes of the Second Arab-Israeli War (1956).

The First Arab-Israeli War

The balance of forces

The formal war began immediately after the state of Israel came into being. The fighting was really just a continuation of that in progress since the United Nations passed its resolution on the partition of Palestine the previous year.

Crude statistics, looking at overall wealth, size of population and so forth, might suggest that the forces of Egypt, Saudi Arabia, Syria, Transjordan, Yemen, Lebanon and Iraq ought to have overrun Israel in a matter of days. But wars are fought by troops on the ground, not numbers, and in reality this was anything but a David versus Goliath conflict.

It is estimated that the non-Palestinian Arabs managed to put about 23,000 troops into the field. The better trained Israel Defence Force (IDF), created by forcing the experienced Haganah, Irgun and Stern Gang to amalgamate, eventually rose to over 96,000. Particularly after the re-armament of the summer of 1948 (when weapons and ammunition of all kinds came in from Soviet-backed Czechoslovakia, France and private US sponsors), the IDF was better armed than the Arabs. It even secretly acquired three US Flying Fortress bombers with which it was able to attack Cairo.

Despite cultural differences between Jews originating from Europe (Ashkenazi) and those from Oriental lands (Sephardi), all Israelis knew that they were fighting for their very existence. This gave them a ruthless determination, sometimes known as the 'Holocaust syndrome'. Israelis had seen what had happened to the meek and conforming Jews who had trusted others – they had been exterminated. The 'fighting Jew' would never let this happen. Their toughness might make them feared – hated even – but it would keep them safe.

To the first generation of Israelis, the end justified the means – even if it meant attacking their own unarmed trucks in order to provoke further fighting with Egypt; even if it meant Haganah troops of future prime minister Yitzhak Rabin killing Irgun fighters who had rejected a unified command (another future prime minister, Menachem Begin, survived the attack); even if it meant extremist assassins commanded by yet another future prime minister, Yitzhak Shamir, killing the UN mediator because he seemed too pro-Arab; even if it meant Moche Dayan's forces terrorizing Arab villages outside Israel so that their inhabitants would learn to live in fear of their neighbours. All of these acts of desperate cruelty actually happened. Understandable but nevertheless abhorrent, they built the wall of hatred and mistrust that has yet to be broken.

Faced with such steely unity, the motley Arab forces stood little chance. As we saw in Chapter 2, their states were largely new creations, politically unstable and not yet able to cope with the strains of full-scale, long-distance warfare. Moreover, although some troops might have been inspired by feelings of Arab or Muslim unity, their leaders were not. The Mufti, sheltering in Egypt, did not get on with the Arab League and refused to allow his Palestinian guerrilla band to co-operate with it. The Egyptians sought as much land as possible on the Sinai side of the Suez Canal. The Syrians wanted fertile land in the Golan Heights and around the Sea of Galilee. The Saudis sent one paltry battalion, the Lebanese and Iraqis were there largely because it was politically less trouble than not being there. Commander-in-chief Abdullah Transjordan, dreaming of one day ruling a Greater Syria, made sure no Arab forces got in the way of his seizure of the land the UN had assigned to the Palestinians on the West Bank of the Jordan.

The course of the war

During the first phase of the war, ended by a UN cease-fire mediated by Count Folke Bernadotte, the Israelis secured their state. When the fighting broke out again a month later they were able to go on the offensive and drive back their dispirited enemies on almost every front. Only in Jerusalem did the British-led Arab Legion hold its own, targeting Palestinians as much as Israelis.

It was a bitty war, punctuated by cease-fires which both sides broke if they felt they could gain an advantage by doing so. The British commander of King Abdullah's Arab Legion called it 'an imitation war'. Its most unsavoury aspect was Israel's Plan D, or Dalet. This strategy, which had been in place before the declaration of independence, was based on the principle of overcoming the enemy within – the Palestinians – before tackling invaders. To achieve this, Israeli forces 'pacified' Palestinian villages and towns. This involved either getting the community to put itself under total Israeli control or driving the population out and destroying the buildings: 360 Arab villages and 14 Arab towns were razed as a consequence of the Dalet. The Israelis said this was the only feasible way of safeguarding their security; to others it looked suspiciously like the insidious form of racism now known as ethnic cleansing.

Despite the murder of Count Bernadotte, the UN continued with its efforts to broker peace. This resulted in a series of separate cease-fires agreed between February (Israel-Egypt) and July (Israel-Syria) 1949. These matured into more durable armistices with every state except Iraq. Totally in command of the military situation by the autumn of 1948, Israeli Prime Minister David Ben Gurion had considered pressing on with the campaign into the Sinai and West Bank. Only international pressure, particularly from the US, had held him back. In a very real sense, the next two Arab-Israeli wars (1956 and 1967) simply picked up the conflict where it had temporarily halted in 1949.

figure 4 Palestine and Transjordan 1947–8

Israel and the Palestinians

The first and most obvious consequence of the conflict, known to the Israelis as the War of Independence and to the Arabs as the Palestine War, was the establishment of the state of Israel. Having absorbed 77 per cent of the UN's proposed Palestinian state, it was some 21 per cent larger than the state envisaged by the UN partition plan. Unlike the UN's Israel, the new one had defensible frontiers – though not as defensible as the military would have liked. The population comprised 717,700 Jews (the ratio of Ashkenazi to Sephardi being 6:1) and 165,000 Arabs (almost one fifth of whom were Christian).

The remnants of the Palestinian state that had only ever existed on paper were divided between Egypt, which occupied the 6.5-km (4-mile) wide strip of Mediterranean coastline around the city of Gaza, and Transjordan, which had seized the West Bank. The international community, Israel excluded, eventually agreed to the West Bank being incorporated within Abdullah's original kingdom to form the Hashemite Kingdom of Jordan, or simply Jordan. Israel and Jordan divided the holy city of Jerusalem between them. Syria got nothing.

So what of the Palestinians? To them the events of 1948 were 'Al Naksa', the disaster. With terrible irony, the establishment of Israel, a country for refugees, had created a new nation of refugees. Precise figures are impossible to come by, but from the start of the fighting to the summer of 1949 perhaps close to 1 million Palestinians had left their homes and fled abroad. They went for many reasons. The Israelis drove out thousands; more fled out of fear, particularly when Arab politicians exaggerated the scale of the Deir Yassin massacre for propaganda purposes; some were pushed aside by invading Arab forces; the better off emigrated in relative comfort to other parts of the Middle East, Europe and America.

In all negotiations the Israelis were adamant that no Palestinian might return. They had either left voluntarily, they argued somewhat obtusely, or they had been removed as a threat to the state. Sprawling, squalid refugee camps ran like a ribbon of shame around Israel's borders. Most were in the West Bank and Gaza, but they also appeared in Lebanon and Syria.

In truth, the Palestinians had not really been a nation. They had never had the chance. But here, where half-naked children played between the cramped tents and insanitary washblocks of the refugee camps, a generation grew up inspired with a new and bitter Palestinian nationalism. As the Jewish founders of the state of Israel had done, so the Palestinians of the camps came to realize that only they could make their dream come true. Tragically, however, like the band of Zionists reporting long ago on the promised land, they too found that, 'the bride is beautiful but she is married to another man'. So began another set of bloody divorce proceedings.

A region of instability

The establishment of Israel, the war, and the flood of Palestinian refugees had a massively destabilizing effect on the Middle East. The humiliation of defeat helped undermine fragile regimes throughout the region. The situation was not helped by the fact that, despite secret talks and the efforts of third-party intermediaries, no peace treaties were signed. This meant that Arabs and Israelis remained technically at war. The Israelis rejected all offers of land for peace, declaring that having just fought for their country they had no intention of giving bits of it away. For their part, the Arab states refused to recognize Israel's existence. Impasse.

The region's problems were greatly exacerbated by the advent of the Cold War. This was the long period of superpower confrontation in which the Soviet Union, the champion of communism, stood toe-to-toe with the USA, the champion of democratic capitalism. It is generally said to have begun with Winston Churchill's famous statement, delivered at Fulton, Missouri, in March 1946, that an 'iron curtain' had fallen across Europe. The rivalry between the two sides of the curtain – communist East and capitalist West – fed wars, coups and terrorism all over the globe. As much by luck as judgement, it never quite escalated into the nuclear Third World War that everyone feared and many predicted.

Two matters tied the Middle East into the Cold War. One was the falling of a second iron curtain across the Palestine region, dividing Jew from Arab. It was inevitable that the superpowers would try to use the Arab-Israeli stand-off to increase their local influence. The reason why they sought this influence brings us to the second factor that made the Middle East such a vital battleground: oil.

The West was now running on oil, not coal, and the Middle East's share of world oil production was rising daily. To the US, which was rapidly taking over Britain's position as the major outside influence in the Middle East, Arab oil was crucial. American policy, therefore, was to keep the Soviet Union out of the region, maintain trouble-free transport routes (both pipelines and seaways), and try to ensure that local governments remained on good terms with the US.

There was one major difference, however, between the way Britain and France had played their part in the Middle East and the way the US would do so. The former had usually dressed their power politics in the clothing of legality – treaties, mandates, and so forth. The US was blessed with no such fig leaves. At that time the media back home did not want the US militarily embroiled in the Middle East, nor did the United Nations or the Soviet Union. Direct, overt interference risked a serious escalation of the Cold War. Therefore, competing with Soviet skulduggery, American administrations had to defend their interests in ways that were sometimes decidedly underhand. In short, that meant using the Central Intelligence Agency (CIA). As a result, the politics of the Middle East, always complex, became a game of bluff and counter-bluff, deceit and counter-deceit that not even the players themselves were able to control.

Syria

After the French withdrawal in 1946, the Syrians were eager to test their shiny new democratic constitution. They were soon disappointed. The country's complicated religious, social and economic diversity made stability unlikely. Defeat and outside intervention ensured its demise.

Shukri al Kuwatli's largely Sunni National Party, deeply corrupt but popular for leading the resistance to the French, clung on to power amid festering discontent. The disastrous defeat by Israel further undermined its already shaky credibility. The US State Department was worried. Like Syria, Russia before the Communist take-over in 1917 had been plagued by poor government, economic hardship and military defeat. Syria, a vital link in the pipeline route from the Gulf to the Mediterranean, might easily go the same way.

The CIA's chosen man was a 'burly Kurd' named Colonel Husni al Zaim, a man of iron will and mind. Kuwatli's elected government was removed and the iron Kurd installed in its place in March 1949. Thus, with supreme efficiency, the CIA had engineered its first coup, overthrown democracy, and given the independent states of the Middle East their first military dictator.

Alas! Zaim proved an unwise choice of puppet. After strutting his stuff like a character out of *Bugsy Malone*, he was shortly removed by another coup. Syria now entered upon a prolonged period of instability marked by a succession of coups by army officers. After changing hands five times in as many years, the baton of government finally ended up with Colonel Faisal al-Atasi, who restored the country's parliament.

Throughout this period a new movement was gathering force in Syrian politics. This was the Arab Socialist Renaissance Party, better known as the Baath Party. It was fiercely anti-Western. Its Pan-Arabist manifesto claimed all boundaries between Arab peoples to be merely inconvenient Western devices. Not surprisingly, the Baathists were also intractably hostile to Israel.

Lebanon

Parliamentary democracy fared better in Lebanon, where the delicately balanced Muslim-Christian constitutional arrangement (see pages 29–30) survived the spat with Israel. The leadership distanced itself from the rest of Israel's enemies by declaring that Lebanon was not really an Arab country and had never wanted to go to war in the first place. A Syrian-backed coup attempt was foiled.

Thereafter, despite an assassinated prime minister and a president removed by a general strike, the system survived. Lebanon did not join the Second Arab-Israeli War and, to the intense annoyance of other Arab nations, refused to break off relations with Israel's allies, Britain and France (see page 5).

Iraq

Iraq fared better than Syria. Boosted by rising oil revenues, the country prospered. Its ragged form of democracy operated after a fashion, although it saw two prime ministers overthrown by popular uprisings and a period of martial law. Behind the scenes regent Abdullah and the army continued to wield considerable power. Sadly, though, the stability and modernization anticipated when the British-educated King Faisal II came of age in 1953 failed to materialize. The young king lacked charisma and political instinct – a dangerous formula at any time, but potentially disastrous in post-war Iraq.

Diplomatically, Iraq's most significant move was entering into the Baghdad Pact just before the Second Arab-Israeli War (1956). The Pact started as an agreement with Turkey over the treatment of militant Kurds. It was then expanded to include Iran, Pakistan and Britain, and became known as the Middle East Treaty Organization (later changed to the Central Treaty Organization or CENTO). Its purpose was to act as a sort of North Atlantic Treaty Organization (NATO) of the Middle East, blocking any Soviet attempts at infiltration there. Pact members came and went, and it was never very effective. Most Arab countries mistrusted it because of British membership.

Jordan

The end of King Abdullah of Jordan – 'the dog who sold Palestine to the Zionists' – might have been predicted. Indeed, the British representative in Aman had warned him that the al-Aqsa mosque in Jerusalem was a dangerous place to visit. But visit Abdullah did, for the site contained the grave of his father, Hussein the sometime Sharif of Mecca.

The king was shot dead at point blank range on 20 July 1951. For a keen chess player, he had made the unusual mistake of not thinking far enough ahead. His killer was a fanatical Palestinian determined to slay the man whom he believed had betrayed not just the Palestinians but the entire Arab nation. There was some truth in this belief.

Two years later, Talal, Abdullah's schizophrenic son, was declared mentally unfit to rule. The crown passed to his son, another Hussein. The young man had been beside his grandfather at the time of his death and had narrowly escaped being killed himself in the wild hail of bullets that the royal bodyguard – too late – had sent in the general direction of the assassin.

The 18-year-old Hussein inherited all of his grandfather's political skills, and more. Educated at Harrow (Winston Churchill's school) and the Royal Military College, Sandhurst, England, he retained an affection for the country that had created his kingdom after the First World War. At the same time, he was too clever to let pro-British sentiment spoil his relations with his fellow Arabs. Though tempted, for instance, he refused to join the Baghdad Pact. After the Second Arab-Israeli War, he proved his Arab credentials by dismissing all British advisors and abrogating his grandfather's post-war Anglo-Jordanian treaty of friendship and co-operation.

Nasser

Defeat in the war with Israel left Egypt ripe for revolution. The shaky constitutional monarchy handed down by Britain had been seriously undermined by the extraordinary figure of King Farouk. In his late teens he had been described by a British High Commissioner as 'uneducated, lazy, untruthful, capricious, irresponsible and vain, though with a quick superficial intelligence and charm of manner' (*History Today*, Vol. 52, no. 7, 2002, page 55). Time had not improved him. Now in his early thirties, his girth and lust for ladies as pneumatic as himself shocked and offended his subjects.

The Free Officers' coup

Worse still, Egypt's bloated playboy monarch dabbled in politics with dangerous ineptitude. The country's corrupt and inefficient government was allowed to run on unchallenged, making the rich richer and the poor poorer. An attempt to suppress the increasingly popular Muslim Brotherhood in the middle of the disastrous war with Israel led to the assassination of the prime minister and the subsequent killing of the Brotherhood's leader by government agents.

For a while, many Egyptians focused their fury on the British. In accordance with the pre-war treaty, Britain still maintained a strong presence in Egypt and full control over Sudan. In the Suez Canal Zone they had no less than ten airfields and two naval dockyards, defended by a large military presence. By the early 1950s, guerrilla attacks on British positions had become commonplace.

When negotiations failed to make any progress, the Egyptian government unilaterally ended its treaty with Britain. This only increased the tension and terrorism. The severity of one British retaliatory raid, which left some 30 Egyptians dead, led to widespread demonstrations in Cairo. Muslim Brothers, Communists and frustrated ordinary citizens joined forces in an orgy of destruction. It began with Madame Badia's emporium for gambling and belly-dancing, and ended with banks, the British Council and other buildings, even cinemas, vaguely associated with the Western way of life. As Cairo burned, King Farouk enjoyed an extended luncheon for 600 guests. Only when it was over did he call out the army to suppress the riots in his capital. Over the next six months he went through four prime ministers. Something had to give.

Enter a group of 89 well-meaning Egyptian army personnel by the name of the Free Officers. Their leader was a tall, handsome veteran of the Israeli war, one of the few men who had emerged from the conflict with his reputation enhanced. His name was Colonel Gamal Abdul Nasser. For the time being, though, the 32-year-old stayed in the background and allowed attention to be focused on the group's nominal head, the higher ranking General Mohammed Naguib.

Officially, the CIA had no links with the Free Officers and there are still Egyptians who refuse to believe that the United States had a hand in the rise to power of one of their national heroes. The evidence, however, suggests otherwise. The coup that drove out Farouk and saw General Naguib installed as both president and prime minister was almost a carbon copy of the Syrian affair of four years earlier. It was welcomed by the State Department, and the US entered into a period of good relations with the Officers' seemingly moderate, pro-Western regime. Considerable sums of American aid found their way into the Egyptian treasury.

Nasser's honeymoon

The Free Officers had come to power with a six-point plan that included free education for all and an end to colonialism. Their international outlook was officially non-aligned and much of their rhetoric was about Arab nationalism spearheaded by Egypt's National Union for Arab Socialism. Other political associations were banned, as was the Muslim Brotherhood. The latter was outlawed after a failed attempt to assassinate Nasser. The driving force behind the Officers' coup had already replaced Naguib and now headed Egypt as chairman of the Revolutionary Command Council, prime minister and president.

So far Nasser had done well. He had abolished the monarchy, redistributed land and initiated a large number of much-needed schemes to regulate and reinvigorate the economy. Foremost among these was the construction of a high dam at Aswan to control the waters of the Nile. For this the Americans and British had promised a hefty $270 million. What had annoyed the Brotherhood was the president's agreement with Britain that allowed Sudan to become independent and the British to leave the Suez Canal zone gradually. Hard-line Islamists and nationalists had demanded union with Muslim Sudan and an immediate withdrawal of all foreign forces from Egyptian soil.

Nasser had never enjoyed good relations with the British, Egypt's former masters, who still clung to the fanciful notion that they were a major power. Any thawing produced by the Canal agreement was immediately re-frozen when Nasser heard of the Baghdad Pact (see page 56). He called it an insult to the Arab nation and a 'festering crime'. He would not join, nor would he countenance Jordan doing so. Britain, he believed, no longer had a role in the Middle East and should quit the region for good – as long as they left behind their contribution to the Aswan Dam.

The successful son of a postmaster from Alexandria had enjoyed something of a honeymoon with the US. Because of the Holocaust and the power of the Jewish vote in certain states, American policy had always been pro-Israel. As President Truman had bluntly put it, 'I have no Arabs in my constituency'. That did not preclude friendship with Arab states, however. Truman's successor, Eisenhower, tried to remain even-handed. As we have seen, the US had offered funds for the Aswan Dam project and after the Qibya Massacre (see page 61) Eisenhower withheld $75 million of US aid to Israel.

Eisenhower's cordial relations with Nasser ended suddenly when the Egyptian premier was tempted into infidelity. The bait was arms. Ever since the war with Israel, Egypt had wished to re-arm. The US and Britain, pledged to try to maintain a balance between Israel and her enemies, had provided some weapons but nowhere near as many as Nasser wanted. Early in 1955 he believed his point of view vindicated when, responding to the death of an Israeli cyclist in an Egyptian intelligence gathering mission, the IDF launched a massive raid on Gaza that left 38 Egyptian soldiers dead.

A chance conversation with the Chinese while on a visit to Indonesia appeared to solve Nasser's problem. Arms? The Chinese never had trouble obtaining arms. All he had to do was ask the Soviets, which Nasser promptly did. Within weeks, with Czechoslovakia acting as an intermediary, he was promised 100 self-propelled guns, 200 armoured personnel carriers, 300 tanks, 200 MIG 15 fighters, 50 bombers ... and all $300 million's-worth in exchange for cotton rather than scarce hard cash. For the ambitious president it was precisely what the doctor had ordered.

As far as the US was concerned, the move was an irritating betrayal that brought the Soviet Union into the heart of the

Middle East. The following year, British and American funds for the Aswan Dam were frozen. Nasser responded with a move that sent shockwaves of disbelief humming around the world. Speaking to an enormous crowd in Alexandria, he announced that he was nationalizing the Suez Canal. The charges collected from the waterway's shipping, he explained, would be used to make up the shortfall on his dam project.

The move made Nasser the darling of the entire Arab world. He expected to be challenged, of course, but not quite as violently as he was.

The Suez crisis

Israel after the First Arab-Israeli War

Life was hard in Israel after the war. Two years later 100,000 of its citizens were still living in tents, and immigration was continuing apace. By the fourth year of its existence, however, things had begun to improve with increased foreign aid, notably from private Jewish foundations, the US and (West) Germany.

Unlike most of its Arab neighbours, Israel enjoyed some political stability under Labour coalition governments headed by the old war-horse Ben Gurion and the more urbane Moshe Sharett. Tension continued between Labour and the hard-line Herut Party, successor to the Revisionists, although Ben Gurion's robust style of leadership attracted less criticism from the right than Sharett's more inclusive approach. Other sources of friction were uneasy relations between the Ashkenazi and Sephardi, and the degree to which the new state should embrace the Orthodox Jewish faith. The problem was partly side-stepped by not producing either a written constitution or a bill of rights.

Tension with Arab neighbours

The state's most serious danger was the continued threat from the surrounding Arab states. Arab governments did what they could to hurt the new state economically, boycotting its products and, where possible, impeding its commerce. Actual terrorist activity was limited. The bulk of the early Arab so-called 'infiltrations' into Israel were tragic cases of desperate Palestinians sneaking back to collect possessions, harvest crops or even just set eyes on the homesteads they had lost.

Aggressive infiltration began in 1950, when a dozen Israelis were killed. Thereafter the number of victims was about 50 a year. Israel responded to all intrusion, pacific or not, with an iron fist. Unmarked borders were mined and suspects shot on sight. The bodies of those slain were booby trapped to kill relatives coming to collect them. Over six years perhaps as many as 5,000 Palestinians, most innocent civilians, had been killed.

Disproportionate Israeli response also took the form of reprisal raids, mainly into Jordan and the Gaza Strip. The most vicious of these destroyed the Jordanian village of Qibya and killed 69 people, half of them women and children. Ben Gurion lied that the atrocity had been carried out by local Jewish settlers provoked by Arab attacks. The Qibya operation had been led by an ambitious young officer named Ariel Sharon. The following year the same man led two IDF commando squads that shot up a Gaza refugee camp, killing 20 civilians.

So the violence was cranked up yet again. By the time of Nasser's arms deal with the Soviets, his relations with Israel had reached a new low. An Israeli attempt to implicate Egypt in anti-Western terrorism – the Lavon affair – was badly bungled, leaving the Israelis exposed as an international menace. Later, in the year of the Gaza raid, Nasser also closed the Strait of Tiran (see page 4). This prevented access to the Red Sea from Israel's southern port of Eilat. The Israelis regarded it as tantamount to a challenge to combat.

The Allies' plan

By the autumn of 1956, it was not just Israel that was itching for a showdown with Nasser. The French were fed up with the assistance that Egypt was giving independence fighters in the French colony of Algeria. (As we saw in Syria, the French rarely gave up a colony without a fight.) They wanted Nasser removed, at almost any price, and Israel was the ideal ally in such an enterprise. They had already supplied arms and were negotiating to build an Israeli nuclear reactor. The British, although less gung-ho, were also sick of the Egyptian premier. Prime Minister Anthony Eden dubbed him 'the Muslim Mussolini' and was furious with the way he had scorned the Baghdad Pact and pressured Jordan in to not joining.

Two-thirds of Europe's oil and one-third of Britain's passed through the Suez Canal. As a commercial enterprise, it was also a source of revenue for the British and French governments.

The sudden nationalization of this vital waterway had been totally unacceptable, despite Egypt's mutterings about compensation. The US put pressure on both sides to come to some sort of compromise but their desultory talks got nowhere. Equally ineffective were attempts by the French, British and Israeli secret services to eliminate Nasser by foul means.

The deadlock was broken by a cunning plan. It brought together France, Britain and Israel – the latter two becoming the most unlikely of allies – in a top-secret anti-Egyptian coalition. The preparations involved a build-up of British and French troops in the Mediterranean and a clandestine visit to France by British Foreign Secretary Selwyn Lloyd (sporting a false moustache) for a meeting with Ben Gurion and Israel's one-eyed Chief of Staff, Moshe Dayan.

Dayan and the IDF were in confident mood. The French had always kept them supplied with more weapons than was made public. As a counter-balance to Egypt's Soviet weapons, France had recently delivered a fresh consignment of tanks and aircraft. Dayan and his fellow hawks were eager to use them before Egypt's re-armament was complete. The prospect of doing so in alliance with Britain and France was even better. In fact, they couldn't wait.

05

war to war

This chapter will cover:
- the Second Arab-Israeli War and its consequences
- the political instability of the Middle East 1957–66
- the plight of the Palestinians
- the re-arming of the Middle East and preparations for another war.

The Suez War

On 29 October 1956, taking up where they had left off eight years earlier, the Israelis attacked across Sinai towards the Suez Canal. Within a week they had captured Gaza and the entire Sinai Peninsular. Meanwhile, Britain and France had expressed mock concern for the security of the canal. The Israelis and Egyptians must withdraw to within 16 km (10 miles) of the international waterway, they demanded. Their ally duly obliged. Nasser, on the other hand, would have none of it: just as the Anglo-French plan had predicted.

Upon Nasser's refusal, British and French fighter-bombers attacked Egyptian positions for almost a week, during which time 95 per cent of the new Egyptian air force was destroyed. One bomb sank a ship in the canal, blocking it. The Egyptians completed the job by sinking concrete-filled hulks alongside it. From now on, whatever the outcome of the campaign, the canal would be useless for some time.

When the bombing stopped, British and French marine and airborne troops landed near the canal; 36 hours later a cease-fire had been negotiated. The assault force was home by Christmas and Nasser remained in possession of the canal. He had won.

The Anglo-French Suez plan had failed for four main reasons. First, the operation had been too slow. A sudden seizure of the canal within, say, three days would have given the attackers the upper hand in further negotiations. As it was, the prolonged bombardment allowed UN and domestic opinion to turn almost unanimously against the venture.

Second, the invasion had taken place with no diplomatic or propaganda preparation. Britain and France's allies, press, electorate and political supporters had not been consulted, and all felt understandably annoyed. Third, the operation brought an overstretched Britain perilously close to bankruptcy. A fuel crisis loomed, too. Not only was the canal blocked but Syria, in a gesture of Pan-Arabism, had also cut the oil pipeline that ran from Iraq to the Mediterranean.

Finally, the US was in the throes of a presidential election in which the incumbent, Dwight Eisenhower, was running on a peace ticket. He was furious that his NATO allies had launched a major campaign without even so much as informing him. The Soviet Union had responded to the aggression by threatening missile attacks on Britain, France and Israel unless the fighting stopped immediately. There was no way Eisenhower was going to risk a Third World War in support of the crude neo-colonial thrashings of his European allies.

Such was America's economic and political power, that when it backed a UN cease-fire and demanded that Britain and France do the same, they had little option but to oblige. Rather, Britain obliged and thereby forced the reluctant French to do the same. How were the mighty fallen.

The consequences of Suez

Israel

Before the start of the Suez campaign, Prime Minister Ben Gurion had dreamed of a new political order in the Middle East. Israel would conquer and assimilate all Sinai and the West Bank. Iraq would be allowed to swallow up Jordan on condition that it made peace with Israel. Egypt, crushed and humiliated, would ditch Nasser and accept Israel's peace terms. The Lebanese would follow suit. Finally, left out in the cold, Syria would be forced to do the same. Then Israel would be at peace with its neighbours behind secure and defensible frontiers.

In the face of US and Soviet hostility, the plan came to nothing. Israel was obliged to return all its conquests, although it did get a UN force (United Nations Emergency Force – UNEF) to patrol the Israel-Egypt border and a US guarantee that the Strait of Tiran would be kept open. More importantly, the flow of US aid continued unimpeded.

Within Israel the campaign was seen as a triumph. In response to Arab terrorism, the Israelis had thumped their bullying neighbour and proved they were the Middle East's superpower. Ben Gurion's philosophy of aggressive defence had triumphed over Moshe Sharett's diplomacy. The impact of this political victory would affect the politics of the Middle East for the rest of the century and beyond.

The West

The Suez campaign was an almost farcical final fling of Anglo-French imperialism. Anthony Eden resigned within weeks and the humiliated French Fourth Republic collapsed the following year. The inhabitants of Britain and France's remaining overseas colonies, noting the weakness of their masters, pressed harder for independence.

The Cold War had long been extending its icy fingers across the Middle East. Oil had brought the US into the region during the Second World War. East and West clashed in Iran immediately thereafter. By the time of Suez, the Soviets had a considerable presence in Baathist Syria. In the meantime, accepting domestic sympathy for the Israeli cause, the US had developed close economic ties with Israel. The Soviet-Egyptian arms deal had then extended Soviet influence to Israel's southern flank. When Soviet Premier, Nikolai Bulganin, threatened attacks on Britain, France and Israel, and Eisenhower responded with the 'Eisenhower Doctrine' (see page 72), the Middle East had become a major theatre of Cold War operations.

Two reservations need to be made lest we get the over-simplified impression of a US-backed Israel battling against Soviet-backed Arabs. First, the Soviet Union was an atheistic state – an anathema to Muslim Arabs. Second, several conservative Arab regimes were strongly opposed to communist or even socialist thinking. In 1956 these included the monarchies of Saudi Arabia, Jordan and Iraq, as well as small sheikhdoms like Kuwait and Oman. One reason why the politics of the Middle East were so complicated is that the Arab-Israeli conflict frequently cut across political and religious boundaries.

Egypt

The Suez War did wonders at home and abroad for President Nasser's reputation. He dismissed his military losses as insignificant. What were they compared with retention of a nationalized Suez Canal? Among Egyptians, fellow Arabs and anti-imperialists everywhere he was hailed as the underdog who had triumphed. Having successfully seen off the fading might of Britain and France, he was the undisputed leader of the Arab world.

Between the wars

Almost 11 years elapsed between the Suez War and the next major crisis in the Middle East, the Six Day War. Technically speaking, throughout this period the Arab nations were still at war with Israel, previous conflicts having been halted only by armistices. Moreover, all Israel's neighbours continued to deny its right to exist. The Saudi government was not alone in meticulously blacking out all references to the Jewish state in maps, books and articles.

In truth, however, most Arab states did not really want another large-scale armed confrontation with Israel. Politicians and generals talked about it, threatened it, even planned and postured for it – but they were unwilling to face the possibility of further defeat, loss and humiliation.

Yemen and Saudi Arabia

That a low-born army officer with links to the Soviet Union might claim leadership of the Arab world was abhorrent to the monarchies of Saudi Arabia and Jordan. The extent of this gulf was vividly illustrated when a civil war broke out in the tiny Yemen Arab Republic (North Yemen).

On one side was the country's conservative ruler, the imam; on the other were rebellious army officers. These forward-thinking young men had been trained in Egypt, where they had picked up republican and socialist ideas. King Abdulaziz having died, the Saudi government was headed by his conservative, palace-building, pleasure-seeking son Saud. Not wishing to entertain a revolutionary republic on his south-western border, he backed the imam.

The issue divided the Saudi royal family. The king's brother, Faisal, who would eventually remove his elder sibling in a palace coup, was a modernizer. He opposed the policy of supporting religious traditionalists. Such men (and they always were men in a strict Muslim society) rigorously resisted the sort of modernization, like setting up television broadcasting, that Faisal sought for Saudi Arabia.

With the Saudis divided, Nasser responded to the Yemeni rebels' request for help with 70,000 troops and a great deal of equipment. This was sufficient for them eventually to win the five-year civil war. There is a further twist to the complex tale. While the Egyptians and Saudis were still fighting a proxy war in Yemen, they found themselves on the same side in the Six Day War with Israel.

Egypt

Nasser's bid for Arab leadership received a major boost when he announced that Egypt and Syria had agreed to flout geography and history and become one country. The 1958 amalgamation was seen as the first step towards the formation of a single Arab nation. Egypt was designated the 'Southern Province' and Syria the 'Northern Province' of a United Arab Republic (UAR). Not surprisingly, after the wedding confetti had been swept away, the new partners took a long hard look at each other and realized that their marriage had been entirely about convenience and not affection, let alone love. Divorce came with yet another military coup in Syria three years later, although the Egyptians retained the grandiose UAR title for a further ten years.

Through all this, Nasser continued to make politically correct anti-Israeli noises – 'I announce from here, on behalf of the people of the United Arab Republic, that this time we will exterminate Israel' (1959) – but took no steps to turn rhetoric into reality. With UNEF guarding his Sinai frontier and economic progress funded by substantial aid from both the Soviet Union and the US, the Egyptian president had no wish to do anything that might rock his even-keeled boat.

Syria

Compared with Egypt's plain sailing, the voyage of the 'Northern Province' – Syria – was tempestuous. Colonel Faisal al-Atasi's Baath Party espoused a curious cocktail of anti-imperialism, non-alignment in the Cold War, pick-and-mix features of Islam, and socialist egalitarianism. Above all, it was authoritarian and highly centralized.

The army cashed in on popular resentment at the state of Syria's economy and its subordinate status in the UAR, and in another coup re-established Syria as an independent country. The new, nominally civilian government soon fell foul of the army Baathists who engineered yet another coup in 1963. Under the strain of all this regime change, divisions were starting to open up within the Baath Party itself. Some members remained avidly pro-Nasser, others had close links with the Baathists in neighbouring Iraq (see page 69). A third group was keen to emphasize the party's specifically Syrian nature.

All factions claimed to have the cause of Arab unity closest to their hearts. In the end, the Syrian Baath Party came out on top, crushed all opposition, set up a police state, and diverted attention from domestic affairs by vigorously playing the anti-Israeli card.

Iraq

Matters were just as chaotic in Iraq. Here, despite extensive public works provided by mounting oil revenues, the rule of King Faisal II failed to hold public support. In the eyes of the bulk of the population, joining a British-backed Baghdad Defence Pact and opposing the formation of the UAR were major political own goals. In 1958, a well-organized military coup removed the monarchy, slaughtering the king and leading members of the royal family. Power was placed in the hands of Brigadier Qasim. He survived for five years until ousted (and executed) by the Baath Party, whose influence had spread east from Syria.

Over the next few years the country was torn between ambitious army officers, passionate Pan-Arabists, socialists, and those seeking to establish stable civilian rule. The Soviet Union waded in and brought Iraq into its sphere of influence with grants of weapons and aid. Nevertheless, given its uncertain domestic situation, Iraq was in no position to do anything but shout from the sidelines during the Six Day War (see page 79).

Jordan

Amid the surrounding mayhem, the young but politically astute King Hussein of Jordan managed to cling on to power. He walked a dangerous diplomatic tightrope. At one stage he was close to a Pan-Arab union with Faisal's Iraq, at another he was maintained in office with the help of US aid ($100 million p.a. by the early 1960s) and British paratroops.

Hussein's most intractable problem was the West Bank and East Jerusalem, the territories his grandfather Abdullah had seized in the First Arab-Israeli War. As well as 400,000 new subjects, they had brought him hundreds of thousands of Palestinian refugees, and a frontier with the sworn enemy of all Arabs. It was across that frontier, snaking along the yellow-brown hills above the River Jordan, that the iron of the Israelis met the flint of the Palestinians. To Hussein's dismay, the collision generated sparks that eventually flared into war.

The Palestinians

In all this sorry saga, the Palestinians remained the losers. They were still the forgotten people, pitied by all, wanted by no one.

By the end of the Suez War, it was clear to some of them that they were unlikely to get anywhere if they left matters in other hands, specifically in those of their fellow Arabs. Despair bred resentment, and resentment bred violence.

As we have seen, guerrillas had been operating in and around Palestine for decades. The tradition continued during the early 1950s when the discredited Mufti of Jerusalem, then established in Gaza as leader of an 'All-Palestine Government', had openly urged young Palestinian Arabs to attack the Israeli usurpers of their land. The sporadic and fairly ineffective attacks of these *fedayeen* ('fanatics' or 'self-sacrificers') had been an excuse for Israel's Suez offensive.

After the 1956 war, as Nasser tightened his grip on Egypt, he clamped down on militant Palestinians as he had previously done on the Muslim Brotherhood. He did not want their enthusiasm threatening his policy of saying one thing while doing another. At the end of the decade – in events that are still, perhaps deliberately, shrouded in mystery – a group of young Palestinians gathered in British-run Kuwait (to this day no one is sure how they obtained visas) to form a new organization dedicated to the destruction of Israel and the formation of a Palestinian state. Its name was Fatah ('Victory' or 'Conquest').

Among Fatah's leaders was a Palestinian engineer and political activist who would play a key role in Middle Eastern affairs for the rest of the century and beyond. His full name was Mohammed Abdel Rahman Abdel Raouf Arafat Al Qudua Al Husseini. To the world he announced himself simply as Yasser Arafat.

Yasser Arafat

At first glance, Arafat did not have a lot going for him as a potential leader of the Palestinian nation. Although from a Palestinian family, he had been born and educated in Cairo and spoke with an Egyptian accent. He was small (1.65 m/5 ft 4 in) and any pretension to good looks was marred by bulging eyes and a protruding lower lip (these were a considerable handicap in the burgeoning age of television). What's more, Arafat was not a distinguished public speaker, tending to rant and repeat a string of ill-assorted facts, observations and exhortations. This reflected his fractured academic training.

All these drawbacks Arafat overcame with an exceptional vitality that combined passion, determination, charm and bravery. There was no better salesman in the business. When meeting Saudi Arabia's King Faisal to request money for Fatah, for instance, he might reasonably have expected the Saudis to match Kuwait's few hundred thousand dollars. In fact, Arafat came away with millions. By the mid-1960s, Fatah was by far the best funded, if not the best organized, of all the Palestinian guerrilla groups.

About Arafat's physical bravery there could be no doubt. As a student he had volunteered to fight in 1948, and in the Suez War he had served in Gaza. Once Fatah was up and running he personally participated in a number of raids. The adoption of the *kuffiya* head-dress (originally a white cloth which later changed to a chequered one), worn by the Palestinians who fought the British in the 1930s, reinforced his warrior image. So too did the assumption of the name 'Yasser' – borrowed in customary Arab style from a doughty warrior friend of the Prophet Mohammed.

To the Palestinians who eked out their existence in squalid refugee camps, Arafat came across as a fighter. He would rather die, he swore, than betray their cause. In return, they gave him their trust. Thousands of young Palestinians flocked to join Fatah. The movement armed them, trained them, filled their heads with anti-Israeli vitriol, and by the mid-1960s was using them on hundreds of pin-prick raids into Israel from bases in Jordan, Syria, Lebanon and Gaza.

Unlike the Mufti, Arafat would let himself become beholden to no Arab state or leader. He would use their territory as a base and take their money, but he would be no puppet in their political games. Shortly after receiving Saudi funds, in an extreme example of this reckless independence, he attempted to blow up the kingdom's oil pipeline to the Mediterranean. Similarly, when the first ever summit of Arab leaders, meeting in 1964, accepted Nasser's idea for an over-arching Palestine Liberation Organization (PLO) and Palestine Liberation Army (PLA), Arafat would have nothing to do with either.

Arafat saw quite clearly that Nasser needed the PLO in order to control the Palestinians and curb their guerrilla activity. Unlike the Egyptian president, Arafat eagerly sought another Arab-Israeli war. Earlier, matching the ruthlessness of his Israeli enemies, he had written, 'Violence is the only solution.' Nasser, more of a realist, accepted what Arafat would not: in open warfare the disunited Arab forces would stand little chance against the well-organized Israeli military machine. In the end, though, Arafat got his war. Nasser was proved right and the Palestinians were left in an even worse plight than before.

Arming the Middle East

There could have been no large-scale Middle East war in 1967 if the rest of the world, particularly the US and the USSR, had not armed Israel and its enemies to the teeth. Soviet arms, including sophisticated MIG fighter planes, had found their way into a number of Arab states. Egypt and Syria were the chief beneficiaries. Sometimes the weapons came direct from the USSR, sometimes via Czechoslovakia or another state belonging to the Warsaw Pact, the Soviet Union's answer to NATO.

By 1967 the forces of the Arab nations facing Israel were 50 per cent larger in terms of manpower and boasted 100 per cent more tanks and aircraft. It was such comparisons, ignoring the forces' scattered disposition and uncoordinated war plans, that persuaded Arafat and his ilk that the Arabs really could overwhelm the Israelis.

Since Israel's foundation, France and West Germany had been among its most reliable arms suppliers. France had taken on this role in order to maintain a presence in the Middle East. German assistance, which paid some 30 per cent of Israel's overseas trade deficit, came as reparation payments for the Holocaust. The hardware the West Germans provided was good, too. When US President Lyndon B. Johnson offered the Israelis American tanks in 1964, they politely replied that they would prefer German ones. The rebuff was ignored and 210 US tanks were delivered the following year, together with 48 Skyhawk bombers.

The US decision to arm Middle Eastern states came after Soviet intervention in the region at the time of Suez. Reflecting upon the crisis, President Eisenhower announced a change in US policy: henceforward his country would give economic and military aid to any Middle Eastern government that felt itself threatened by Communism. Some $200 million was allocated to this fund.

The 'Eisenhower Doctrine' led to US troops being sent to Lebanon in support of President Camille (see page 95), and to an increase in US arms and funds for Israel. President Kennedy, helped to office by the Jews of Massachusetts, also felt obliged to assist Israel. Although the State Department remained wary of falling out with oil-producing Arab states, by the time of Kennedy's death a special relationship was developing between the US and Israel.

US backing gave the Israelis a feeling of security. America, they believed, would never allow the Arabs to overwhelm them. That, and President Johnson's remark that the Israelis would 'whip the hell' out of their enemies if war came, was in the minds of the Israeli government as it contemplated a massive pre-emptive strike.

The path to war

The waters of Galilee

Israel had fought its neighbours over the waters of Lake Galilee and River Jordan since Biblical times. The issue arose again the moment the new state was founded in 1948. The US tried to find a compromise solution in the early 1950s, but Ariel Sharon's attack on Qibya so poisoned Arab-Israeli relations that the plan failed (see page 61).

Not long afterwards, the Israelis devised a bold and technically challenging scheme to pump water from the Sea of Galilee and carry it in a vast conduit the entire length of the country. After many years' work, the pumps were switched on in the summer of 1964.

Meanwhile, the Syrians had been working on counter measures. As the Israelis built their conduit, so Syria had constructed dams across two rivers feeding the Jordan. These barriers, when their sluices were closed, would divert a considerable flow of water into the Jordanian River Yarmouk, by-passing the Jordan and Sea of Galilee.

The Israelis were not amused when, as they began taking water from the Sea of Galilee, the Syrians severed the streams that fed it. For two years the new dams were regularly bombed and shelled by the Israelis, forcing the Arabs to abandon their irrigation project. When Israeli forces captured the Golan Heights in the Six Day War, the rest of the world mistakenly assumed they did so for their strategic importance. As Israeli commanders were to admit later, the true importance of the Heights was not military but economic – more specifically, aquatic.

Mounting tension

We are now in 1965. Israeli planes are attacking Syrian installations. The Golan Heights reverberate to repeated artillery exchanges. To the south and west, Arafat's Fatah are stepping up their raids into Israel, not doing great damage but increasing Israeli demands that the government of Prime Minister Levi Eshkol, Ben Gurion's successor, take firm action.

Matters are not improved when the Syrians find an Israeli spy – Eliahu Cohen – in the higher echelons of their government. He is hanged, but the fall-out of the scandal helps topple the Syrian government the following year. This brings into power a group of vigorously pro-Palestinian Baathists. Fatah, temporarily excluded by the previous regime, is welcomed back, re-occupies its bases and renews its attacks on Israel across the Syrian border.

Given the increasingly bellicose rhetoric against which this is happening, it is clear that all-out war is not far away. It will not come, however, without Egypt – and Nasser is not keen. There is little chance that Arafat and the Palestinians will be able to persuade him to change his mind.

IDF provocation

The first of two crucial Israeli actions took place towards the end of 1966. The previous months had witnessed a number of guerrilla attacks on Israel and some strong IDF reaction. Its retaliation of 13 November, however, was without precedent. In response to a terrorist bomb in Hebron that had destroyed an Israeli military vehicle, killing three soldiers and injuring a further four, a large Israeli force, including many tanks, descended on the West Bank village of Samu in broad daylight.

Reports of the massive destruction vary, but perhaps 5,000 villagers lost their homes, their clinic, school and mosque. Several were killed and injured. Jordanian forces rushing to investigate were ambushed and more than 50 of them were killed and wounded. A plane of the Royal Jordanian Air Force was shot down. Other villages in the area were badly damaged.

World opinion swung sharply against Israel. Its cruel bullying of defenceless civilians was roundly condemned by the UN Security Council. More significantly, Israel lost the confidence of King Hussein, who had come close to being overthrown in the furious rioting that followed the Samu debacle. The attack had taken place on his birthday, killing one of his friends. It was scant reward, he mused bitterly, for all his efforts to keep Fatah out of the West Bank. He wanted war with Israel no more than Nasser did, but the Israelis had to show him some respect.

With the US now wedded to Israel, it suited the Soviets to throw their weight unequivocally behind the anti-Israeli movement. While not getting anywhere with Saudi Arabia or Jordan, they had found Nasser's Egypt and Baathist Syria receptive enough to their blandishments and offers of aid. Against his better judgement, at the end of 1955 Nasser had allowed Soviet diplomats to steer him into a defensive alliance with the UAR's former 'Northern Province'.

The Egyptian premier probably believed this would enable him to dampen down Syrian war talk. In fact, the opposite occurred. Instead of pulling back his partner by the handcuffs that linked them, Nasser found himself dragged into positions he did not wish to adopt.

The second act of IDF tactless overkill – or deliberate provocation – took place the following spring. When an Israeli tractor ploughing land within the demilitarized zone between Israel and Syria was fired upon, the Israelis began an artillery duel. Shortly afterwards, Syrian Soviet-built MIGs and Israeli French-built Mirages appeared in the skies overhead. An unequal dogfight took place in which four MIGs were swiftly downed. When the rest fled inland, the Israelis followed and shot down two more within sight of the Syrian capital. The Arab male is not well equipped, either by temperament or upbringing, to accept humiliation. The air battle of 7 April 1967 was a massive humiliation for which the Syrian government and its people wanted revenge.

Soviet misinformation

At this point, the Soviets made an already dangerous situation worse by lobbing a diplomatic hand-grenade into the mêlée. Anwar Sadat, a senior Egyptian aide, was told on a visit to Moscow that Israeli forces were massing on the Syrian frontier in preparation for an invasion. The Soviets urged Nasser to take steps to assist his ally. The reason for issuing such a blatantly false report (the Egyptians saw through it straight away) remains a mystery. Explanations range from the influence of vodka to a wish to promote a Middle East war that might further embarrass the US as it was wading deeper into the Vietnam mire.

Whatever its intended purpose, the Soviet warning was Nasser's Catch 22: either act in support of his ally or massively lose face before the entire Arab world. For the self-appointed leader of the Arabs the second option did not bear thinking about. With a heavy heart, therefore, he asked the UN to withdraw the protective UNEF from part of Egypt's Sinai border with Israel. The reason was clear: if Israel attacked Syria, he would be free to launch a counter-attack from the south.

Closing the Strait

The UN, led by Secretary General U Thant, conducted a series of delicate negotiations with both Israel and Egypt. After various options had been rejected, U Thant tried calling Nasser's bluff. Instead of a partial withdrawal, UNEF was pulled back from all its positions in Sinai, Gaza and Sharm al-Sheikh, the position that guarded the narrow Strait of Tiran. The ploy failed. With UN forces out of the way at his request, Nasser felt obliged to re-occupy Sharm al-Sheikh. In May 1967 he declared the Strait of Tiran closed to Israeli ships and those of other nations carrying military supplies to Eilat. It was the Suez Crisis all over again.

Nasser backed up his action with yet another salvo of verbal aggression: 'The Jews threaten war; we tell them: Welcome! We're ready for war.' It was not really what he meant at all. The high-blown phrases and flamboyant action were a calculated gamble intended to please his Arab audience without pushing Israel over the edge. Sadly, although he knew his own people, Nasser misjudged his enemy. In the eyes of the Israeli government the closing of the Strait was tantamount to a declaration of war.

It was a war that Israel's military establishment had sought, too. They wanted defensible frontiers; they wanted the land they had taken 11 years earlier but had been forced to abandon; they wanted to show their enemies once and for all that the humble, meek, subservient Jew was a creature of the past.

The Soviet Union threatened retaliation if Egypt were attacked. King Hussein of Jordan flew to Cairo and made a defensive pact with Nasser. Other Arab nations expressed solidarity. Nevertheless, US President Lyndon B. Johnson stood by Israel – he had little choice when American public opinion was united in hatred of the 'Hitler of the Nile'. Even so, Johnson continued negotiations, although with little hope of a successful outcome.

'They're going to go,' he said of the Israelis. 'Yes they're going to hit. There's nothing we can do about it.' He was particularly fearful of what the Soviets might do if their client states were hard pressed.

In Israel the mood was tense. 'Live or perish' was the watchword. Perhaps reluctantly, Prime Minister Eshkol was carried along with the nationalistic tide and handed the post of Minister of Defence to the piratical militarist Moshe Dayan. The cabinet knew that Nasser had no intention of starting the fighting. His hostile words, though, were enough to lead the outside world to believe that he might. What was needed, therefore, was an Israeli 'anticipatory counteroffensive' – doublespeak for an attack.

At 7.45 a.m. on Monday, 5 June 1967 the Israelis launched an offensive of Blitzkrieg dimensions. By lunchtime the war was as good as won.

06

divisions and developments 1967–73

This chapter will cover:
- the course and consequences of the Third Arab-Israeli War
- the Arab world 1968–73
- the rise of Palestinian militancy
- the causes and course of the Fourth Arab-Israeli War.

The Six Day War

Israel's victory in the Six Day War of June 1967 was one of the most startling in modern military history. As with the first two Arab-Israeli wars, however, it is important to separate the myth from the reality. The map (Figure 5, page 81) shows a tiny Israel surrounded by vast expanses of Arab-held territory: surely this time Goliath would crush the puny David?

But Israel was not a puny David. By 1967 it was more an outpost of the West. The governments and people of the US, France and West Germany sustained, armed and guarded it. Israel was a state created by war and preserved by war. It had been fighting in one form or another since its inception, often as the aggressor. Its commanders knew exactly what they were doing. If they called for war, as they did in 1967, it was because they knew they would win.

The air assault

The war began with a massive unannounced Israeli air strike against Egypt, Jordan and Syria. Its purpose was to gain immediate air superiority by destroying as many enemy planes as possible while they were still on the ground. The mission's success was almost total.

Taken utterly by surprise, the Arabs lost 189 planes in 80 minutes. In all, 393 of their 416 aircraft were destroyed and Israeli air space was never once penetrated. Virtually the entire Jordanian and Egyptian air forces were wiped out, and those of Iraq and Syria rendered ineffective.

The Israelis cynically insisted, falsely, that their strikes had been in retaliation for threatening Arab moves. The aggressors, intent on a massive land-grab, also kept the extent of their success secret. The last thing they wanted was for the watching world to pressure them into an early cease-fire. The general mood in the US, the most important spectator, was one of admiration for 'plucky little Israel'. Memories of Pearl Harbor had apparently long since faded.

The Sinai campaign

The rapid Israeli advance across the Sinai towards the Suez Canal and Sharm al-Sheikh was more target practice than war. Deprived of air cover, in the barren terrain Egyptian tanks, guns, vehicles and troops were sitting ducks for Israeli warplanes laden with cannon shell, high explosives and terrifying napalm bombs.

In little over three days Sinai was in Israeli hands. They had destroyed 80 per cent of the equipment of the Egyptian army, including about 700 tanks. Up to 11,500 Egyptian soldiers had been killed, many incinerated by napalm. The Israelis lost about 300 troops and 60 tanks. Nasser, his reputation in tatters, had little option but to accept a cease-fire on 8 June.

Jordan

King Hussein of Jordan requested a cease-fire the moment he knew what had happened to his air force. Resistance, he knew, would mean merely slaughter. The Israelis rejected his plea and overcame the West Bank and East Jerusalem in three days.

The West Bank was put under military occupation while East Jerusalem was swiftly joined with its counterpart in the west and incorporated into the state of Israel. Palestinian homes were flattened and their occupants driven out to make way for Israeli settlers.

Syria

After destroying its capacity to fight in the air, Israel left Syria alone while it concentrated on its more southerly targets. For their part, the Syrians made no move. However, by the time the Israelis were ready to shift their campaign to the north and make an attempt on the Golan Heights, the UN was waking up to what was happening and demanded that hostilities stop immediately.

Soviet Prime Minister Alexei Kosygin made the new Kremlin-White House hot line glow red with his threats and denunciations. President Johnson, who had enough on his plate with the Vietnam debacle, urged the Israelis to comply with the wishes of the international community. Further conquest, he warned, might force the Soviets to intervene militarily.

But the Israelis had not quite finished. They wanted the Golan Heights with their precious water supply. Outrageously, to prevent the US learning that their attack on Syria would be unprovoked, they attacked and rendered inoperative the US intelligence-gathering vessel USS Liberty that was patrolling in the Mediterranean. It was all a 'sad accident' they explained to their unconvinced paymaster. Deeply embarrassed, President Johnson had the incident hushed up. His most important unofficial ally had all but sunk an American warship, killing and wounding 205 of its crew – and no one outside the US Navy or the Pentagon knew.

With the US blind and deaf to reality, the IDF made up an excuse to attack Syria and overran the Golan Heights in two days. As many as 115,000 refugees fled the region. With US and Soviet warships on a collision course in the Mediterranean, a cease-fire came just in time.

figure 5 Israel's borders after the Six Day War

The consequences of war

Israel's gains

The war had cost the lives of perhaps 20,000 Arabs and 766 Israelis. In six days of fighting the latter had captured the entire West Bank, Sinai (closing the Suez Canal again) and the Golan Heights. This more than doubled the amount of territory they controlled. It did not increase the size of Israel itself by much because, of the land it had captured, only East Jerusalem was officially assimilated. The rest was simply occupied.

The reason for this was straightforward. Although some 323,000 more Palestinians had become refugees, in the West Bank alone more than twice that number had not fled or been driven out and so were now under Israeli governance. If their land became part of Israel and they were given the vote, the Palestinian Arabs would gain sufficient political power to threaten the concept of the Zionist state. On the other hand, if the Israelis absorbed the conquered territories but denied the inhabitants political rights, they would be guilty of apartheid.

No progress

The war had settled nothing apart from giving the Israelis what they believed were more defensible frontiers. This was purely a military matter because neither the 1948–9 frontiers nor the new 1967 ones had been enshrined in international treaty. They had been declared unilaterally and therefore were still theoretically open to negotiation. The Palestinians, inside Israel and without, remained an unwanted, stateless people.

As the Arabs were still technically at war with Israel, they continued to deny its existence. Armed with thick black pens, armies of clerks all over the Middle East went on scrubbing out Israel from all imported books, maps, magazines and brochures. Their superiors refused to accept that resultant blotches only made the reader more aware of the censored enemy.

Total Israeli victory and total Arab humiliation was no recipe for negotiation. US President Richard Nixon's Secretary of State, William Rogers, hoped otherwise and tried unsuccessfully to persuade the Israelis to accept a land for peace deal as outlined in UN Resolution 242 (see page 83). In 1970, Nixon responded by handing the situation over to Henry Kissinger, his national security advisor.

Instead of trying to bring Arabs and Israelis together, Kissinger's prime concern was to keep Soviet influence in the Middle East to a minimum. To this end, he believed that the best Middle East policy for the US was preservation of the status quo. He hoped that this would show the Arabs that, as had happened to Egypt and Syria in 1967, friendship with the Soviet Union could offer no lasting benefit and might even bring disaster. All forms of US support for Israel grew appreciably.

As we will see, Kissinger's policy was only partly successful. By failing to support peace moves, particularly that of Anwar Sadat, he unwittingly promoted yet another war.

Resolution 242

After months of discussion, in November 1967 the United Nations Security Council agreed Resolution 242 as a framework for solving the Arab-Israeli situation. At its heart was the concept of land for peace. It also said that it was illegal to obtain land by war, and that each nation in the region had the right to live at peace within secure boundaries. Finally, it called for a 'just settlement' of the problem of Palestinian refugees.

Land for peace would, years later, form the basis of Arab-Israeli agreements. For the time being, though, the balance of power between the two sides was too uneven for progress. Moreover, Resolution 242 did nothing for the Palestinians, who rejected it out of hand. This heralded one of the major changes in the Middle East situation over the next 15 years: the gradual collapse of Pan-Arabism and the increase of Palestinian nationalism as the main threat to Israel's security.

Enter Sadat and Assad

The Six Day War dampened down talk of 'liberating' the Palestinians. Humiliation in three wars had proved that the Arab states were simply not militarily strong enough to tackle Israel. Instead, the rhetoric of Arab governments tended to reflect what had always been the reality – that national self-interest came before all else.

Egypt

Of all the Arab countries, Nasser's Egypt had suffered most. Its army and air force had been annihilated, it had lost vast swathes of territory, and the potentially remunerative Suez Canal remained closed. Most significant of all was the damage done to Nasser's personal credibility as leader of the Arab world. When great words are followed by feeble actions, the audience is not inclined to heed the speaker a second time.

Because the Israelis wished continually to remind the Egyptians of their inferiority, and because Nasser wished to show that he had lost a campaign but not the war, in 1968 a fresh 'War of Attrition' began between the two countries. Fought in a spasmodic manner across the Suez Canal, it led to heavy casualties on both sides before being brought to a halt in 1970. While it was in progress the Soviets rebuilt Egypt's armed forces with modern technology, including powerful SAM 3 anti-aircraft missiles, and even permitted Soviet pilots to fly Egyptian jets against Israeli aircraft.

Nasser died of a heart attack in 1970. He was greatly mourned in the Arab world. Despite the disaster of 1967, he more than anyone had worked to ensure that the Arab peoples were respected beyond the Middle East. He was no dictator, and behind occasionally bombastic speech lay a heart that genuinely cared for the welfare of his people.

The same might be said of Nasser's successor, Anwar Sadat, although he did not go in for the same hyperbolic rhetoric. He was a thinker and a realist – during the Second World War he had even flirted with the Nazis in the hope that they would drive the British from Egypt. Shortly after coming to power he offered Israel a peace treaty on the basis of Resolution 242. Prime Minister Golda Meir and her cabinet thought about the suggestion then rejected it outright. So did the US.

When vice-president to Nasser, Sadat had not been taken seriously at home or abroad. He now set about raising and improving his profile. First he began undoing Nasser's cramping socialism. Then, as we have seen, he made overtures of peace towards Israel. When these were rejected, fed up with the level of support offered by the Soviets, he ended Egypt's partnership with them and ordered their advisors from the country.

Sadat made little headway in improving the unresponsive Egyptian economy. Discontent was widespread. Despite initial failures, the president was sure that the answer to all his country's problems was a permanent and lasting peace with Israel. This would enable him to divert millions of dollars from the military to schemes of more obvious benefit. But with Israel unwilling to talk and the US, thanks to Kissinger, happy to let things rest as they were, what was Sadat to do? With his patience running out, he came up with a desperate plan to prove that Israel was not the invincible military behemoth everyone believed it to be.

Syria

Not surprisingly, military defeat and loss of territory had undermined yet another Syrian government. The coup came in 1970 when the minister of defence, Hafiz Assad, quietly removed the government and inaugurated a series of measures that led to his election as president the following year.

Assad's early training as a night fighter pilot ideally suited his style of rule. A member of the Shia minority Alawite community, he remained largely in the dark, an unseen, low-profile figure who pulled the strings of power with total ruthlessness. In this he was not unlike his Israeli opponents, except that his aim was different. Above all, the unsmiling dictator sought to remain in power. After that came recovery of the Golan Heights, the expansion of Syrian power, and the crushing of Israel. When Sadat cut his links with the Soviet Union, Assad was content to become the Soviet's primary client state in the region. It was not communism that appealed to him but arms.

Palestine militant

The Six Day War and UN Resolution 242 marked a major turning point in the history of the Palestinian people. Divided between exile, crowded refugee camps and a stateless life in the occupied territories, they now knew for certain that there was little or no chance of fellow Arabs coming to their rescue. If anything was to be done, they had to do it themselves.

Palestinian organizations

It is estimated that in 1970 there were at least 30 Palestinian groups operating in Jordan alone. A few were independent; most were backed by one or more Arab states or by an outside power such as the Soviet Union or Communist China. Many were infiltrated by the Israelis, the CIA or both.

The leading Palestinian, Yasser Arafat, was unable (or, some say, unwilling) to provide a centralized leadership. He made matters still more complex by founding a Muslim splinter group of his own – Islamic Fatah. The confusing diversity and complexity goes a long way to explaining why the Palestinians rarely spoke with one voice or followed a consistent strategy. For this particular failing Arafat was primarily responsible.

The Palestinian umbrella organization was the PLO, established in 1964 under Egyptian auspices to co-ordinate Palestinian activities. It had a president, a legislature (the Palestine National Council), a charter and, in 1968, the Palestine Liberation Army. Before the 1967 war it had been very much in the pocket of its Arab League paymasters. Thereafter it took a more distinctively Palestinian line. Yasser Arafat was elected PLO chairman in 1969.

Fatah was Yasser Arafat's guerrilla organization that had been in existence since the late 1950s. Based in Damascus, it operated mainly out of Syria, Jordan and Lebanon. Following Arab humiliation in the Six Day War, the next year it gained considerable prestige by the way it fought off an IDF attack on Karameh, Fatah's Jordanian headquarters. By 1970 Fatah was the largest and wealthiest of the Palestinian organizations, dominating the PLO.

Al Sa'iqah ('Thunderbolt') was a small Syrian socialist guerrilla group established in 1968. The Popular Front for the Liberation of Palestine (PFLP), led by the uncompromising Marxist George Habash, attacked Israel and Western interests in general from the late 1960s onwards. It specialized in aircraft hi-jacking and rejected all negotiation with Israel ('that lap dog of capitalist imperialists') or its supporters. The Democratic Front for the Liberation of Palestine (DFLP) was an extreme left-wing political movement established by the Jordanian Christian Marxist Naif Hawatmeh. It worked with the PLO and by the 1970s was engaging in particularly indiscriminate acts of terrorism.

Black September

In the late 1960s, Arafat and other Palestinian leaders took a two-pronged approach. They continued the guerrilla attacks on Israel while at the same time building up a sense of Palestinian nationhood by providing schools, clinics, training centres and other practical assistance. The Israelis rejected out of hand

Arafat's serious proposal that Israel and the occupied territories should become a single, secular, democratic state. In fact, Israel refused even to recognize the PLO, dubbing it an illegal terrorist organization.

Nor was King Hussein of Jordan enamoured of the PLO and its multifarious branches. He disapproved of their left-wing politics and their refusal to contemplate accord with Israel. Most of all, he objected to their lawless ways within Jordan. They have been described as a state within a state. More accurately, they resembled malcoordinated gangs of armed ruffians who terrorized, raped and pillaged the local population. Thousands were killed in regular clashes between Palestinian militants and the Jordanian army.

At one stage Hussein tried to bring the Palestinians on side by offering to make Arafat his prime minister. The PLO chairman was flabbergasted. Prime minister? Run a government? Non-plussed by the offer and alarmed by the thought of respectable and accountable responsibility, he turned it down. Compromise rejected, the king determined to bring the Palestinians to heel by less delicate means.

Arafat knew Hussein despised him. Nevertheless, he felt that Assad's Syrian and Iraqi forces still based in Jordan would come to his aid if there was a showdown. The crisis came in September 1970.

The PFLP hi-jacked four Western airliners. One was blown up at Cairo, the other three were flown to Aman where they too were eventually destroyed. The passengers were subjected to a crash course of lectures in Palestinian politics, but were physically unharmed. The purpose of the hi-jackings was to free captive Palestinians in an exchange and draw the world's attention to the Palestinian cause.

For Hussein this was the last straw. Using his capital's airport for anti-Western terrorist activities – and even renaming it in the process – was totally unacceptable. Either he or the whole rag-bag of Palestinian activists had to go. The king declared martial law, stopped all rights of political expression and sent in the army. Arafat called for Hussein to be deposed and the Palestinians to lead the revolution.

The fighting was tough. Reinforced with some deserters from the Jordanian army, at first the Palestinians were on top. The Iraqis did not get involved, however, and advancing Syrian armour was swiftly recalled when the US and Israel made it clear that it would not reach Aman intact.

By the end of the month ('Black September' in Palestinian parlance) the Palestinians had been defeated. Arafat and some 4,000 supporters eventually made their way to Lebanon, where they would cause even greater civil upheaval (see Chapter 7). The PLO leader himself claimed to have fled Jordan in disguise. The Jordanian authorities said they knew all along who he was and where he was headed. They were only too delighted to see the back of him. The whole unsavoury incident reflected badly on Arafat, the Palestinian militants and the Arab world as a whole.

Sadat's patience runs out

Terrorism and counter-terrorism

As after previous wars, there were those in the Israeli establishment who believed that after the 1967 conflict the security of their land depended on constantly reminding the Arabs that Israel was all-powerful. Their political spokesperson was Menachem Begin, while in the military they were best represented by the ruthless Ariel Sharon. As far as this duo was concerned, Israel should never hand back any of the land it had taken in the Six Day War.

Prime Minister Golda Meir, who had replaced Eshkol in 1969, was more moderate. Heading a conservative Labour coalition (because of the country's proportional electoral system, all Israeli governments were coalitions), Meir felt that Israel should keep hold of Gaza and East Jerusalem, but that there might be room for negotiation over other occupied areas. This division in Israeli ranks was in part due to the pressures ordinary Israelis felt at living in a land constantly under siege.

The feeling of siege arose from continual terrorist attacks. These, as always, drew massive reprisals. Sharon was the foremost exponent of these, 'thinning out' Palestinian refugee camps, clearing away Arabs to make way for Jewish settlements and, on occasion destroying entire villages. The devastation of the Syrian village of Dail in January 1973, for instance, left an estimated 500 dead.

The previous September, Fatah had carried out its most daring mission. The motive was Arafat's desire to raise the profile of his group after recent headline-grabbing PFLP missions. His target was the Munich Olympic Games, about as high profile a target as one could get. Like many of Arafat's projects, the attempt to take Israeli athletes hostage was poorly planned and bungled in operation. Eleven Israelis and five Fatah terrorists were killed. In the predictably terrifying IDF reprisals perhaps 500 Palestinians, Syrians and Lebanese lost their lives. Neither side came out of the episode with their reputation enhanced.

The Arab plan

Without drawing attention to what was going on, Sadat had rebuilt Egypt's armed forces. In particular, his anti-aircraft defences could now cover an area extending 16 km (10 miles) beyond the Suez Canal. Simultaneously, the Soviets had been pouring arms into Syria, giving Assad's army a considerable but unnoticed tank advantage on the Golan Heights. Golda Meir's government, on the other hand, could not believe that the Arabs posed a real threat. Certainly Israeli intelligence, normally so efficient, had reported nothing alarming.

In the south, Israeli confidence was based on a gigantic wall of sand, steel and concrete topped with blockhouses. This supposedly insurmountable 'Bar Lev' ran for 160 km (100 miles) beside the Suez Canal. To make doubly sure, the Israelis were ready to pump oil into the canal and set light to it, producing an impassable barrier of fire. Egyptian engineers studied the problem carefully. Yes, they informed their president, they could almost certainly tackle both the firewall and the Bar.

Sadat was not looking to recapture Sinai, let alone march to Jerusalem. All he wanted was a symbolic victory to show the world that the Israelis were not invincible. Then, he believed, a realistic negotiated peace might be possible. Assad, with whom Sadat made a secret military pact, had much narrower aims. He wanted to retake the Golan Heights. He had been Syria's defence minister at the time of their capture, and was eager to expiate this slur on his manhood.

The Fourth Arab-Israeli War

The synchronized Egyptian-Syrian attack began on 6 October 1973. This was the Jewish holiday of Yom Kippur. For once, surprise was with the Arabs. Egyptian frogmen blocked the pipes through which oil was to be pumped into the canal. High-pressure hoses blasted away sufficient sand from the Bar Lev for

Egyptian tanks to storm through. Above, Soviet-made anti-aircraft missiles downed scores of Israeli aircraft attempting to halt the advance.

In just over two days the Israelis lost 500 tanks and 49 planes, and a despairing Dayan told his prime minister, 'We are heading for a catastrophe.' For the first time, Arab forces had inflicted a major defeat upon the Israelis. 'You have made us all proud,' King Faisal of Saudi Arabia told a smiling Egyptian premier.

Sadat, his point made, would have been happy to end the war there and then. Unfortunately for him, his ally Assad had fared less well. After significant initial advances, his forces were being driven back down the Damascus road. To help him, Sadat ordered an advance beyond the screen of the air defences. The result was a predictable slaughter as superior Israeli aircraft shot up unprotected men and armour.

When the fighting began, Iraq sent 20,000 men to Syria. Jordan, Kuwait, Morocco, Algeria and Saudi Arabia sent only token forces to the front. The PLA, though not under Arafat's command, had operated on both fronts. More significantly, the US and the USSR swiftly reinforced their respective sides.

US President Richard Nixon assisted Israel despite a warning from King Faisal that the Arab oil-producing states might be forced to impose an oil embargo on states supporting Israel. This became a reality when Nixon went further and gifted Israel a staggering $2.2 billion. He had to make sure Israel could defend itself without having to resort to nuclear weapons. The Israeli nuclear capability, though never used, always hung ominously over Middle East crises.

Sharon had now rallied the southern Israeli forces and was planning to cross the canal into Africa. The manoeuvring of a gigantic bridge into position was poorly handled and in the end only a comparatively small number of Israeli tanks made it to the other side. Here they met with stiff Egyptian resistance. Meanwhile, Sadat had admitted that he could not fight the Israelis and the United States together and accepted a cease-fire.

The Israelis broke the agreement, repeatedly. Soviet leader Leonid Brezhnev called for a UN peace-keeping force, provided by himself, to stand between the opposing armies. Nixon refused to accept Soviet troops in the Middle East. The nuclear arsenals of the two superpowers were put on alert. Fortunately, before anyone could press the button, a compromise solution was agreed. Troops were not needed as United Nations' observers would monitor the cease-fire outlined in Resolution 338.

Once again, a Middle East crisis had threatened to plunge the world into nuclear catastrophe. This time all concerned – Americans, Russians, Israelis and Arabs – were keen that it should not happen again. The conditions for a settlement were much more favourable, too. In defeating the Israelis on the battlefield, albeit temporarily, and bringing the West to its knees with the oil embargo, the Arabs had finally won the right to be taken seriously.

The oil weapon

On 17 October 1973, the Organization of Petroleum Exporting Countries (OPEC), a mostly Arab group, raised the price of crude oil by 70 per cent. At the same time it cut production by 25 per cent and banned all sale of its products to the US and the Netherlands (prominent supporters of Israel). Scarcity sent oil prices even higher. In 1972 a barrel of crude oil had cost $3.00. By the end of the following year, the price had risen to $18.00.

The effect was devastating, far greater than OPEC had anticipated. Most obviously, there was a worldwide oil shortage. British industry was put on a three-day week to save fuel. Many Western nations imposed speed limits on their roads to cut the consumption of petrol and diesel. Filling stations ran dry and long queues formed outside those still operating. There were reports from the US of angry motorists shooting each other as they fought for a place in the line.

The global economy stagnated. Unemployment soared as many countries went into recession. Inflation, caused by rapid price rises, hit at the same time. The resultant 'stagflation' caused widespread misery, hitting the poor hardest. It was a full ten years before the worldwide recession finally lifted. By then the West had made considerable efforts to diversify its sources of energy, developing nuclear power and exploiting oilfields of its own, such as those in Alaska and the North Sea.

Political reaction

OPEC's use of the oil weapon presented the West, and the US in particular, with a tricky dilemma. For many years they had maintained close ties with Saudi Arabia because it controlled an estimated 30 per cent of the world's oil deposits. But there had always been those who had questioned this friendship because of the Saudis' domestic tyranny and support of Palestinian terrorism. This problem was now dragged into sharper focus.

By and large Western governments turned a blind eye to what was going on within oil-producing countries like Saudi Arabia, claiming that a state's domestic affairs were its own responsibility. At the same time, they were liberal in their criticism of what was going on inside Communist states. One rule for the rich ... That said, the oil crisis did make Kissinger's Middle Eastern policy of upholding the status quo no longer realistic. OPEC action might not have helped the Palestinians (it was hardly intended to help them, anyway), but it did initiate the process that eventually produced a lasting peace in some areas.

The image of the Arab

The world's image of the Arab had undergone a dramatic make-over. OPEC action made oil-producing states even more fabulously rich than they had been before. Millionaires, whose fathers had herded camels and whose mothers had been born in a tent, wore their robes with pride as they were driven around Western cities in vast limousines, buying up property and funding all kinds of commercial enterprise.

The Saudi oil minister, Sheikh Ahmed Yamani, was lampooned in some areas of the Western press as a highwayman who demanded 'Yamani [Your money] or your life.' The irony behind the jest was that it was true. Love them or hate them, the Arabs mattered.

One story illustrates well the power of the new image. A small, run-down seaside town in Britain wished to boost its economy by developing its port. Capital for the project was hard to find. The enterprise needed a sponsor, someone whose participation would assure others that the idea was sound. Enter an actor in a chauffeur-driven car, wearing Arab clothes. He emerged at the port, was shown around the site, chatted to officials, smiled, nodded, and was driven off again. Immediately the rumour mill started running: an Arab billionaire was backing the project. Before long sufficient funds were found for work to begin.

On a more solemn note, back in the Middle East the oil crisis widened two significant rifts. One was between the oil-producing states and the rest; the other was between those who embraced the Western-style liberal secularism that came with prosperity and those who adhered to the more puritanical ways of Islamic fundamentalism. From these twin chasms dragons would soon emerge to plague the ravaged Middle East still further.

07

Lebanon bleeds

This chapter will cover:
- the gradual erosion of Lebanese stability during the 1960s and early 1970s
- the Lebanese civil war
- Israel's invasion of Lebanon, the expulsion of the PLO and the refugee camp massacres
- Lebanon's slow recovery in recent years.

Uneasy peace

We saw in earlier chapters how Lebanon was created when the French divided up the Ottoman province of Syria after the First World War. The ancient Syrian links are important for they have re-emerged to play a major part in Lebanese history since 1945. We also saw how the country's constitution, linked with an inter-community power-sharing agreement, enabled the diverse but comparatively prosperous little state to weather the storms that beset so much of the Middle East after the Second World War.

During the 1950s, President Camille Chamoun fell foul of his Arab neighbours for Lebanon's perceived pro-Western, pro-Israeli stance. The political acumen of General Chehab, commander of the Lebanese army and, perhaps, the short-lived appearance of US marines prevented serious unrest. Chehab then took over the premiership. Under his presidency and that of his successor the country's stability held, enabling it to prosper as a vigorous entrepôt and financial centre serving the entire region.

'Welcome to Beirut,' declared a young Lebanese greeting a Western visitor in 1973. 'Our city is the Paris of the Middle East. Everyone is happy here. We have open minds and tolerate everything.' A charming city Beirut might have been, but not everyone was happy and minds were closing fast. Barely two years later the place had become hell on earth.

Sources of instability

The key to Lebanon's stability was harmonious relations between the Christian and Muslim communities. More specifically, it meant the country's four main socio-religious groups – Christians, Druze, Sunnis and Shia – sharing power. Tragically, the conditions allowing this to continue had been gradually breaking down.

Rapid urbanization had led to 40 per cent of the population living in the Beirut conurbation. This had widened the gap between the largely Muslim countryside and the urban Christians. In Beirut itself the separate ethnic and religious communities lived in distinct quarters. When trouble did flare up, the security services were notoriously heavy-handed.

Lebanon refused to join the Arab cause against Israel in the Six Day War of 1967 and the Yom Kippur War of 1973. The decision had led to hostility towards Lebanon in the Arab world, and within the country towards the Christian minority (40 per cent of the total population) that controlled the most influential positions. Among the Christians, the Maronites (about 23 per cent of the total population) were particularly prominent. There was talk of secret agreements between the Christians and Israelis. Ironically, the opposite was true: unbeknown to the Lebanese, Ben Gurion and Dayan had actually talked of invading Lebanon and dismembering it.

The influx of around 270,000 Palestinian refugees, driven out by war and Israeli policy, had greatly added to Lebanon's difficulties. By 1973, ten per cent of those living in the country were Palestinian. Some had done well. For example, the country's largest construction company, CCC, was Palestinian owned. The majority, however, were poor and landless. They shared many of the same grievances as the impoverished rural Muslims.

Then came Black September, bringing the PLO leadership and their many followers from Jordan (see pages 86–7). They came with weapons, their own organization and, above all, an independent, aggressive attitude. To many Lebanese, especially the Christians, they were unwelcome swaggerers. Just as in Jordan, they were a law unto themselves, collecting taxes, setting up road blocks and generally behaving as if they owned the place. In Beirut it was made worse by plentiful money and the city's cosmopolitan, easy-going atmosphere. The PLO bureaucracy became huge and corrupt – some of its workers grew rich by selling arms to the Christians. Arafat kept PLO accounts in a small notebook in his jacket pocket. He even found time in his life for women. It was all a long way from the rugged simplicity of Fatah's early years.

The chaotic reality of Beirut did not match the outside world's image of the PLO. The international profile of Arafat and his organization was rising. For some years Arafat had been playing down his terrorist image and presenting himself as a peacemaker. Although the change cut little ice with the US administration, elsewhere it bore fruit. A PLO plan for solving the Palestine-Israel problem by the creation of two states was generally well received. In 1974 an Arab League summit at Rabat declared the PLO to be 'the sole legitimate representative of the Palestinian people'. Later that year Arafat addressed the United Nations and the following year the PLO was given UN observer status (see Chapter 8).

By a previous agreement signed in Cairo, the Lebanese government had given the PLO virtually a free hand in organizing the Palestinians in southern Lebanon – as long as it did not interfere in national politics. However, Palestinian attacks across the border into Israel, drawing heavy Israeli responses, inevitably involved the Lebanese government. The PLO's help with local medical, educational and other facilities also gave it political status. Its natural ally was the Lebanese National Movement (LNM). Led by Kamal Jumblatt, this was a largely Shia party dedicated to improving the lot of the impoverished Muslim majority.

The spring of 1975 found the confrontation between the country's militia groups growing rapidly. Apart from the non-sectarian Lebanese army and the PLO, the most prominent military-political organization was the Christian Phalange. The motto of these inflexible, European-orientated and right-wing paramilitaries was 'God, the Fatherland, and the Family'. Regarding themselves as descendants of the ancient Phoenicians, not Arabs, the Phalange strongly rejected Pan-Arabism and hated the PLO. Their 10,000-strong militia was well armed and ruthless.

The story of the many horrifying conflicts that tore Lebanon apart in the last quarter of the twentieth century is indescribably complex. Furthermore, the nation's deep wounds are still not fully healed, so history merges with politics. The narrative that follows, therefore, is by necessity much simplified. It is also based on current thinking and knowledge, factors that may well change with the perspective of time.

Civil war

The horror of war

Arguments about who was responsible for the outbreak of the civil war persist to this day. The conflict did not start suddenly. Rather, Lebanon slid into war: the fishermen of Sidon went on strike; clashes with the authorities turned violent; Maronites fired on Palestinians, Palestinians fired on Maronites; the PLO joined with the LNM after a Maronite attack on refugees; the Phalange of Bashir Gemayel clashed with the Phalange of his brother Amir; Sunni fought Shia fought Druze. By May 1975, Lebanon was in total, bloody chaos.

One story among many illustrates the random, senseless nature of the killing. Christian militiamen were in the habit of stopping cars to check whether they were carrying Palestinians. As forged papers were easy to acquire, they set the occupants the language test. 'What is red and juicy and eaten with salad?' The terrified interogatee replied 'tomato'. If they did so using the Lebanese word, 'banadoura', they were allowed to go free. If they said 'bandoura', the Palestinian version of the word, they were instantly killed, or worse.

Central government collapsed and local warbands imposed what order they could. Arms poured into the country from around the world, particularly from Syria and Israel. The factions stockpiled sophisticated weaponry like rocket launchers and artillery as well as the rifles and grenades by the container load. There had never been a civil war like it. The firepower in daily use was awesome, terrifying. Thousands of Lebanese fled abroad. Dwellings were shattered, businesses wrecked, communications cut. Around 70,000 people lost their lives, most of them innocent civilians.

Foreign players

Many governments kept a close eye on the Lebanese situation. A significant number intervened with arms and money, some in a most unexpected way. The majority of the Arab oil producers, for instance, aided the Christians because they feared the Communist leanings of some Palestinians. Israel and the CIA also helped the Christians. Iraq supported the PLO.

No one watched what was going on more closely than Syria's president Assad. Until the end of 1975 he gave support to Muslim groups, mainly the LNM-PLO. By early the next year he was having doubts: if the Muslims won, as now seemed likely, Lebanon would either be divided or become a left-leaning state dominated by the PLO. Neither situation would be acceptable to Israel, which would certainly intervene.

To prevent this happening, Assad switched support to the Christians. This produced the extraordinary situation of Israel and Syria – sworn enemies and still technically at war – both backing the same side in a civil war on their borders. Assad received US assurance that the Israelis would not object, and sent 20,000 Syrian troops into Lebanon from the east. To the west, Israeli warships blockaded the coast and reinforced their strong links with Bashir Gemayel.

The Lebanese civil war sounded the death knoll of Pan-Arabism. It presented a most distressing image of Arabs to the outside world. Moreover, it played into the hands of Israel, giving it ample excuse to expand its northern frontier if considered expedient. Finally, the civil war was being exploited by Assad. At a time when he was vying with Egypt for leadership of the Arab world, it enabled him to pose as a defender of Muslims and a peacemaker.

Eventually, acting on a Saudi-Kuwaiti-Egyptian initiative, a cease-fire was agreed. Very roughly, the Muslims (LNM-PLO) and Druze were left controlling the south. Until his assassination the following year, Jumblatt was their overall political leader. The north was in Christian hands. A 'Green Line' ran through the centre of Beirut dividing the Christian east from the Muslim west, and 30,000 Arab League troops, mostly Syrian, patrolled as peacekeepers.

Israeli intervention

Incomplete cease-fire

The cease-fire agreed in October 1976 brought a reduction in the violence but not its complete cessation. The Phalange were still under arms, as was the LNM, and clashes between them and smaller groups persisted. Syrian forces remained in the country, too. In the north and in East Beirut Bashir Gemayel had combined most Maronite groups to form a fiefdom of his own. He was happy to receive Israeli support.

Operation Litani

The PLO's strength was predominately in the south of the country. After the Lebanese civil war it had increased its governmental role, using some of the funds provided by supportive states and organizations to help restore electricity, water and communications in areas shattered by the conflict. The less corrupt PLO operatives also sought to build for a better future by expanding the network of schools and medical clinics in Palestinian areas. Furthermore, Arafat had agreed with the Lebanese and Syrian governments to cut back on Palestinian attacks on Israel (the Shtaura Accord). Despite his poor organizational ability, Arafat was trying to put forward the PLO as a viable government for a separate Palestine.

This tied in with three developments beyond Arafat's control, two alarming, one potentially favourable. The former were the growing accord between Egypt and Israel (see Chapter 8), and the election of Menachem Begin as Israel's prime minister (1977). This ex-Irgun commander now headed the Likud Front, a right-wing, nationalist coalition. These two setbacks were to some extent balanced by the election of Democrat Jimmy Carter to the US presidency in 1976. One of his first actions was to declare himself in favour of a 'Palestinian homeland'.

Arafat's state-building efforts with the PLO were a total anathema to Begin. Like its Labour predecessor, the Likud government maintained pressure on the PLO by constant and fairly indiscriminate cross-border attacks. These were not just retaliatory. Rather, in the light of the PLO's restraint, they were intended to be provocative. (The Israelis themselves called them 'preventative' – rather like the Anglo-American invasion of Iraq in 2003. See page 198.) The Israeli government did not want the PLO quiescent – it wanted it removed, disbanded, liquidated. It therefore sought to provoke PLO attacks on Israel as an excuse for further missions of its own.

Arafat was never consistent, nor did he have control over all Palestinian terrorist activity. In March 1978, an 11-man Fatah hit squad made their way down the coast and landed near Haifa. They had intended to reach Tel Aviv and were confused by their surroundings. In due course, finding the main road between Haifa and the capital, they decided to make the most of their opportunity. Their attack on a bus left 37 dead and a further 78 injured.

This was just the excuse Begin needed. He ordered the IDF to advance into southern Lebanon and destroy the PLO bases there. Arafat led the resistance in person, fighting, as he always did, with immense bravery. It was to no avail. Two thousand people were killed, almost all of them Palestinians and Lebanese. Around one quarter of a million people were rendered homeless. Operation Litani, as it was called, established a security zone south of the River Litani patrolled by an Israeli-backed South Lebanese Army. This accomplished, the IDF withdrew. Henceforward the PLO had to tread more warily in the south, although its bases further north were unharmed.

Israeli invasion

The advance of the right

The positions of extreme Israelis and Palestinians had much in common. Each rejected compromise and denied the right of the other to exist. Both saw the conflict between them as a fight to the death. By 1980, however, the bulk of Palestinians, including Arafat, realized that they would never be able to wipe Israel from the map. Hence Arafat's 'two state' solution – Israel and Palestine as separate, independent countries. In the circumstances, it was the best he could hope for.

It was not the best the Israelis could hope for. Their deal with Egypt (see Chapter 8), exchanging land for peace, was still the desired template of most mainstream politicians. It involved handing back some land to those from whom it had been taken – Jordanians and Syrians – but not to the Palestinians. To this end, hard-line Israelis were prepared to go to almost any lengths to reduce the power and influence of the PLO.

In the early 1980s the Israeli right was riding high. First, Begin was re-elected as prime minister. Second, two hard-liners, Yitzhak Shamir and Ariel Sharon, entered the government as foreign and defence ministers respectively. Third, Jimmy Carter had fallen foul of the media and the new militant Iranian regime of Ayatollah Khomeini (see page 127), and failed to get re-elected. His place had been taken by Ronald Reagan. The Republican president and his slow-witted secretary of state Alexander Haig regarded Israel as a 'strategic asset' in their battle against Communism. This meant publicly supporting the Likud administration in almost all it did, even though it might disagree in private.

Israeli provocation

In 1981, Begin's government officially annexed the Golan Heights. Next, showing how ruthless it was prepared to be in defence of its country's interests, it ordered the destruction of an Iraqi nuclear plant that was under construction at Osirak. In Operation Babylon, Israeli F-16 fighter-bombers, with F-15 fighter protection, completely destroyed the site with 900-kg (2,000-lb) bombs. Israeli planes then tackled the PLO headquarters in Beirut, leaving 300 civilians dead. A US-promoted cease-fire was declared, broken, and agreed again.

Shamir and Sharon were determined on an all-out invasion of Lebanon. Its purpose would be three-fold: final destruction of the PLO, the establishment of a pro-Israeli government in Lebanon (headed by Bashir Gemayel), and a war with Syria that would force it to accept peace on terms similar to Egypt's. Jordan would have no choice but to follow suit, they reasoned, leaving Israel secure, the PLO feeble and homeless, and non-Israeli Palestinians obliged to become citizens of the states in which they lived.

Arafat refused to play ball. Despite repeated Israeli incursions into Lebanon, the PLO did not retaliate. The Israeli command was finally relieved by events in London, England.

figure 6 the division of power in Lebanon before the 1982 Israeli invasion

On 3 June 1981, the Israeli ambassador to Great Britain was shot and wounded outside the five-star Dorchester Hotel. The gunman belonged to Abu Nidal, a terrorist gang whose leader had been expelled from the PLO for attempting to assassinate Yasser Arafat. Begin had no time for such details: to him all Arab terrorists were the same. Three days after the London shooting, 1,240 Israeli tanks roared over Israel's northern border into Lebanon.

Peace for Galilee

The Israeli invasion was named Operation Peace for Galilee, although there had been little or no fighting in Galilee for years. It was just another example of skilful Israeli propaganda: however unjustified the assault, the combination of 'peace' and 'Galilee' instinctively warmed the hearts of Christians the world over, not least those of mainstream America.

In military terms the advance was a blistering success. The invaders did not stop in the south, as they had said they would, but powered on to Beirut to link up with the Maronite forces of Bashir Gemayel. Resistance from the PLO, Muslim groups and the Syrians was crushed, the Syrian air force losing dozens of planes. Thousands were killed, mostly Arabs and many of them civilians. Assad accepted a cease-fire almost immediately and the Lebanese government soon followed suit.

The international outcry against the invasion was loud and virtually unanimous. Words, however, were not enough. The only country with the power and influence to limit Israeli policy, the US, was reluctant to ditch an ally pursuing a policy to which it had given tacit approval. US funds that permitted Begin to pay for his $1 million-a-day venture remained largely intact. As a gesture, though, supplies of some US-made weapons, such as deadly cluster bombs, were cut.

Short of military intervention, there was little anyone else could do. Certainly the Arab states were not prepared to get involved. We have seen before how they had little love for the Palestinians, nor were they willing to risk much for a country that had stood on the sidelines in 1967 and 1973. Egypt, at peace with Israel (see Chapter 8) and expelled from the Arab League, did nothing. Jordan saw no point in intervening. Saddam Hussein's Iraq, already at war with Iran, had neither the desire nor the means to get involved (see page 133).

Beirut under siege

By 1 July, the PLO fighters were holed up in West Beirut, surrounded by Israeli-Maronite forces. The Israelis did not want to get involved in deadly street-to-street fighting. Instead, as previously agreed, they asked their ally Gemayel to go in and root the enemy out. Gemayel refused. The Israelis began to realize that they had underestimated the man: he wanted to govern a fully independent Lebanon, not a puppet state. He no more wanted his country dominated by Israel than by the PLO.

The siege of West Beirut intensified with regular bombing, artillery and rocket attacks. Supplies of water and electricity were cut. Prime Minister Begin, it seems, was under some sort of illusion that the heart of Beirut was akin to Hitler's bunker in Berlin during the Second World War. 'I feel as a Prime Minister,' he telegraphed President Reagan, 'empowered to instruct a valiant army facing "Berlin" where amongst innocent civilians, Hitler and his henchmen hide in a bunker deep beneath the surface' (Avi Shlaim, 2001). By equating Arafat with Hitler, this remark demonstrates just how rigidly men of Begin's generation were tied to their hideous past. They were unable to see the present for what it was, regarding it instead as a form of nightmare, endlessly repeating what had been.

In this most desperate of situations, once again Arafat showed extraordinary bravery and a remarkable instinct for survival. The Israelis wanted him dead. Time and again their spies marked the building where he was supposed to be – in came the warplanes – the building was destroyed – he emerged somewhere else, smiling, his shoes defiantly polished, his distinctive head-dress intact. Journalists and soldiers alike testified to his unique ability to rouse the shattered Palestinian forces, taking men by the arm, encouraging them, assuring them that in the end victory would be theirs. 'Beirut will be the Hanoi and Stalingrad of the Israeli army' he quipped with irrepressible optimism.

Once, when it was certain the PLO was on the verge of surrender, a group of high-ranking Lebanese officials came to wish Arafat bon voyage. Introducing them, a Palestinian official told his leader that the delegation had come to say goodbye. 'Ah!' Arafat replied, 'Where are they going?' The whole room burst out laughing. The remark itself was not particularly amusing. What so attracted those present was the sheer joyful indestructibility of a man whose immediate prospects were just about nil.

Eventually, on 12 August, President Reagan called Prime Minister Begin in person. The fighting in Beirut had to stop at once, he warned. Did the victims of the Holocaust really wish to be the perpetrators of another such horror? The guns fell silent almost immediately. An international peace-keeping force of mainly American, French and Italian troops was called in to supervise a cease-fire. The PLO and its supporters were escorted from West Beirut and into exile in any country that would take them. Arafat, a sad and lonely figure, sailed away to Tunisia where he re-established his PLO headquarters.

Massacre

In order to get elected as president of Lebanon, Bashir Gemayel had denounced the Israeli presence in his country. Begin's policy was clearly beginning to unravel. True, the PLO had been driven from Lebanon, but there was nothing to stop them or similar groups returning, and the economic and political cost had been enormous.

The vast reservoir of international sympathy for the Jews, present since the Holocaust, was rapidly running dry. US friendship had been sorely tested. Syrian forces remained in eastern Lebanon, supporting PLO remnants in the al-Biqa Valley. Unnecessary Israeli aggression had made enemies of the Druze and the Lebanese Shia. The creation of Hezbollah ('Party of God'), an Iranian-backed terrorist organization that would prove even more intractable than the PLO, can be traced directly to Israeli attacks on previously neutral Shia villages. Worse was to come.

The removal of the PLO had left the Palestinians alarmingly vulnerable to attacks from their Maronite enemies. One spark would be enough to re-ignite the fire and inspire the Christian militia to another orgy of slaughter. What came, in fact, was not a spark but a bonfire: president-elect Bashir Gemayel was blown to tiny pieces by a bomb that destroyed the Phalange headquarters. His body was so mutilated that his wife had to identify him by a wedding ring on a severed hand.

The Phalange were rocked to their very core. Many of them refused to believe that their leader, the man who symbolized all they stood for, was dead. Rumours soon circulated that he had been seen walking uninjured from the ruins of the building where the bomb had gone off, making his way to a mysterious ambulance. One day, when his people were in great danger, he would return like King Arthur to save them.

For the time being, the Phalange sought revenge. Everyone in Lebanon knew this. The Israeli forces knew it, too, as did their political masters back home.

What happened next is still disputed. Nevertheless, it seems clear that Sharon and Israeli military leaders on the spot approved the entry of armed Phalange bands into the Palestinian camps of Sabra and Shatilla. As their escorts were well aware, it was not a social call. They remained there for three days, engaging in a ghastly orgy of slaughter, torture, mutilation and rape. The IDF, knowing full well that something terrible was happening, did not intervene until they tired of the screams. The death toll will probably never be known, but it is thought to amount to around 2,000 men, women and children.

Israel's Lebanese policy was in tatters. An estimated 400,000 Israelis filled the streets of Tel Aviv to protest at the IDF's role in the killing, passive or otherwise. Their government condemned the massacre, too, but denied all responsibility. Public pressure eventually forced Sharon to leave his post in the Defence Ministry, although he remained in the cabinet. A government enquiry exonerated the IDF from blame. The Sabra and Shatilla massacres were investigated by many others, including international bodies and Israeli journalists. None of their reports supported the view that Sharon and his forces were entirely innocent.

Towards settlement

Chaos returns

In the May following the Sabra and Shatilla massacres, Israel negotiated an armistice with President Amin Gemayel, brother of the assassinated Bashir. It lasted only a year until abrogated under Muslim and Syrian pressure. In that time the increasingly unpopular IDF, subject to violent and persistent attacks from all sides, had begun its painful withdrawal to the southern security zone which it had established during its previous invasion.

Meanwhile, the international peace-keeping force was also coming under attack. In the spring of 1983 a number of Americans, Italians and French were killed by a group whose name meant nothing at the time: Islamic Jihad. Within weeks it would be on everybody's lips. In April an Islamic Jihad suicide bomber drove a truck laden with explosives into the American

Embassy in Beirut and blew away the central section of the building. Human remains were found floating in the Mediterranean. In total 63 people died, including all the leading CIA agents in the region. A telephone message to a press agency announced with great clarity: 'The operation is part of the Iranian revolution's campaign against the imperialist presence throughout the world.'

President Reagan, would-be gunslinger that he was, immediately went on the offensive. His men were no longer in Lebanon as part of a peace mission. They were there to defend President Gemayel and crush his enemies, the Druze, Syrians and Shia. All of them used Soviet-made weapons, Reagan argued, so they must be Communist sympathizers. This was not just a civil war in Lebanon, it was part of the US's worldwide crusade against the Evil Empire of the red flag.

The crusade failed, despite the best efforts of the American forces in the area. Nothing symbolized American impotence more than the massive 40-cm (16-inch) guns of the battleship USS New Jersey pounding Druze positions from a safe distance offshore: a great deal of sound and fury only served to make the enemy more determined. Shia suicide bombings increased, killing over 300 American and French peace-keeping soldiers in their bases. Bewildered, hurt, and humiliated, the international forces left the country in 1984.

The withdrawal of external forces led to five more years of turmoil. The remnants of the PLO fell out with the Shia, the Syrians gradually increased their hold on the country while the Maronites, when not squabbling among themselves, did their best to resist them. The economy went from bad to worse.

When Amin Gemayel's term of office ended and it proved impossible to choose a new president, the country found itself with two prime ministers. The more forceful of them, General Aoun, announced a War of Liberation against the Syrians in an attempt to bind all Lebanese together.

The Taif Accord

Following a cease-fire, in 1989 the Saudi government invited the Lebanese parliament to meet in the hill town of Taif to work out a new power-sharing agreement. The multi-billionaire Lebanese businessman Rafiq al-Hariri, a prominent member of the Shia community, funded the visit. It eventually produced a fresh compromise – but no immediate end to the instability or the fighting. A new president was elected and promptly assassinated. General Aoun rejected the Taif Accord, giving Syrian forces a reason to re-enter the country. This time they were regarded by most parties as a necessary inconvenience.

The country was exhausted. Over 25 per cent of its population had fled abroad. About 150,000 had been killed. Hundreds of thousands had been made homeless. Not a family in the land had escaped suffering and loss. Hariri, now prime minister, set about getting the country back on its feet again. His wealth, business acumen and worldwide contacts made him in many ways the ideal man for the task. Nevertheless, the probity of all the deals made by 'Mr Miracle', as Hariri was known, did not always bear scrutiny.

Although there was a definite decline in violence and a marked economic recovery in northern Lebanon, less progress was made in the south where the borders of Lebanon, Israel and Syria met. Eventually, though, the IDF left the region in May 2000. The withdrawal left some issues unresolved. Among these were ownership of an enclave on the Golan Heights known as the Sheba Farms, the continued presence of Syrian forces in Lebanon, and the ongoing anti-Israeli activities of Hezbollah and Islamic Jihad (see page 147). At the dawn of the twenty-first century, real and lasting peace was still a long way off.

08

Camp David

This chapter will cover:
- how the conditions at the end of the 1973 war made Arab-Israeli peace talks possible
- US Secretary of State Henry Kissinger's shuttle diplomacy
- President Sadat's historic visit to Israel
- the Camp David agreement and its repercussions.

'We can negotiate'

At the end of the Fourth Arab-Israeli or Yom Kippur War, the Egyptian chief of staff addressed the Israeli deputy chief of staff with the remark, 'Look, this is the first time a war between us has ended in equality ... From here we can negotiate.' The comment was as prophetic as it was perceptive. Five years later Israel and Egypt reached an historic agreement that marked the beginning of what has been called the Middle East peace process.

Post-war Israel

Both Egypt and Israel claimed to have won the war. Technically speaking, since it was advancing into Egypt and Syria when President Nixon and Secretary of State Kissinger ordered a halt to the fighting, Israel was the victor. Politically, though, the victory was Egypt's.

The IDF had lost 3,000 men and women. Some had been captured, others were missing in action. The mightiest power in the Middle East, the state built by war and for war, had been caught napping and was driven back. Although an inquiry into what went wrong did not finger out the political leadership, Prime Minister Golda Meir's tarnished Labour government resigned the following year.

The new Labour administration was led by Yitzhak Rabin, the first Israeli-born politician to head the country's government. A native of Jerusalem, he had fought with the Haganah against the Palestinians and, briefly, against the dissident Irgun of Menachem Begin (see page 49). After independence he had attended staff college in Great Britain and made a name for himself as chief of staff in the 1967 war. On retiring from the army he had served as ambassador to the United States. Having been elected to the Knesset (the Israeli parliament) only in 1973, he lacked political experience. An awkward manner made his job even more difficult. Henry Kissinger remarked in *Years of Upheaval* (Little Brown & Co, Boston, 1982), that Rabin 'had many extraordinary qualities, but the gift of human relations was not one of them'.

Because of the oil crisis and the world economic recession (see page 91), Rabin predicted seven lean years for Israel. He was correct. Inflation and unemployment rose. Overseas friends, notably the apartheid regime in South Africa, fell away under threat of an Arab oil embargo. Internal divisions widened, not just between Ashkenazi and Sephardi (see page 49), but between an emerging peace movement and extreme nationalists who sought a 'Greater Israel'. Among the latter was the Gush Emunin movement which encouraged the building of Jewish settlements on occupied territory close to areas populated by Palestinians.

Rabin's government was supported by a small majority in the Knesset and frequently divided over policy issues. Its slogan 'continuity and change' was an attempt to appeal to as many Israelis as possible. Sometimes Rabin was hawkish, as when he approved the successful 'Raid on Entebbe' (a daring mission by Israeli commandos to rescue the passengers of a hi-jacked Air France plane). At other times, as in his relations with Egypt, he was more accommodating.

Egypt, Syria and the PLO

Life was no easier on the other side of the Suez Canal. Sadat's personal status rose dramatically as a result of his country's efforts in the Yom Kippur War, but this did not help him with Egypt's immediate economic difficulties. These were deeper rooted than those of Israel. Within a few years, the popularity of the 'hero of the crossing', as Sadat was known, had given way to violent anti-government demonstrations and unrest. Further dismantling of the repressive Nasser regime and an attempt to introduce limited democracy had little immediate impact. As far as Sadat was concerned, much depended on the anticipated 'peace dividend' of his foreign policy.

Syria's President Assad had lost further territory in the Golan Heights area as a result of the 1973 war, although this was never admitted to his people. In the words of his propaganda, 'He led the Liberation War of October 1973 in which our Armed Forces and people achieved great victories and emancipated the will of the Arabs and destroyed the enemy's arrogance' (taken from the Syrian government website, http://assad.org). Unlike Sadat and Arafat, Assad was not prepared to woo the Americans. Instead, he preferred to remain in the Soviet camp, giving moderate support to the Palestinians and pressing his case to be seen as leader of the Arab world.

Assad's erstwhile client, Yasser Arafat, was trying to move in a different direction. In keeping with his new, non-aggressive stance, the PLO had kept a relatively low profile during the Yom Kippur War. As it continued to embed itself into Lebanese political and economic life, its international standing rose with official recognition by the Arab League and the UN. The recognition that Arafat really wanted was that of the US State Department. Here he met with no success at all. Three times before the war and even in the middle of it, Arafat tried to contact Secretary of State Kissinger. The best he got was a warning not to employ his terrorist activities against US interests. He – and with him the Palestinian people – were being frozen out.

Shuttle diplomacy

Paradoxically, Sadat had gone to war in 1973 because he wanted peace. He wanted to open the Suez Canal, he wanted to cut back on military expenditure, he wanted himself and his people to be able to concentrate on making their country stable and prosperous, not always looking over their shoulders in the direction of Sinai. The first step towards achieving all these things was to settle Egypt's differences with Israel.

The first attempt to find a peaceful post-war settlement was a grand conference in Geneva, Switzerland, co-hosted by the UN, the USSR and the US. Neither Syria (self-excluded) nor the Palestinians (not invited) were present. After a few days of grandiose-sounding statements from all sides, the conference fizzled out. A comprehensive peace for the Middle East was beyond anyone's capacity to organize. Enter Henry Kissinger.

President Nixon's indefatigable and infinitely patient Secretary of State, Henry Kissinger, was keen to defuse the situation in the Middle East as swiftly as possible. The region's tensions were expensive and dangerous. Besides, a US-brokered settlement would enhance his country's position in the world and leave the Soviets looking like warmongers.

Having witnessed the Geneva fiasco, Kissinger abandoned the 'big plan' idea in favour of a step-by-step approach towards implementation of UN Resolution 242. To this end he spent many months flying backwards and forwards between the capitals of the Middle East, relaying offers and counter-offers, making suggestions of his own, and, when he felt it appropriate, using the big stick of US economic power to bring the parties round to his way of thinking.

Sinai I and II

Assad, as might be expected, proved the most intractable. It took almost a year to work out terms of disengagement on the Golan Heights. There negotiations ground to a halt. Neither Israel or Syria would contemplate the sort of concessions necessary for a fully fledged peace treaty. The question at the back of both sides' minds was water – as we have seen (page 73), whoever controlled Golan had their hands on a vital water supply.

Negotiations between Israel and Egypt went better. Rabin went along with Kissinger's suggestions as long as it did not look to his electorate as if he was bowing under pressure. In private the Israeli prime minister was also prepared to admit that in the end his country would have to release not just land taken from Egypt but also that taken from the Palestinians. For his part, Sadat played the 'crossing' card with skill: Egypt's initial breakthrough on the Suez Canal had seriously undermined Israeli self-confidence, making them more amenable to compromise. Rabin was also softened by Kissinger's pledge that he would never include the PLO in negotiations until it renounced all violence and recognized Israel.

Under Kissinger's auspices two far-reaching disengagement agreements were reached, Sinai I and Sinai II (1974 and 1975). The armies pulled back, peacekeepers went in, and the Suez Canal was opened for the first time since 1967. After this the talks lost momentum.

According to Kissinger and President Gerald Ford, who had replaced the disgraced Nixon following the Watergate scandal, it was Rabin's tactlessness and inflexibility that blocked progress. This is not strictly true. The astute, French-educated King Hassan II of Morocco agreed to act as a secret go-between in Rabin-Sadat approaches that by-passed the Americans. Rabin took up his offer. Heavily disguised, he sneaked into Morocco with a message for the Egyptian president. It was taken on by Hassan's trusted commander of the royal guard, but evoked no response. Sadat would do nothing without US backing.

Early the next year it was Egypt's turn. Hoping to break the diplomatic deadlock, Sadat's vice-president approached Rabin's deputy, Shimon Peres. This time it was Austria's Jewish chancellor, Bruno Kreisky, who acted as an intermediary. Again, nothing came of the initiative. The peace process was stalled.

Elections in the US (1976) and Israel (1977) brought Act I of the peace drama to its anti-climactic close. At the time no one was even sure that there would be an Act II. Nevertheless, the curtain did rise again, and with different actors in key roles the second act was even more momentous than the first.

A moment in history

Jimmy Carter

In the autumn of 1976, Republican President Ford was defeated in the polls by Democrat Jimmy Carter. Carter was an idealist, a 'big picture' man. Not for him the cautious shuttle diplomacy of Kissinger with its piecemeal results that left the major questions unanswered. To Carter's way of thinking, the longer the Arab-Israeli problem remained unsolved, the more intractable it would become. Not only that, but Carter was a reader. Before taking office in January 1977, he did his homework, brushing up on the relative merits of each side. In the course of this swotting, he decided that the Palestinians had a case.

Early in his presidency Carter met with Yitzhak Rabin and said that he believed that Palestinians would be better off with a homeland of their own. The word 'homeland' set alarm bells ringing in Rabin's mind. Like all Israelis, he remembered every detail of his people's struggle towards statehood. He knew full well the British Foreign Secretary's famous Balfour Declaration of 1917, in which he had supported the idea of a 'homeland' for the Jews in Palestine. Just as the Jews had interpreted Balfour's use of 'homeland' as codeword for 'state', so Rabin interpreted Carter's remark as backing for a Palestinian state. The shutters came down.

Menachem Begin and Likud

The situation was saved in a most unexpected way. Rabin's wife had illegally kept open a US bank account she had opened when her husband was ambassador in Washington. The scandal came on top of others and Rabin resigned in the midst of the 1977 Knesset elections, handing over leadership of the Labour coalition to Shimon Peres. Rabin's resignation was not enough to save Labour. After the elections, for the first time in Israel's history, Labour was unable to form a government. Its place was taken by a right-wing coalition known as Likud.

Likud had been formed four years earlier in an effort to break the Labour monopoly of power. At its heart were the old Liberal and Herat ('Freedom') Parties. Likud's intellectual position was inherited from Russian Jewry, notably Jabotinsky's revisionist and Greater Israel philosophy (see page 100). In practical terms, its foreign policy might take the same course as that of Labour. The difference between them was intellectual. Both made national security their number one priority. For Labour, though, it was essentially a pragmatic issue, while to Likud it was ideological. As we have already noted, Rabin understood that one day Israel's security would be best served by handing back some of the West Bank and Gaza. To Likud this was impossible – a hideous betrayal of the solemn trust imposed upon them by the 6 million victims of the Holocaust.

Leadership of the Likud fell upon Menachem Wolfvitch Begin, sometime leader of the Irgun terrorists who had once exchanged fire with Rabin. Begin had been born in Poland in 1913. He had trained as a lawyer and was an active Zionist before fleeing to Soviet territory to escape the Nazis at the start of the Second World War. One of his brothers and both his parents failed to get away and died in concentration camps. After being held in Siberia by the Russians, in 1941 he joined the Free Polish Army and was taken with them to Israel. Here he became the first head of Herut, the party he helped found.

The experiences of the first 40 years of his life had left a deep imprint on Begin's thinking. As we saw in the last chapter, his mind automatically linked opposition to Israel with anti-Semitism on the Nazi scale. His was a siege mentality. Embattled Israel, surrounded by enemies, had to defend itself within an iron wall.

The metaphorical wall encompassed both the West Bank and Gaza. Over those two pieces of land there could be no discussion. This was a point of view Begin shared with Ariel Sharon, his minister of agriculture. In many administrations the agriculture portfolio might not be a position of great importance. Not so in Begin's. Agriculture meant water and that meant retention of the Golan Heights, the West Bank and Gaza. Beneath the latter two lay about one half of the area's underground water.

Likud retained power with the support of ultraconservative religious and nationalist groups. They supported the government's refusal to negotiate over Gaza and the West Bank for different reasons. These lands, together with much of Jordan, had been part of the ancient realm of King David which they, the Jews of the twentieth century, were gloriously recreating. God's chosen people were coming into their own once more. To hand away what God had given would be sacrilege. With Sharon's blessing, the number and scale of Jewish settlements in the occupied West Bank grew markedly.

Sadat's finest hour

It was widely believed that Begin's election marked the end of the Middle East peace process for the duration. To the surprise of many, however, he declared himself willing to talk. At this point, President Carter, intellectually sound but still diplomatically naïve, set the process back by suggesting the Soviets be involved. The idea was not well received in the US, Israel or Egypt.

Sadat and Begin took up the running on their own. Once again Hassan II acted as clandestine facilitator. Begin found that he and the king, a prominent figure in the Arab world, shared certain key opinions. When the subject of Yasser Arafat and his organization was raised, the king declared bluntly, 'The PLO is a cancer in our midst. Their fate does not concern me at all'. Begin could only nod in total agreement.

After some initial exchanges, it was clear to Anwar Sadat that his Israeli counterpart was dragging his feet. What was needed was some dramatic, very public act that would force Begin into moving the process forward. Just as he had gambled by ordering an attack across the Suez Canal four years earlier, Sadat gambled again by laying his cards squarely on the table in full view of the whole world.

Speaking before the Egyptian National Assembly on 9 November 1977, Sadat pronounced these historic words:

> You heard me saying that I am prepared to go to the ends of the earth if my doing so will prevent any of my officers or men being killed or wounded. I really am ready to go to the ends of the earth and Israel will be amazed to hear me say that we do not refuse – I am prepared to go to their very home, to the Knesset itself and discuss things with them …

(Kirsten E. Schulze, *The Arab–Israeli Conflict*, page 110)

It was a brilliant move. The world applauded and awaited Begin's response. He had to accept. Sadat was invited to Israel and asked to address the Knesset, just as he had said he would. His speech called for an 'overall peace', not just one between Egypt and Israel. This 'durable peace based on justice' would involve Israel handing back the conquests of 1967 in return for full recognition by the Arab world and binding peace treaties with its neighbours. The Palestinians should be granted self-determination, establishing a state of their own if that was what they wished.

Begin refused to be carried away by the emotion of the moment. The tone of his speech in reply was a stark contrast to that of the Egyptian president. His tone was tight and mean. He talked of the past, of injustices done to the Jewish people. There could be talks, he agreed, but with no pre-conditions. He gave away nothing and did not once mention the Palestinians. Clearly, there was still a very long way to go.

Just how far apart the Arabs and Israelis were became apparent over the next few months. Begin suggested a partial Israeli withdrawal from Sinai, then promptly allowed further Jewish settlements to be built on occupied territory there. At the same time, more settlements were appearing in the West Bank and Gaza. Sadat was at his wits' end. To make matters worse, hostility against him was rising in the Arab world. It was feared that he was prepared to go it alone, abandoning the united Arab front that had more or less held firm since 1948.

The deadlock was broken by Jimmy Carter. In a move that was almost as dramatic as Sadat's speech to his parliament, he sent personal invitations to the president of Egypt and the prime minister of Israel. Would they please visit him at the presidential country retreat of Camp David, Maryland, to discuss their differences? It was an invitation neither man dared refuse.

Camp David

The Camp David talks marked a fundamental milestone in the recent history of the Middle East. Before the agreement, the Arab-Israeli story had been one of hatred and wars; afterwards, solid and enduring peace was at least a possibility. Camp David showed the way by cutting two knots. One had bound Arab to Arab in a solid front against Israel, the second had tied Israeli to its conquests. On their severance, much of the rest of the bitter tangle could begin to unravel.

The exception, as so often, was the Palestinian problem. This difficulty was glossed over at Camp David because Sadat knew that he could not have peace with Israel if he tried to fight the Palestinians' cause as well as the Egyptians'. Later, other Arab states were to follow his pragmatic example. One by one the Palestinians' Arab allies fell away, until they were faced with a reality that many of them had known in their hearts all along: whatever they wanted they had to get for themselves. Precisely the same realization had motivated the founders of Israel in the middle of the century.

Shangri-La

Camp David is situated within the elevated and densely wooded reaches of the Catoctin Mountain Park in Maryland. Established by F. D. Roosevelt as a summer refuge from the heat and humidity of Washington DC, its original name of Shangri-La had been changed by President Dwight Eisenhower to the more prosaic one it bears today.

Three features of the camp were important for the talks' success. The first was its air of informality. This meant the negotiators could behave as if on holiday, dressing casually and wandering or cycling around the extensive grounds as they wished. There was not a reporter or a press camera for miles. Aliza Begin and Kihan Sadat were invited to attend with their husbands, although Mrs Sadat was unable to accept. The wife of the US president, Rosalynn Carter, accompanied her husband and played a key role in maintaining a cordial, relaxed atmosphere.

Camp David is just what it says it is – a complex of many buildings spread out over several acres. This gave each party separate and discrete accommodation where they could retire to put their feet up or hold private discussions. Finally, Camp David is remote. Except in thick fog, access is by helicopter. The site is surrounded by a high and heavily guarded protective fence to keep out intruders. This isolation and security also make the camp a difficult place to leave. Begin described it as an 'elegant jail'. Had it been possible simply to walk out, it is quite likely that the talks would have failed as at one time or another both parties felt that a resolution was unobtainable.

All this made President Carter's choice of venue for the talks a masterstroke. Once he had got the two parties to his dacha, isolated from outside pressures and influences, he was determined not to let them go until agreement had been reached.

His role was more than just that of a facilitator – at times he was almost an enforcer.

Chemistry and quotation

Carter's unusually united team was headed by himself, his Secretary of State Cyrus Vance, and his National Security advisor Zbigniew Brzezinski. Vice-President Walter Mondale was brought in at the end because of his perceived friendship with Israel. As well as Begin, the Israeli delegation also contained Foreign Minister Moshe Dayan, Defence Minister Ezer Weizman, and Attorney General Aharon Barak. Prominent among Sadat's delegation were Foreign Minister Muhammad Ibrahim Kamil and Osama El-Baz.

The chemistry of the assembled parties was complex and at times explosive. There was no love lost between Sadat and Begin. Their initial discussions ended up as shouting matches. Fortunately, Sadat liked and trusted Carter. His favourite member of the Israeli party was the ex-RAF fighter pilot Weizman.

Perhaps because they were both of Polish origin, Begin and Brzezinski seemed to get on well. On the evening of the fifth day of the talks the two sat down to a game of chess. Begin sighed and confessed that the game brought back vivid memories: the last time he had played was just before his arrest and deportation to Siberia by the Soviet secret police. His beloved Aliza let him down. Entering the room some time later and seeing the game still in progress, she announced with delight that Menachem loved to play chess. He had obviously been playing all his life and the story about the game at the time of his arrest was just a ploy to gain sympathy.

Chess was not the only diversion. To lower the temperature, on day six Carter took his guests to visit the Gettysburg battlefield. Sadat, who as a cadet had studied the battle in great detail, was delighted. To Begin it meant nothing until they came to a memorial of President Lincoln's Gettysburg Address. 'Fourscore and seven years ago our fathers brought forth on this continent a new nation ...' began the Israeli prime minister. He knew the speech by heart and continued right through to its famous ending: '... that this nation under God shall have a new birth of freedom, and that government of the people, by the people, for the people shall not perish from the earth.' It looked as if Lincoln and Begin shared the same dream.

To the brink and back

The talks lasted 14 days. Two basic issues were at stake. One, the return of Sinai and the normalization of Israeli-Egyptian relations; two, the return of other occupied territories, specifically the West Bank and Gaza, and the right of self-determination for the Palestinians living there. From the outset, Begin's position was the strongest. He had something to give (Sinai) and would not lose too much face back home if he returned without agreement. Carter was eager for a foreign policy triumph to bolster his flagging presidency. Sadat, having been the prime mover in the peace process, had the most to lose.

During days one and two each side set out their positions. Sadat showed his lack of experience as a negotiator by revealing to Carter the concessions he was willing to make. The face-to-face meetings of Carter, Sadat and Begin on days three and four produced little but hostility. Thereafter the Americans acted as shuttle diplomats, ferrying messages and suggestions between the sides. By now it was clear there could be no firm agreement over the Palestinian question, so it was set aside for the time being. On strictly Israeli-Egyptian business, Begin's unwillingness to hand over settlements and airfields in Sinai was proving a major obstacle to progress.

By day ten the two sides were still unable to agree and Carter feared the talks would fail. Begin, at his most adamant, had declared, 'My right eye will fall out, my right hand will fall off before I ever agree to the dismantling of a single Jewish settlement'. Later, Carter retorted that the Israel prime minister was throwing away peace for 'a few illegal settlers on Egyptian land'.

On day 11 Sadat and his entourage packed their bags and announced that they were leaving. Carter put on a jacket and tie and went to confront the Egyptian delegation in their lodge. If the talks collapsed, he warned, he could not guarantee that US aid to Egypt would be maintained. Moreover, Sadat would have made a fool of himself before the Arab world. Was he sure he wouldn't stay, just for a few days?

From then on the end was in sight. The US agreed to build new airfields for the Israelis and to guarantee their access to Sinai oil – but the Sinai settlements had to go. US aid to Egypt amounted to about $1 billion a year during the 1980s.

The fate of the Palestinians was left in the air. The final text of the Camp David Accords spoke of what should happen to give the Palestinians their rights as outlined by Resolution 242, but there was nothing about what would happen. Although the Accords said that the 'peaceful and orderly transfer of authority' should begin when a 'self-governing authority … in the West Bank and Gaza [was] established', they contained no timetable for this to happen. Negotiations on the Palestinian issue dragged on long after all parties had left Camp David, but little substantive progress was made.

The aftermath

Back at the White House, all parties signed the Camp David Accords on 17 September 1978. Sadat and Begin shared the Nobel Peace Prize for their ground-breaking agreement, a reward perhaps more deserved by Jimmy Carter. After a further seven months of detailed negotiation, Israel and Egypt signed a formal treaty. By its terms Israel agreed to withdraw from 80 per cent of Sinai over three years, retaining rights to the area's oil. A UN observer force would patrol the new border. Most significant of all, Israel and Egypt established full diplomatic relations.

Although the abandonment of the Sinai settlements drew down the wrath of conservatives on Begin's head, many Israelis welcomed the treaty as the first step towards full international recognition and an eventual all-embracing peace. The more cynical saw it simply as a ploy to secure Israel's southern frontier, leaving the IDF free for a full invasion of Lebanon in 1982 (see Chapter 7).

Israeli strikes against the PLO continued, notably the assassination by a hit squad of Arafat's most trusted subordinate and adopted son, Ali Hassan Salameh. Jewish settlements went on being built on the West Bank, where local Palestinian leaders had met roundly to denounce the treaty. Likud and Begin were re-elected in 1981. The year before, disappointed that the Camp David process had not been taken further, Ezer Weizman had resigned. Leaving Begin's office for the last time, he had noticed a peace poster on the wall. Ripping it down, he shouted, 'No one here wants peace!'

Sadat had a rougher ride. His fellow Arabs accused him of abandoning the Palestinians for the sake of Sinai. Egypt was expelled from the Arab League, which moved its headquarters from Cairo to Tunis, and was subjected to an Arab boycott. Interestingly, of all the Arab nations only the PLO maintained diplomatic relations with Egypt, albeit in secret. Arafat was still eager to cosy up to America.

In Egypt itself the reception of the peace treaty was mixed. Much would depend on the 'peace dividend' that Sadat had set so much store by. To his intense frustration and disappointment, despite all the US aid and cuts in military expenditure, the Egyptian economy showed few signs of a significant recovery. As the class gap widened still further, popular unrest grew. In an attempt to mollify his people, the president introduced an element of popular participation in the political system and announced that henceforward Egyptian law would be based on the Islamic Sharia Law. It was too little, too late.

Still the discontent rumbled on. In September 1981, Sadat took action to forestall a possible coup, arresting over a thousand of the country's political élite. The next month a massive military parade was organized to celebrate the anniversary of the crossing of the Suez Canal during the Yom Kippur War. Here, on 6 October, before thousands of his people, Anwar Sadat was shot dead by a Muslim extremist.

Among his own people Sadat was not liked. He had promised much but delivered little, and his regime was intolerably harsh. The West, however, saw a different Sadat. The title 'hero of the crossing' had taken on a double meaning. He had not just crossed the canal. With a great leap of faith he had crossed cultures, striding over a gulf of misunderstanding and mistrust to shake hands with the enemy. It was as brave an act as any on the battlefield.

09
revolution and war

This chapter will cover:
- Iran's White Revolution
- the overthrow of the Shah of Iran in the revolution of 1979
- the rise of Saddam Hussein in Iraq
- the Iran-Iraq War.

Our attention now moves east, to the Persian Gulf. Iran and Iraq had as much impact on the late twentieth-century world as Israel-Palestine, but for very different reasons. Iran underwent a unique political, social and religious revolution, the impact of which was felt right across the Middle East and beyond. Iraq came under the rule of a dictator as ruthless as any we will meet. These two states, each representing a distinct form of tyranny, then clashed in one of the most senseless and costly wars of recent times.

King of Kings

In Chapter 2 we saw how the absolute but well-intentioned young ruler of Iran, Mohammed Reza shah Pahlavi, was trying to modernize his oil-rich state along Western lines. Opposition came principally from a traditional landed élite, often called the notables, and the Shia Muslim hierarchy. Domestic support, at first, came from a tiny group of Western-educated intellectuals and business people, and the landless rural majority.

International backing was always available from the West, eager for Iranian oil and keen to support a friendly bulwark against possible Soviet expansion. In 1953, for example, US support enabled the shah to recover his authority after it had been briefly undermined by Prime Minister Muhammed Mosaddeq. Thereafter the shah was very much America's man.

The White Revolution

Shah Pahlavi carried out what was termed a 'White Revolution' from above. The key was land reform: obliging wealthy landowners to hand over their land to impoverished tenants. One estimate suggests some 12 million Iranians benefited from this move, increasing the proportion of owner-occupied land from 26 per cent to 78 per cent over a 12-year period. Those who lost land were compensated, sometimes in shares.

The profit-sharing principle was introduced into industry, and co-operative ventures were encouraged. Government grants and direct injections of capital came largely from the profits of the National Iranian Oil Company, a Western consortium led by BP. Mosaddeq had briefly nationalized the oil industry but the restored shah reversed the decision.

In an effort to diversify the economy, government help was given to vehicle and steel manufacture, mining, and construction. Dams were built and irrigation projects completed in double-quick time. Gross national product was rising at almost eight per cent a year by the mid-1970s. It has been estimated that the average per capita income rose from $170 to $2,500 in just 18 years.

The White Revolution was about more than economics. All sectors of education were expanded and university-level students encouraged to study abroad. Malaria was eliminated and the benefits of modern medicine extended. Literacy and health corps were established to benefit the many remote villages and smaller towns. A range of Western experts, from language teachers to civil engineers, flooded into Iran at the shah's behest. Iranian women were urged to set aside their traditional subservient roles and play prominent parts in all aspects of life. Pictures of the shah with his third wife, Farah Diba, adorned every loyal enterprise, from bazaar stall to ministry. This was not just royalist propaganda, but an effort to portray a woman as a working partner. The conscious effort to make Iran a Westward-looking country also brought all the peripheral glitz of Euro-American life: the flashy cars, the night clubs, the movies, rebellious teenagers, and so forth.

White tyranny

A list of the achievements of the White Revolution looks impressive. Its cost, however, was unpleasantly high. First, there was the toll it took on the shah himself. He became a living example of the corrupting effect of power. In 1967, in a ceremony of vast expense and magnificence, he had himself crowned Emperor of all Iran and King of Kings. At the same time, Farah was created 'Shahbanoo' or Empress. The move was justified as necessary to promote the royal family as a unifying force. Within Iran and abroad, it was mocked as pompous tomfoolery.

The 1971 celebration of 2,500 years of Persian monarchy drew equally sceptical responses. The elaborate and costly show was staged amid the spectacular ruins of Persepolis, once the capital of the ancient Persian Empire. The site was chosen to link the Pahlavi dynasty with the country's glorious past. In the light of what was to happen to him, the shah might have been better advised while at Persepolis to reflect upon the transitory nature of earthly power.

Associating the ruling dynasty with a pre-Islamic past did not do much for his already acrimonious relationship with his country's Shia hierarchy. Nor did another of the shah's attempts at self-glorification: replacing the Islamic calendar with an 'Imperial' one that began with the foundation of the Persian Empire some two and a half millennia before.

In carrying out his policies, the increasingly autocratic shah rode roughshod over the country's constitution. Ministers, in theory representative of the people, were merely his appointees. He talked of introducing democratic reforms but took no practical steps to do so. Savak, the state intelligence and security organization, rooted out opposition and dealt with its perpetrators with summary ruthlessness. Distorted by the power he wielded, the once-handsome shah came to look cold and cadaverous. It was as if the lymphatic cancer that eventually killed him had begun by attacking his soul.

The Iranian revolution

Mounting opposition

There were two strands of opposition to the shah. One comprised those who supported his Westernization policy but believed it did not go far or fast enough. They sought more participation in the political process, for instance, and less state interference in business and industry. The second group was the Islamists, opposed to Westernization and calling for a return to Sharia (see page 124). It is a measure of the shah's political ineptitude that he managed to unite these seemingly irreconcilable parties.

By the mid-1970s, the fairly apolitical bulk of the population, although they had benefited from the shah's rule in many ways, found their confidence in him melting away. As elsewhere in the world, rising oil prices fuelled inflation. This cut the value of wages and savings. Against this background the shah's massive military spending programme was criticized as tactlessly inappropriate. Most Iranians felt that too much oil wealth flowed into the pockets of the few rather than the many. No one outside the royal inner circle had a good word for Savak.

Informed of his people's unease, in 1977 the shah made the mistake of slightly relaxing his political control. One measure in particular – reducing the powers of the censor – served only to fuel demands for more reform. Public protests at the end of the year resulted in several deaths at the hands of the security forces.

The following January popular unrest surged again. Students in Qumm protesting against a visit by US President Jimmy Carter were fired on by the police; 70 were killed. The Shia branch of Islam has a particular respect for martyrdom. One of its traditions is that martyrs are commemorated 40 days after their death. So, 40 days after the Qumm slaughter, fresh protests broke out. This time the city of Tabriz saw more than 100 protestors slain. After another 40 days a similar number was shot at Yazd. By mid-summer almost the entire country was consumed by protest.

The shah vacillated. After trying conciliatory tactics, in early autumn he ordered a crack down. In Tehran hundreds were shot dead on what was immediately dubbed 'Black Friday' (8 September 1978). Martial law was introduced and thousands of arrests made. Public protest gave way to strikes and within a short space of time the country's key industries ground to a halt.

Ayatollah Khomeini

By this time the protest movement had coalesced around the austere figure of Ruhallah Khomeini. Few late twentieth-century figures were more controversial than this scholar-dictator. Born around the turn of the century in the town of Khomeyn, from whence he took his name, he came from a long line of mullahs (Shia religious leaders). A learned but humourless student of Islam, in his fifties he was proclaimed an ayatollah – important religious leader – and ten years later a grand ayatollah.

Khomeini used his position as one of the country's leading Shia clerics to speak out against the shah's rule. For his opposition to the forced reduction of religious estates he was imprisoned then sent into exile. As the unsmiling firebrand was now in his mid-sixties, the shah must have thought he had seen the last of him. Not so – the older Khomeini grew, the more active he became. Moving from Turkey to Iraq and eventually Paris, France, the ayatollah kept up a constant barrage of criticism of the shah and his regime. By the late 1970s, illegally copied recordings of his unrelenting, earnest speeches were in popular demand throughout Iran.

Reason alone cannot explain Khomeini's popularity. Many of the things he advocated – women re-veiling, bans on alcohol and Western music, for example – had little obvious appeal to the students of both sexes who so adored him. He was certainly helped by his absence from Iran. Without the intrusion of awkward reality, his image became fantastically embellished in the popular imagination: Ayatollah Ruhallah Khomeini developed into the long-lost saviour who would one day return to rescue his people. Khomeini's nationalistic Shia roots contrasted favourably with the shah's pro-Western secularism, too. In short, Khomeini was everything the shah was not. The obverse of popular hatred for the shah was hysterical love of Khomeini. The two were part of the same tidal wave of emotion that swept across the nation. What elevating the revered mullah meant in practical terms people only discovered when it was too late to do anything about it. By then they had given the unyielding puritan supreme authority for the rest of his life.

The flight of the shah

Stirred up by Khomeini's vision of an Islamic republic, Shia fundamentalists became the most prominent and outspoken of the shah's opponents. At their head were the Mujahedin, 'Dedicated Fighters'. As 1978 came to an end, appeals to Khomeini to return to his native land multiplied. Waiting until such a move would be unopposed as well as universally welcomed, he refused to come home as long as the shah remained in the country.

During the especially holy month of Muhurram, beginning on 2 December, anti-shah protests reached a crescendo. The strikes escalated and literally millions took to the streets. Government buildings were occupied and ransacked, and officials assassinated. To the Mujahedin no task was too dangerous – if it led to death, so be it: there was no greater honour than martyrdom. In such conditions the government could not operate.

Accepting the inevitable, on 16 January 1979 the shah left the country. At the time officials announced that he was going on holiday. This was later changed. The new version said he had left Iran to prevent further bloodshed. Neither explanation was particularly convincing. The regency government that the shah left behind was unable to cope. By now the loyalty of the armed forces and police was shifting from the shah to Khomeini.

The saviour finally arrived on 1 February. Amid scenes of extraordinary mass hysteria, he made his way from the airport to Tehran through a crowd of several million. There seemed nothing he could not do. When the official government fled, he appointed a new one in its place. By the end of the year, Iranians had voted in a referendum to make their country an Islamic republic on a new model devised by their religious and political leader.

Under the Khomeini constitution the secular and the religious were merged. All government actions, from the passing of laws to making treaties with foreign powers, were subject to the scrutiny of a Guardian Council comprising the country's most learned Shia clerics. This reverend body was charged with ensuring that the government acted in accordance with the Koran. At the head of the Council, on the very pinnacle of the theocratic power pyramid, sat Ayatollah Khomeini. Against his judgements there was no appeal. In practice, therefore, Iran had come close to swapping one dictator for another.

The new Iran

Mercy was not Khomeini's favourite attribute of the Almighty. He gave his blessing to bands of young enthusiasts who patrolled the streets looking for backsliders, possible royalist sympathizers, or anyone just showing an interest in Western culture. Thousands of ex-royalists were reportedly executed. Women were beaten for not covering their faces, shopkeepers for being found in possession of Elvis Presley tapes. Thousands of better-off Iranians fled abroad. Human rights were no more respected than they had been under the previous regime.

One of the most destabilizing effects of the Iranian Revolution stemmed from Khomeini's determination to export it. Central to this process was an often declared fight with the 'corrupt' West and its 'evil' sympathizers. Since straightforward battle was not an option, Iran became a training ground for Muslim terrorists prepared to embrace martyrdom. Thus international terrorism entered a new and more violent phase that would bear its most vicious fruit in the early years of the next century.

Meanwhile, an incident had occurred that turned nearly all democratic states against Iran's new government. When the shah visited the US seeking treatment for his cancer, Khomeini demanded his extradition. This was refused – the US had no extradition treaty with the new regime in Iran. In response, a gang of student extremists seized the US embassy in Tehran and took captive the 66 US citizens working there. President Carter demanded their immediate release. Backed by the frenzied anti-Americanism of the streets, Khomeini refused.

Carter applied economic pressure, freezing Iranian assets in the US and placing an embargo on the country's oil. Still the hostages were not released. Growing desperate, the president authorized a clandestine rescue attempt by helicopter. Incompetence and a sandstorm caused the mission to be aborted before it reached Tehran – by which time eight Americans had been killed in the chaos of collision and fire. The world watched in disbelieving disgust as elderly ayatollahs gloated gleefully over the charred bodies. Following the death of the shah, Carter's defeat by Ronald Reagan, and the outbreak of the Iran-Iraq war, the hostages eventually came home in January 1981.

The rise of Saddam Hussein

The monarchy of the British-created state of Iraq was overthrown in 1958. The consequent five-year rule of Brigadier Qasim was bloody and troubled. After only a year in power, for example, he narrowly escaped assassination at the hands of Baath Party machine gunners. The wielder of one of these weapons was hit in the leg by a bullet but managed to make a daring escape on horseback and by swimming fully clothed across the Tigris. The hero of this adventure, which would one day be recounted ad nauseam in prose, verse, song and film, was a 22-year-old Sunni Muslim from the Tikrit district named Saddam Hussein.

The advance of the Baathists

Saddam Hussein, son of a peasant farmer who died around the time of his birth, was brought up in a tribal society which espoused loyalty and cruelty in almost equal measure. Single-mindedly ambitious, he joined the Baath party while a student. He was not particularly attracted to the organization's socialist or nationalist principles, but saw it as a means to power.

After the failure of the 1959 coup attempt, Hussein fled abroad to Damascus then Cairo. His part in Iraq's next coup – if indeed he did have a hand in it – is obscure. Qasim had incurred the disfavour of the West by nationalizing part of Iraq's oil industry, threatening to invade Kuwait and leaving the Baghdad Pact. It is not surprising to learn, therefore, that the CIA played a significant role in his fall from power in 1963. The coup was carried out in the name of the Baath party, with army assistance. Many of the conspirators were from the Tikrit region.

figure 7 Iraq

Shortly after pictures of Qasim's bullet-riddled body appeared on television, General Arif expelled the Baathists and took the reins of government into his own hands.

Hussein learned several lessons from each of the coups he witnessed. Two were particularly important: one, total control was possible only with the support of the army, security services, party and a strong local (tribal) power base; two, the first priority of anyone taking power was to eliminate all possible rivals as quickly as possible.

General Arif's failure to apply this last lesson cost him his position. In 1968 he was overthrown in yet another coup, organized by the Baath Party with the backing of Colonel al-Nayif, head of military intelligence. Had Arif been more ruthless and eliminated the Baath Party leader and deputy leader (the cousins Ahmed al-Bakr and Saddam Hussein) after he had arrested them in 1966, his period of power might have been longer. As it was, Hussein persuaded the guard ferrying him from the court house to prison to stop by a local restaurant. Here, with extraordinary good fortune, he escaped by simply walking out of the back door of the building.

President Saddam Hussein

The fall of Arif left al-Bakr as head of state and Hussein as his lieutenant, the strong man behind the scenes. Over the next ten years, Hussein eliminated possible opponents. Nayif, for example, who had helped the Baath come to power, was personally escorted to the airport by Hussein and told never to return to Iraq. Later, unsure that exile was sufficiently secure, Hussein had him shot dead in London. Ex-Defence Minister General al-Tikriti was assassinated in Kuwait. Many others simply disappeared. Membership of any opposition party was punishable by death.

Hussein struck on 10 July 1979. Prompted by his eager successor, al-Bakr announced to a meeting of the Revolutionary Command Council (RCC) that on account of his poor health he was stepping down as president. Hussein would succeed him. There was some opposition within the Baath Party and talk of a Syrian-backed coup. Barzan, Saddam's half-brother, investigated the rumours with torture-assisted thoroughness. One-quarter of the RCC were executed, along with 16 other possible opponents of the new regime.

The new president did not stop there. He wanted the purge to be a public warning to anyone who even thought of standing in his way. Suspects from all over the country were rounded up and killed. In many instances – a new departure this in Iraqi thuggery – their families were punished too. The prominent journalist Patrick Cockburn (2002) tells how the tortured body of one prominent Baathist was dumped back at his house with a note saying that he had died of a heart attack and mourning was forbidden.

Hussein did not want power simply for its own sake. He was determined that Iraq, hitherto little more than a somewhat chaotic second-rate Gulf state, should become the premier force in the region – a country to be reckoned with at the high table of nations. Immediate events in Iran seemed to play straight into his hands.

Glancing to the east, Hussein saw that the Khomeini regime had plunged Iran into chaos, considerably weakened its armed forces with fanatical purges, and severed all links with its previous backers in the West. Moreover, there was no chance of Shia fundamentalists doing a deal with the atheistic Soviet Union. Since both the West and the Soviets viewed with horror what was going on in Iran, Hussein reasoned, they might well support an attempt to unseat the ageing ayatollah. Besides, an attack would be the best way of preventing Iran's religious plague from infecting the Iraqi Shia, who comprised about 60 per cent of the population.

Confident of success but with no formal military knowledge or experience whatsoever, Hussein ordered a full-scale invasion of Iran in September 1980.

The Iran-Iraq War (1980–8)

Animosity between Iran and Iraq went back a long way. The Bakr-Hussein regime's Friendship and Cooperation Treaty with the Soviet Union in 1972, for instance, placed Iraq on the opposite side in the Cold War to the US-backed regime of Shah Pahlavi. In 1973–4, the shah, with tacit US support, backed separatist Kurdish rebels in northern Iraq. Equally serious was the conflict over the Shatt al-Arab waterway, the broad estuary formed by the confluence of the Tigris and Euphrates Rivers.

Iraq's coastline is only 40 km (25 miles) long. The Shatt al-Arab, at its eastern end, is the country's vital link with the Gulf. A treaty made before the Second World War gave control to Iraq. After this had been abrogated by Iran, the Algiers Agreement (1975) between Hussein, then vice-chairman of the RCC, and the shah gave their two countries joint control over the waterway. Following these Iraqi concessions, Iran stopped supporting the Kurds in their struggle for independence. As a consequence, the Kurdish war soon ended.

This was the situation when Khomeini and Hussein came to power in their respective countries. A more contrasting pair of dictators it would be hard to imagine, so it comes as little surprise to learn that they were soon at war. Nevertheless, for a few months Hussein had gone out of his way not to react to his new neighbour's fiery taunts.

The Khomeini regime refused to recognize Saddam Hussein's secular and therefore unholy government. The ayatollah himself called on Iraq's Shia majority to rise up against a president whom he dubbed 'the main obstacle to the advance of Islam in the region'. Hussein, with rare humour, mocked the dusty old mullah as 'that mummy'. Shia assassins, recruited by Iran, slew numerous Baath Party officials, and Iranian support for Kurdish rebels began to flow once more.

We cannot be completely sure why Hussein did not react more swiftly to such blatant provocation. The most likely answer is that he wished to secure his rule before engaging in any dramatic foreign adventure. He had plans to spend some of Iraq's fast-growing wealth on large-scale projects that would boost his popularity, such as irrigation and health care. War would divert these funds into unproductive arms purchases.

Towards the end of 1979, Hussein's mind began to change. He expelled 100,000 Iraqis of Iranian stock and began supporting Iranian Sunni opposition to Khomeini. With fine irony, while battling against the Kurds at home, he backed the Kurdish independence movement within Iran. When these signals drew forth no response, military clashes along the Iran-Iraq border escalated. After Iraq had unilaterally abrogated the Algiers Agreement in September, all-out war was all but inevitable.

The course of the war

The story of one of the most costly, cruel and protracted of modern wars is simply told. It began with an Iraqi operation intended to deliver a knockout blow, rather like that launched by Israel at the start of the Six Day War. Iraqi planning and execution fell far short of the Israelis', however. Although initial gains were made, Iran's armed forces remained very much operational. In fact, far more damage had already been done by Khomeini, whose purges had deprived the Iranian army of 12,000 officers and the air force of one half of its pilots.

After the first clashes, during which the Iraqi army had advanced a relatively short distance into Iran, a period of stalemate ensued. This came to a close in the autumn of 1981. The Iranians launched an offensive that eventually retook much of the land they had lost and threatened Kirkuk in northern Iraq and Basra in the south.

In a significant development, the Iraqis first used poison gas in the defence of Basra. Delighted at the weapon's efficacy, it was thereafter employed on all fronts, especially against the Iraqi Kurds. In an attempt to hit the Iranian economy, Hussein stepped up the so-called 'Tanker War', striking at Iranian oil tankers and their port facilities.

By the time the war dragged into its sixth year, the situation for Hussein was looking extremely gloomy. Khomeini even issued a fatwa – religious command – demanding that his people win the war within the next 12 months. Iraq was saved by several factors, including massive foreign arms shipments and, paradoxically, a near-mutiny in its own army. The latter occurred when General al-Rashid was summoned to the presidential palace to explain why he had failed to make headway against the Iranians in the south. Normally, such a summons meant only one thing: removal and probable execution.

Rashid's officers were aware of this. They also knew that their commander had been unable to conduct the war as he would have wished because of continual amateur meddling from Baghdad. Before Rashid arrived at the palace, the officers sent a message to Hussein saying that if anything happened to him they would not be able to continue the war. When Rashid arrived at the palace he found a smiling Hussein waiting to decorate him. Thereafter the president left the conduct of the war largely in the hands of the professionals.

The seventh year of the conflict saw Iraq on the offensive again and the UN Security Council voting unanimously for a cease-fire. Iraq accepted it but Iran wavered. Directed by US intelligence, which identified the weakest points in the Iranian line, the Iraqi army made notable gains. For the first time for years they found themselves on Iranian soil. The Iranian president, Ali Akbar Hashemi-Rafsanjani, implored the ailing Ayatollah Khomeini to call a halt to the slaughter. The old man was not yet ready.

Khomeini's mind was changed by a terrible accident. On 3 July 1988 the *USS Vincennes*, on duty in the Gulf, accidentally shot down an Iranian passenger jet with 290 people on board. The US offered compensation but would not apologize. Rafsanjani persuaded Khomeini that the incident demonstrated Iraq's alliance with the US, which was about to attack Iran. Saying it was like taking poison, Khomeini agreed to call a halt to the slaughter. His decision was also influenced by near-rebellion at home and Iraq's development of missiles that could rain chemical and biological warheads on Tehran and other major Iranian cities. Not even Khomeini was sure he wanted martyrdom on that scale.

The terrible price

The Iran-Iraq war was remarkable for a variety of unpleasant reasons. One was the extent of the slaughter. Around half a million people were killed, well over 50 per cent of them Iranians and their Kurdish allies. The number of wounded was at least twice as many. The war had cost an estimated $800 billion dollars, leaving both countries heavily indebted. Iraq, for example, owed Saudi Arabia $25.1 billion, Kuwait $10 billion and the rest of the world another $40 billion. Hussein seems genuinely to have believed that as he had been defending the Arab world against Iranian fanatics, his fellow Arabs would forgive his debts. They did not.

In the thick of the slaughter were Iran's Revolutionary Guards, the Pasdaran, and its youth movement counterpart, the Basji. Both were imbued with their leader's extraordinary passion for the cause, even to the point of death. Believing that victory could be won only by 'blood ... and strength of faith', Khomeini advocated the murderous 'human wave' tactic – thousands upon thousands of foot soldiers pouring towards the enemy lines and eventually overcoming them by sheer weight of numbers.

The antics of the Basji particularly horrified those who encountered them. Drawn mainly from deeply religious, rural families, these young boys (some only 12 years old) carried on their person tokens of their coveted martyrdom: a piece of white cloth symbolizing their shroud and a plastic key (a gift from the ayatollah) to remind them that their entry into paradise was guaranteed. Lightly armed, if at all, they were used as human minesweepers or as decoys to draw enemy fire. They were shot down in their thousands.

The international dimension

The international repercussions of the war were extremely complex. On the surface, the West, headed by the US and France, joined with the Soviets in support of Saddam Hussein. The French built up especially strong commercial links with Iraq. America, estranged during Bakr's premiership, re-established diplomatic relations with Baghdad during the war. The CIA regularly supplied Iraqi generals with invaluable reconnaissance material.

Of the handful of states siding with Iran by far the most surprising was Israel. The reason was simply that they did not want Hussein, with his capacity to reach Tel Aviv as well as Tehran with his lethal warheads, emerging as a major power in the Middle East. We have already seen how the Israeli air force got in a pre-emptive strike against Iraq's nuclear plant in 1981 (see page 101).

As so often the case in the murky world of diplomacy, the picture was less straightforward than it at first seemed. Britain, for instance, sold Iran spare parts for its tanks. In what is known as the Iran-Contra Affair, the chicanery of the US administration was even more cynical. During 1985–7 it emerged that senior US officials, possibly with the knowledge of President Reagan and Vice-President George Bush Sr were selling arms to Iran via Israel. These weapons then found their way to Islamic terrorists operating in Lebanon, who in return freed Western hostages held there. The profits from the arms sales were used to fund the Contras – anti-Communist guerrillas fighting in Nicaragua.

The Tanker War also brought the international community into the conflict. By the end of the war more than 50 warships were patrolling the Gulf to defend Iraqi, Kuwaiti and other tankers from Iranian air strikes. Meanwhile, Iraqi planes were free to attack Iranian shipping at will.

Post-war Iraq

From almost every viewpoint, the Iran-Iraq war was a costly, tragic exercise in futility. By the time the two sides had finally finished haggling in 1990, the terms of their settlement were virtually the same as those of the previous Algiers Agreement. Strategically, therefore, all that bloodshed, all that misery, all that expenditure had achieved precisely nothing.

Billions of dollars of oil revenue that might have been spent on education, health or transport had been wasted on armaments. As far as Hussein's personal ambitions were concerned, however, the war had not been entirely a waste. It had allowed him to tighten his stranglehold on Iraq, eliminating thousands of Shia dissidents and innocent Kurds. His Kurdish policy came wickedly close to genocide. The chemical attack on the city of Halabja, for instance, left 5,000 men, women and children dead within 30 minutes.

By the close of the war the Iraqi army boasted 55 divisions and 4,000 tanks. This fulfilled another of Saddam Hussein's ambitions: he now ruled perhaps the most powerful state in the Gulf. His neighbours watched anxiously to see how he would exercise that power.

Intifada

This chapter will cover:
- unsuccessful attempts to solve the Israel-Palestine problem in the 1980s
- the emergence of Palestinian nationalism
- the First Intifada
- the election of Yasser Arafat as president of the state of Palestine
- the Madrid Conferences and renewed hopes of a settlement.

Fruitless negotiation

Time of strife

During the early 1980s the Middle East was as strife-torn as it had ever been. In the east, to satisfy the ambitions of their dictator-rulers, the people of Iran and Iraq were dying in their tens of thousands. Iranian fundamentalist fervour was beginning to seep across the region, bringing with it a new wave of unstoppable terrorism in the form of the suicide bomber. Egypt's discontent had manifested itself in the assassination of its well-intentioned president.

The Israeli invasion of Lebanon had gone horribly wrong. It brought none of the political or strategic gains intended, and ended in a shameful withdrawal. The massacres at Sabra and Shatilla left the Israeli government in deep disgrace and the nation bitterly divided. The PLO had been defeated and its leadership now languished in distant Tunisia. The people it purported to help remained stateless, impoverished and largely hopeless. The only beam of light, appearing in the middle of the decade, was the emergence of Nicholas Gorbachev as leader of the Soviet Union. His leadership would end the Cold War that had so often fuelled the Middle East's bitter quarrels.

Lebanese endgame

At about the time that Saddam Hussein was wondering whether war with Iran was such a good idea after all, several thousand miles away Yasser Arafat was also contemplating the future with some alarm. Now based in Tunis, for the first time in its existence the PLO had no common frontier with Israel. The armed struggle to replace Israel with a single democratic Palestinian-Jewish secular state had clearly failed.

Arafat, as PLO chairman and instigator of its policies, was inevitably blamed. Senior figures within the Palestinian National Council were tired of his inefficiency, favouritism and corruption. They wanted him removed. Back in Lebanon, open fighting broke out in the Baqa Valley between remnants of Fatah loyal to Arafat and Syrian-backed PLO dissidents. Keen to be at the front, Arafat shaved off his beard, donned a smart suit and dark glasses and sneaked into the battle zone via Cyprus.

After Shia bombs killed 241 US marines and 59 French paratroopers, mediators were eager to restore some semblance of order to the battered country. They eventually managed to separate the warring Palestinians and once again Arafat sailed off into the sunset with a US guarantee that the Israelis would not interfere with his flight.

Talks about talks

The bewildering details of the criss-cross network of proposals and talks going on at this time, some secret, some open, are too obscure to be relevant here. Many were simply talks about talks – efforts to decide an agenda and who would be allowed to participate before the negotiations proper began. The Israelis and the USA, for example, would not talk with the PLO because they regarded it as a terrorist organization. For this, Arafat had only himself to blame. Because he claimed, arrogantly and inaccurately, to speak for all Palestinians and control their paramilitary activities, he was also held responsible for their actions. This sometimes rebounded unpleasantly on him.

In 1985, for instance, a PLO hit squad – acting with or without Arafat's knowledge – killed three Israelis on a yacht in Cyprus. The Israeli government reacted by bombing the PLO HQ in Tunis, killing 56 Palestinians and 15 Tunisians. Small wonder several Arab states had said they were unwilling to harbour the PLO when it was expelled from Beirut. Arafat miraculously survived the raid on his compound. He was, he said, out 'jogging' at the time. Those who knew him smiled. Arafat was never a jogger – he had been simply taking a walk.

A few weeks later Arafat was again put in a difficult position. This time it was by his friend Abu Abbas, the pro-Iraqi bandit and leader of the Popular Front for the Liberation of Palestine. Abbas arranged for four young, frightened and poorly trained would-be freedom fighters to hi-jack the cruise liner *Achille Lauro* as it sailed from Alexandria. On board were 556 passengers and crew, including some Americans. Arafat immediately took responsibility. He would, he told the world, sort the matter out peacefully and discipline the hi-jackers. In fact, he did neither.

The hi-jackers shot dead a disabled American passenger and dumped his body overboard. When the ship returned to Egypt, an Egyptian aircraft was ready to fly the hi-jackers and Abu Abbas to Tunis. US fighter aircraft intercepted it en route and forced it to land in Italy. The Italian authorities, not wishing to get involved, eventually released all the hi-jackers.

Not only were the Israelis and the Americans unwilling to talk to the PLO, but the PLO itself refused to accept the crucial UN Resolution 242 (backed by the 1973 cease-fire Resolution 338) which the US made a central pre-condition for negotiation. Arafat's understandable objection was that 242 talked of peace between the 'states' of the Middle East and not of self-determination for the Palestinians. Even when Arafat said he would accept Resolutions 242 and 338 in return for Palestinian self-determination, US president Ronald Reagan rejected the offer out of hand.

When Israel went into Lebanon for a second time there were three peace suggestions in the air. The Reagan Plan wanted to take matters on from where they had been left at Camp David. Another plan, drawn up at an Arab summit at Fez, suggested a return to the two-state solution envisaged by the UN in 1947. The third idea was that somehow Jordan should merge with Palestinian-inhabited territory to form a state or confederation. Something on these lines was agreed between Arafat and King Hussein in 1985. Two years later Hussein made another agreement, this time with Israeli Prime Minister Shimon Peres. Along with all the other proposals, neither produced any lasting or tangible result.

Israel's National Unity

Depressed by the death of his wife and haunted by what was happening in Lebanon, Prime Minister Begin resigned in 1983. He was briefly replaced by Yitzhak Shamir, the one-time Stern Gang member. After the following year's elections neither the Labour nor the Likud coalitions were able to form a stable government. With the country under pressure from its friends over Lebanon and inflation running at 400 per cent a year, a political crisis was the last thing Israel needed. A way out of the difficulty was found by establishing a Labour-Likud Government of National Unity. Labour leader Shimon Peres became prime minister, while Likud leader Shamir acted as his deputy and foreign minister. Then, 25 months later, their roles were reversed.

Peres initiated the phased withdrawal from Lebanon (see page 107), leaving a security zone in the south of the country under the nominal control of the South Lebanese Army. Under both Peres and Shamir the policy of planting Israeli settlements in the occupied territories, especially the West Bank, continued apace. Indeed, Shamir refused even to talk of the 'West Bank' – to him it was 'Judea and Samaria', two provinces of the Old Testament Kingdom of David. The Jewish population in the area tripled between 1982 and 1986, bringing perhaps half of the land there and over 80 per cent of the water into Israeli hands.

The motives for this were two-fold. First, settlements appealed to the ultraconservatives to whom the Likud was increasingly beholden for political support. Second, with each settlement built it became more difficult for Israel to abandon its conquests of 1967. By the end of the 1980s, the government could claim with some justification that things had changed so much since the Six Day War that proposals made immediately after it were no longer relevant. The answer, they suggested somewhat cynically, was not for the Israelis to leave the territories, but for the Palestinians to do so.

At this point, for the first time in the long and unhappy saga, the ordinary Palestinians took matters into their own hands. They had had enough of being a political football kicked about by Israelis, the PLO, the Americans, the Soviets, the Egyptians, the Syrians, the Jordanians, the Iraqis, and just about everyone else who took a passing interest in the Middle East. Despairing of ever being listened to amid the hullabaloo of international politics, they let out a long, instinctive, heart-rending scream of pain.

The Palestinians

The West Bank and Gaza Strip

The Palestinians of the West Bank and Gaza Strip called their uprising the Intifada, meaning 'trembling' or 'shaking off'. With the benefit of hindsight, it is perhaps surprising that they endured so much for so long before losing patience. It may help, therefore, if at this stage we remind ourselves just who these people were.

When the state of Israel had been created out of the mandated territory of Palestine, the area contained some 1.3 million Arabs. Few of these people regarded themselves as Palestinians. Rather, their loyalties were to clan, tribe, faith, and the wider Arabic-speaking community. The enormous upheaval caused by the First Arab-Israeli War left around 150,000 Arabs within the new state of Israel. Although technically Israelis, they were very much second-class citizens. For almost 20 years they lived under military controls. To discourage the development of a distinct

Arab identity, the administration referred to them not as Arabs but as 'Druze', 'Bedouin' and so forth.

The remaining 1.15 million Arabs from the Palestinian mandate were scattered three ways. Over 20 per cent went to live in neighbouring Arab lands, settling either in refugee camps just over the border or in the towns. The largest group, around 100,000, went to Lebanon.

A second group fled to the West Bank, joining the Arabs already living there to swell its population to about 700,000. In this rugged region, with the city of Jerusalem on its south-western edge, they lived as shepherds, farmers, craftspeople, labourers and managers of small businesses. The hills of the north-west received sufficient annual rainfall for grazing and the harvesting of cereal crops. Elsewhere, water from the River Jordan or pumped from beneath the ground irrigated fields of fruits and vegetables.

The third group of Palestinian Arabs pressed into the Gaza Strip. Its boundaries determined by a 1949 cease-fire line, this was an area of 363 sq km (140 sq miles) that had surrounded Egypt's 1948 military headquarters. Only 8 km (5 miles) wide at its broadest, it was an arid band of poor and desperately overcrowded territory with little to recommend it. The bulk of the refugees lived in camps managed by the United Nations. Here, as on the West Bank, it was more than ten years before all the tents had been replaced by concrete huts. Water and sewage provision were poor. Education and medical facilities were generally rudimentary, and employment opportunities extremely limited.

For most of the time until the Six Day War the West Bank was administered, though not formally annexed, by Jordan. Egypt ruled the Gaza Strip with considerable harshness. Its inhabitants, for example, were not given Egyptian citizenship. Jordanian rule in the West Bank was reasonably sympathetic.

The emergence of a nation

Both the Gaza Strip and the West Bank were overrun by the Israeli army in 1967 and thereafter administered by Israel. Some Arabs fled the Israeli advance, others were forced to leave. Those who remained behind rapidly developed a national consciousness, becoming the first generation of true Palestinians.

Two factors helped the emergence of Palestinian nationalism. One was the PLO, with its network of semi-independent affiliates. The organization gradually became more than just a resistance movement. Recognized as the voice of the Palestinian Arabs of the West Bank and Gaza Strip, it came to regard itself as a government in waiting. Its pronouncements and propaganda filtered through to the crowded dispossessed, instilling in them a sense of what they believed ought to be and hoped one day would be.

The second influence on the growth of Palestinian nationalism was the behaviour of the Israeli conquerors. For ten years, guided by Moshe Dayan, the occupied territories were governed with a comparatively light hand. Those dwelling in the West Bank benefited from new roads (built for military purposes but useful for getting goods to market), better housing, and improved medical services. This changed dramatically with the formation of Begin's Likud government in 1977.

Israeli oppression

The most obvious sign of the Israeli government's new approach to the occupied territories was its settlement policy. In ten years the number of Jewish settlements rose from 36 to over 100. Most were small and the soil they farmed was generally poor, but to their Arab neighbours they were an obvious affront. The Israelis said the land they built on was either barren or not owned by anyone. The Arabs complained that, barren or not, the land was not just there for the taking. Furthermore, much of the land for whom no owner could be found had belonged to Arabs who had fled during the various wars. New settlers dug bore holes that drew upon the West Bank's precious underground reserves of water. Some sources say the average Israeli was allocated 12 times as much water as the average Palestinian.

Israeli settlers were given grants and tax advantages, and provided with good roads, schools and medical services. Their Arab neighbours looked on with increasing resentment. The settlements attracted some of the most intolerant and racist elements of Israeli society, too. Vigilante groups, like Gush Emunim, attacked Arab shops and houses. When apprehended, the perpetrators of this anti-Arab terrorism were generally let off lightly. Arab resentment grew still more bitter.

Life was made difficult for the Arabs in all kinds of little ways, too. They were subjected to road blocks and strict searches of their vehicles and property. Large-scale meetings were prohibited and taxes were increased. Failure to pay led to imprisonment. If Palestinians tried to get redress, the legal system was weighted against them. Verbal and minor physical abuse were commonplace, adding to the general feeling among the Palestinian Arabs that they were an unwanted and despised people.

In 1985, the Israeli cabinet voted to tighten the screw still further. Its 'Iron Fist' policy, devised by Foreign Minister Rabin, had a double aim: to destroy all opposition to Israeli rule, and persuade Palestinians that life would be better for them outside Israeli-governed territory. This tied in with the 'Greater Israel' policy of gradually absorbing the occupied territories into the state created in 1948.

Iron Fist led to an increase in so-called 'administrative punishments', which included deportation and preventative detention. The latter meant holding people without trial or appeal on suspicion that they might commit a crime. The use of physical intimidation increased, too. Palestinian youths were regularly rounded up, beaten, tortured and made to confess to crimes they had never committed. The courts turned a deaf ear to accusations of malpractice.

One comparatively mild example is illustrative of thousands of similar cases. The Palestinian lawyer Raja Shehadeh recalls the case of a 14-year-old shepherd boy who lived near Ramallah. One day, as he was grazing his sheep on the hills near Jenin, an anti-Israeli demonstration took place which involved throwing stones at Israeli soldiers. When he returned to Jenin, the young shepherd was arrested and taken to a special prison for youths that occupied a former British army barracks in the Faraa Valley.

He had done nothing, the boy told his interrogators. He had been out on the hills with his sheep all day. 'Confess!' screamed his persecutors. The lad did not even know to what he was supposed to confess. He was beaten until one of his arms fractured, then released. The Israelis believed such behaviour would break the back of Palestinian resistance. Not surprisingly, it had the opposite effect.

All this took place against a background of high unemployment (as much as 50 per cent in the Gaza Strip), poverty and lack of hope. The way the world's rich and powerful glibly discussed the fate of the Palestinians at high tables only served to unite the 'people nobody wanted' in their fury. They were not numbers or tokens, they insisted – they were people with as much right to a decent life as any one else.

There were, needless to say, acts of cruelty on both sides. With the PLO advocating talks for a peaceful settlement, more militant Palestinian groups continued along the path of violence. These included the Syrian based PFLP, which organized the hang-glider attack on northern Israel in 1987 that led to the death of six Israelis. A new organization, Islamic Jihad, brought Iranian-style Shia fundamentalism into the equation.

The spark that ignited the bonfire flashed on 6 December 1987. On that day, Shlomo Sakal, an Israeli trader, was stabbed to death in a Gaza market. The next day an Israeli military truck ran into Palestinian workers at the Erez checkpoint between Gaza and Israel, killing four and injuring seven. The Israelis said it was an accident. The Palestinians did not believe them, claiming that it was deliberate revenge for the stabbing.

Rioting broke out on the Gaza Strip. The Israeli security forces reacted harshly. On 9 December, Hatem Sissi, a resident of the Jabaliya refugee camp in Gaza, was shot dead by Israeli soldiers chasing stone-throwing youths. More Palestinians took to the streets, more police and soldiers confronted them. The conflagration spread to the West Bank and before long the whole of the occupied territories was caught up in the protest. The Intifada had begun.

Intifada

Violence

The Intifada was a spontaneous, violent, revolutionary movement not dissimilar to that which had overthrown the French establishment in 1789. A major difference was that the Palestinian movement involved a high proportion of children. Wearing the distinctive kuffiya head-dress that Arafat had made the symbol of the Palestinian cause, they came out in their thousands to taunt the occupying forces with words and stones. The stone-throwing was also symbolic, being a traditional Islamic way of warding off evil spirits.

The children of the Intifada were a new and desperate generation. Raised amid violence and cruelty, they too were violent. Without a sense of a better future – at least on earth – they were fearless, too. Mobile, organized, knowing the terrain infinitely better than their enemy, they were an impossible target. If the Israelis used force, the world condemned them as child murderers; if they hung back, the protests escalated as the attackers believed they were winning. It was one war in which the Israelis, for all their military might, could not triumph.

Backed by $40 million from Iran and Iraq, at the local level the Intifada was organized by the Palestinian United National Leadership (or Unified National Command – translations vary). This organization had come into being a few weeks after the start of the uprising. At the heart of its 14-point plan of action was self-determination for the Palestinians. Islamic Jihad also emerged into the open, organizing relief as well as anti-Israeli activities.

Another child of the Intifada was the Islamic Resistance Movement, commonly known as Hamas. Led by Sheikh Ahmed Yassin and Dr Abdulaziz al-Rantisi, Hamas had its roots in the Muslim Brotherhood (see page 57). It was organized into military and relief sections, responsible, respectively, for attacks on Israelis and assistance for the Palestinians. Like Islamic Jihad, it rejected all possibility of compromise with a state that it regarded as both illegal and an infidel virus within the body of a holy Muslim society. Ironically, the Israeli government had for a while been encouraging the growth of such Islamic groups as a counter-balance to the PLO. The policy's shortcomings were now apparent.

At first the PLO leadership in Tunis and Baghdad, where Arafat moved some offices in the late 1980s, was unsure what to make of the Intifada. When it became clear it was not just a flash in the pan, Arafat gave it his wholehearted support. He handed over daily responsibility for the PLO-Intifada operations to his lieutenant Abu Jihad. This competent and tireless administrator co-ordinated and assisted the uprising as best he could from remote Tunis. Elsewhere, the reaction of most Arab leaders, apart from President Assad, was the opposite to Arafat's. At first welcoming the Intifada, they were soon playing it down. Such an inspiring example of people power was not quite what the unelected heads of largely corrupt Middle Eastern regimes wanted plastered all over their national TV screens.

On the ground, the stone-throwing of the children was accompanied by demonstrations by women, illegal flying of the Palestinian flag, a tax strike, boycotts of Israeli goods and a host of other activities that rendered the occupied territories ungovernable. The movement was widely covered by the world's media which was almost universally shocked by Israeli tactics and sympathetic towards the Palestinians. The anger of ordinary people had drawn the world's attention to their plight far more effectively than their leaders had ever done.

Counter-violence

To begin with the Israeli cabinet saw the Intifada as just another Arab disturbance that they would soon quell with the usual tactics. Curfews were imposed, arrests and detentions increased, and the security forces urged to use appropriate tactics to cow the rioters. Within a few weeks, it was clear that what was happening was more than just another round of troubles.

Seeking to break the resistance with what Rabin called 'might, power, and beatings', the government declared a state of emergency and called up reservists. Mass arrests were made, tear gas used to disperse crowds, universities and schools closed. Houses used by suspected leaders were blown up. Arabic newspapers were heavily censored. It is said that a deliberate attempt was made to break the fingers and legs of the stone-throwers.

Within two years, 626 Palestinians died, 37,500 were wounded, and around 40,000 were arrested – yet the fires of the Intifada blazed as fiercely as ever. A considerable number of Israelis began to view the occupied territories in a new light. Instead of being essential to the security of Israel, they were actually weakening the country. Three-and-a-half million Israelis were just not physically capable of holding down one-and-a-half million Palestinians. The cost to the Israeli economy was enormous. It was not just a matter of expenditure, either. The call-up took people from productive work, and when the crossing points into Palestinian lands were closed, as often happened, Israeli businesses were deprived of labour.

Abroad, the reputation of Israel sank to an all-time low. At home, national morale collapsed. Comparisons were made between the racist behaviour of the IDF and other security forces, and the Nazis. A Peace Now movement gathered strength, calling for an immediate settlement with the Palestinians. The ultraconservatives reacted with renewed defiance and determination never to surrender to those perceived simply as terrorists.

In April 1988 the Israeli cabinet agreed a dramatic attempt to destroy the Intifada by eliminating its leadership. A submarine landed an Israeli hit squad in Tunisia. Aided by spies and aircraft, it sought out the organizing mind behind the Palestinian uprising. Before the horrified gaze of his wife and young child, Abu Jihad's body was shot through with 150 bullets. The action was condemned by governments around the world, while a funeral attended by thousands in the streets of Damascus announced the creation of yet another Palestinian martyr.

The state of Palestine

Diplomatic advances

Diplomatically the Intifada had dramatic consequences. When it had been active for about seven months, King Hussein of Jordan announced what had been a practical reality for years: he had no claim either to the West Bank or to represent the Palestinians. This significantly enhanced the authority of the PLO and Chairman Arafat.

Armed with his new prestige, Arafat determined to use the Intifada as a springboard for a diplomatic triumph. In June 1988 one of his officials announced at an Arab summit that the PLO would accept UN Resolutions 242 and 338 in return for a Palestinian state. The offer evoked no dramatic response.

In November Arafat went even further. Appearing as the Intifada's triumphant commander, he told a meeting of the Palestine National Council that the state of Palestine now existed. Jerusalem was its capital and he was its president. (His position would be confirmed by election the following year.) He went on to accept a two-state solution to the Palestine-Israel problem. Although the US and Israel remained sceptical, the UN invited Arafat to address its General Assembly. As US Secretary of State Schultz would not grant Arafat a visa to speak at the UN in New York, the General Assembly adjourned to Geneva. Here Arafat spoke on 13 December, making sweeping concessions.

A comprehensive Middle East peace settlement was needed, Arafat declared. He talked of the 'state of Israel', recognizing its existence. He accepted Resolutions 242 and 338. He renounced terrorism. At a news conference the next day he went even further. Israel, he admitted, should be permitted to live in peace and security. When questioned further, he underlined the extent of his concessions with the famous words, 'Enough! Do you want me to do a striptease?'

At last, in renouncing violence and accepting Israel's right to exist, Arafat had uttered the words the US wanted to hear. Its response was immediate: American negotiators would begin talks with the PLO at once. Israeli premier Yitzhak Shamir, however, insisted that his country would not negotiate with terrorists. Coming from someone who had himself fought as a terrorist against the British, it was hardly a convincing argument. His real reason for stalling was an unwillingness to hand back 'Judea' and 'Samaria'.

The First Gulf War

Under American pressure, cracks began to appear in Israel's National Unity government. Defence Minister Rabin, Labour, came out in favour of talks with the Palestinians. Prime Minister Shamir, Likud, then put forward a plan of his own that offered the Palestinians almost nothing. Despite the efforts of Secretary of State Schultz and his successor James Baker, no progress was made. The Israelis would not negotiate with Arafat, nor would they stop their programme of settlement building. The latter entered a new and more vigorous phase with the appointment of Sharon as Minister of Construction and Housing.

Two acts of violence only made matters worse. The first was the shooting dead of seven Palestinians in the occupied territories by a young Israeli. The second was when the *Achille Lauro* hijackers, now with Iraqi backing, landed on a beach near Tel Aviv and were shot dead by Israeli security forces. On 13 June 1990, James Baker stormed out of talks with the Israelis shouting, 'Our telephone number is 202–456–1414. When you're serious about peace, call us.' A week later he announced that he was breaking off talks with the PLO as well.

Surprisingly, the deadlock was broken by Saddam Hussein. Over the past few years Arafat had become increasingly dependent upon the Iraqi dictator. This led him to make one of the biggest mistakes of his career. In the summer of 1990,

Saddam Hussein's forces invaded and occupied Kuwait (see Chapter 11). The action was condemned by just about every country in the world, including the wealthy oil-producing Arab states. Arafat, however, went the other way and sided with Iraq. In doing so he tied himself to an international leper. Worse still, the next year an American-led coalition drove the Iraqi forces from Kuwait and destroyed much of Hussein's military capacity. This left Arafat and his PLO isolated, impecunious and impotent. The only option left to them was to return to the negotiating table.

Hopes of settlement

As soon as the First Gulf War ended, US President George Bush Sr announced a new initiative to settle the Israeli-Palestinian question once and for all. Secretary of State Baker put forward a nine-point plan as the basis for an international conference. Arafat rejected it.

Arafat's move was little more than a gesture of independence. His position was considerably weaker than it had been before the war. His oil-rich backers had cut his funding, leaving the PLO close to bankruptcy. The image of Palestinians dancing at the sight of Israeli civilians killed by Saddam Hussein's Scud missiles had not gone down well internationally, either. Moreover, the Israelis had improved their tarnished reputation by not reacting to Iraq's unprovoked attacks.

Therefore, when peace talks co-hosted by George Bush and Soviet premier Mikhail Gorbachev were announced, Arafat had little choice: he could either attend or be cast into outer diplomatic and political darkness. To meet Israeli sensibilities, the Palestinians were represented by delegates from the occupied territories. The PLO went as part of the Jordanian delegation, though without Arafat himself.

A series of conferences was held in Madrid, Spain. Not surprisingly, they soon ran into difficulties. The usual sticking points arose: Israeli settlements in the occupied territories, and the Palestinian desire for full statehood rather than just a vague autonomy. The Israeli hand was strengthened by the arrival in Israel of thousands of Jews from the collapsing Soviet Union. Where could they be housed, pleaded Shamir's government, if settlement was not permitted on the West Bank? Shamir was in no hurry to reach agreement, and the Soviet development made a useful bargaining point.

After a few months, as the talks were bogging down, elections were held in Israel. The Labour leader, Yitzhak Rabin, campaigned on the manifesto of bringing peace with the Palestinians within a year. From the man who had been an unflinching hard-line defence minister, this was difficult to believe. Nevertheless, the electorate placed the Labour coalition in charge of the Knesset. It was now up to Rabin, prime minister of Israel for a second time, to deliver on his pledge.

Desert Storm

This chapter will cover:
- the state of Iraq after the Iran-Iraq War
- Saddam Hussein's invasion of Kuwait and the international reaction to it
- the First Gulf War, 1991
- the repercussions of the war.

Saddam bankrupt

By the end of the Iran-Iraq War in 1988, it is estimated that Iraq owed almost $100 billion to overseas agencies and governments, and that it would take a further $180 billion to repair the damage done to the country's infrastructure. With an annual income from oil revenues then running at around $10 billion, it would be almost a quarter of a century before the country was back on its financial feet again. In other words, Saddam Hussein's regime was to all intents and purposes bankrupt.

Financial worries were only one source of the dictator's headache. At home there were grumblings from the Shia majority in the south, which had suffered decades of Sunni domination and persecution by Hussein's secular government. At the other end of the country, the Kurds – the largest national group in the world not to have their own state – remained as dissatisfied as ever with their lack of autonomy.

In the country at large the deprivations brought on by the war fuelled discontent within a regime that totally disregarded the rule of law and human rights, and maintained itself by fear and torture. Some sources say there were no less than four attempts to assassinate Hussein in the two years following the ending of the war with Iran – one from within his army's élite Republican Guard.

Sensing the weakness of his position, Hussein made grand announcements about liberalizing his government. He established a committee to prepare a new constitution that guaranteed multi-party government and freedom of the press. Given Hussein's abhorrence of any opposition, there was no evidence that the words of the document would bear any relation to practical reality. At the same time, he made efforts to improve relations with his Arab neighbours. He concluded non-aggression pacts with Saudi Arabia and Bahrain, and joined with the non-oil-producing states of Egypt, Jordan and North Yemen to form an Arab Co-operation Council.

The continued existence of the massive army raised during the Iran-Iraq War was another of Hussein's problems. A rapid reduction in its size was a strategic, social and economic impossibility: a sudden influx onto the streets of large numbers of unemployed young men would be a recipe for disaster. Hussein knew only too well that his term of unenlightened government had not made the country any less susceptible to violent upheaval than at the time of the 1958 and 1963 coups. The answer to the problem of the army, he decided, was to use it rather than lose it.

Increasing isolation

The West, headed by the US, had been prepared to back Iraq during the 1980s as a bulwark against the fiercely anti-Western Islamism of the Ayatollahs' Iran. Even so, Hussein's dictatorial regime was hardly a natural ally of democratic capitalism, and support for it was seen very much as the lesser of two evils. Nor was the relationship easy. In 1987, for example, the Pentagon and Washington were forced to exercise considerable restraint when a stray Iraqi Exocet missile hit *USS Stark*, killing 37 of the crew.

Immediately after it had enabled Hussein to claim victory over Iran, the US began to pull back from its close relationship with him. It had not been best pleased by his use of what came to be known as 'Weapons of Mass Destruction' (WMDs) against Iranians and Kurds. Israeli reports that he was attempting to fit nuclear warheads to Soviet-built Scud-B missiles were also worrying. In 1988 there was a mutual expulsion of diplomats from Washington and Baghdad.

Two years later, the administration of President George Bush Sr took Iraq to task over the misspending of agricultural credits. His former allies were even less impressed when Hussein boasted that he was developing a three-stage rocket capable of carrying a warhead 1930 km (1,200 miles), bringing the entire Middle East within range. Nevertheless, at the start of 1990, US-Iraq trade was still worth some $3 billion.

The French also had strong commercial links with Iraq, especially in the arms trade. True to their pragmatic and independent approach to world affairs, the administrations of President Mitterand were not often willing to let political niceties stand in the way of economic advantage. The closeness of the relationship between President Hussein and right-wing Prime Minister Jacques Chirac gave the French media plenty of opportunity to mock the affair between the phonetically-united Chirac and Iraq.

On the other hand, Soviet support for Iraq was on the wane. Thousands of Soviet advisors remained in Iraq but their numbers were being reduced all the time. Caught up in the spirit – and economic necessity – of détente, President Gorbachev was eager not to annoy the US. The collapsing Soviet economy obliged him to reduce international aid on every front. By the autumn of 1990 the Soviet Union itself was on the way out and in no position to play a major role in an international debacle in the Gulf.

The government of Britain, Iraq's third largest trading partner, was also having second thoughts about backing the regime of a man whom its tabloid newspapers were calling the 'Butcher of Baghdad'. Two issues brought the matter to a head. One was the discovery that British firms were secretly manufacturing parts for a 'super gun' and illegally exporting them to Iraq. The mysterious assassination of the weapon's Canadian inventor added to public disquiet. The second issue was the arrest and execution on false spying charges of the British journalist Farzad Bazoft. It seems that Saddam Hussein, furious at attacks on him in the British press, called personally for the death penalty.

Threatening Kuwait

Against this background of debt, potential unrest and worrying international isolation, in February 1990 President Saddam Hussein attended a meeting of the newly-formed Arab Co-operation Council. The price of oil had dropped the previous month, making his country's economic plight yet more precarious. Nevertheless, even when in trouble it was beneath the dignity of a proud man from Tikrit to plead for help. Saddam spoke of himself as the saviour of Sunnis from Shia extremism. He had, he said, borne on his own shoulders the entire weight of defending the Arab world. It was only right, therefore, that he should be rewarded with a cancellation of his war debts and a strict adherence to agreed production quotas in order to push up the price of oil.

The requests fell on deaf ears. The robed aristocracy of the Gulf had no desire to help an aggressive and vulgar parvenu from upcountry Iraq. Hussein was humiliated.

Pressure on Kuwait

The Iraqi president was seriously handicapped by a lack of objective and honest advice. The problem was entirely of his own making. Surrounded by a phalanx of fawners and sycophantic relatives, he rarely heard the truth and was never offered unpalatable policy suggestions. Thus isolated within a cocoon of fear, during the first half of 1990 he searched desperately for a way out of his troubles.

One obvious solution lay on Iraq's very doorstep: Kuwait. Hussein's plan was to cajole and frighten the tiny Gulf sheikhdom into helping him out. It is worth remembering that the state of Kuwait, like Iraq, had been created by British imperialism. Although frontiers had appeared on the map, on the ground they had yet to become an established part of the political scene. As we saw at the start of the Iran-Iraq War, several boundaries were still disputed. Indeed, on a number of occasions in the recent past Iraq had laid claim to the whole of Kuwait. Until only days before he gave the command, however, the Iraqi dictator did not intend to invade. He simply did not think it would be necessary.

Hussein made three claims. Kuwait had 'stolen' Iraqi oil worth $12 billion from the Rumaila oilfield; it had allowed too much oil to come on to the world market, forcing down the price; it had contemplated seizing territory from the Iraqis while they had been combating Iranian Islamic fundamentalism. All of these serious misdemeanours, Hussein announced, could be settled amicably with a little Kuwaiti generosity. They simply had to cut their oil production, hand over financial aid and suspend Iraq's debts.

Kuwait's ruling al-Sabah family was not impressed. Around 100,000 Iraqi troops moved up to their narrow southern border. Believing this to be merely the usual Hussein bluff and bluster, on the other side the Kuwaiti leadership stood their forces down. A visit from US ambassador April Glaspie failed to convince Hussein that his attitude towards Kuwait was leading him into dangerous waters. Another visit, this time from Egypt's widely respected President Hosni Mubarak on behalf of the Arab League, left the Iraqi leader unchecked but his fellow Arabs believing that he would never dare attack Kuwait.

Crisis talks

On 31 July 1990, the Saudis invited the Iraqis and Kuwaitis for high-level crisis talks. The oil price had recently risen, swelling Iraq's income. Compromise seemed close: Iraq asked for $10 billion, Kuwait offered $9 billion. The two sides were almost there. At this stage, unfortunately, the conversation became personal.

On one side was Hussein's cousin, Ali Hassan al Majid. Known as 'Chemical Ali', this was the man who had supervised the murderous gas attack on the village of Halabja (see page 138). Opposite him was the Crown Prince of Kuwait.

The cultural and social gulf between the two men was much wider than the economic one. Neither was an experienced negotiator at this level. Unwilling to make the final concession necessary for a compromise, their remarks grew acrimonious, then heated. Before long they were shouting at each other. Alarmed, Saudi guards hurried into the room to find them close to blows.

Chemical Ali pleaded that the Iraqis, fellow Arabs, were in dire poverty. Surely Kuwait could not deny alms to the poor? The Crown Prince snorted. If the Iraqis were hard up, he retorted, they should send their women out on to the streets to earn a bit of cash. The insult, hinting at rumours that Saddam Hussein was of illegitimate birth, was as pointed as it was tactless.

In such a poisonous atmosphere compromise was impossible. When the Crown Prince's words were reported to Hussein, his fury knew no bounds. On 2 August, 100,000 Iraqi troops and 2,000 tanks entered Kuwait. The invasion had begun.

Operation Desert Shield

Saddam Hussein's attack on Kuwait took the world by surprise. Mubarak's assurances had created a false sense of security. Few observers believed that Hussein would actually do something quite so outrageous or so foolish. He had talked proudly of fighting Iran to defend the Arabs; he had recently proposed an anti-imperialist and anti-Zionist coalition with Kuwait; he had openly touted for leadership of the Arab world. Now, in stark contrast to all he had said, he had perpetrated an act of naked aggression against a virtually defenceless Arab neighbour.

Politicians everywhere, accustomed to endless rhetoric of Arab unity in the face of Israeli aggression, were deeply perplexed. The action seemed so irrational. But Hussein the dictator had become divorced from reason and logic. Cut off from reality, he was incapable of forming a coherent or long-term strategy. He governed instead by cunning and instinct. That is why the invasion of Kuwait was not widely predicted – it was essentially a spur of the moment, irrational act.

The rape of Kuwait

In the face of the overwhelming Iraqi onslaught, Kuwait fell in a matter of hours. The Emir's half-brother made a brave but hopeless last stand with some loyal troops, but the rest of the royal family fled to Saudi Arabia in a fleet of sleek Mercedes. The remaining population, native Kuwaitis as well as many thousands of foreign workers, were virtually imprisoned within the emirate.

The al-Sabahs had run Kuwait as a private fiefdom. The administration, headed by the royal family, was unelected. The National Assembly, wielding only very limited powers, had been suspended for the previous four years. It was hardly the sort of place that democrats normally rushed to assist.

Kuwait, however, had oil. It was also a vital Iraqi bridgehead into Saudi Arabia. Between them these two Gulf states controlled some 40 per cent of the world's known oil reserves. If that was not enough, Hussein horrified decent-minded people the world over by the brutal way he treated his new 'province' – he had formally annexed Kuwait as a province of Iraq on 8 August. Foreigners were not allowed to leave but held as hostages. Kuwaitis were subjected to a plague of rape, murder, beatings, and systematic looting. The neat, tidy and well-ordered little state soon deteriorated into an enclave of sordid cruelty. Although their activities provoked ferocious reprisals, it is estimated that the Kuwaiti underground resistance killed some 100 Iraqis.

The coalition forms

Resistance within Kuwait was the least of Hussein's worries. If he had wondered before how the international community would react to an invasion, he was quickly left in little doubt. Iraq's action was condemned throughout the world. The West's response was led by the British Prime Minister Margaret Thatcher. Nearing the end of her premiership, she was more prone than ever to seeing issues as either black or white. Britain had guaranteed Kuwait's independence 30 years previously, so it had to do its duty. Nevertheless, it could not act without the US. Schoolmistress Thatcher is allegedly to have cajoled the more cautious US President Bush Sr with, 'Now, George, don't go wobbly on me!'

Bush did not go wobbly. Furthermore, skilful diplomacy enabled him to go to war on the cheap. The US had plenty of material left over from the Cold War era, and the bulk of the eventual cost of the campaign would be met by its Arab allies. Once the Americans had moved, Soviet President Mikhail Gorbachev had little option but to go along with them. With his country in turmoil, the last thing he needed was a confrontation with the world's one remaining superpower.

The majority of Arab nations joined the chorus of condemnation. To King Fahad of Saudi Arabia, who genuinely feared that his kingdom might be next on Hussein's hit-list, it was, 'the ugliest aggression in human history'. Syria's President Asad was equally disapproving of his neighbouring Baathists. Egypt's President Mubarak used more cautious language. The most widely respected Arab leader, he had to make sure the oil producers and West paid a fair price for his backing. They did. When the affair was finally over, generous foreign subsidies had reduced Egypt's international debt by 75 per cent.

Within the region, only Jordan, North Yemen, Sudan, Libya and the PLO registered any approval of Hussein's action. At that time Libya's maverick President Gaddafi would support any anti-American cause. Jordan's King Hussein personally disliked President Hussein but felt obliged to go along with the overwhelmingly pro-Iraqi mood of his people. The political, military and economic clout of Yemen and Sudan were negligible.

As we have seen, the decision of Yasser Arafat to throw in his lot with the Iraqi dictator was one of the most unfortunate he ever made (see pages 151–2). Hussein tried to use it to his advantage by linking his action with events in Israel and the territories it occupied. Ten days after the invasion of Kuwait he agreed to pull out of the emirate if Israel withdrew from the territories it had occupied in 1967. Such crude bargaining deceived no one, nor was the reputation of the Iraqi leader much enhanced in Arab eyes by equating his actions with those of the Israelis. Later, at war with the United Nations' coalition liberating Kuwait, Hussein again made an unsuccessful effort to bring Israel into the equation.

The build-up

For years the US had been anxious about the vulnerability of the Saudi oilfields. It already had a plan (codenamed 1002–90) to defend them and was eager to move swiftly lest Hussein continue his southward thrust. First, it had to get permission to build up forces on Arabian soil. The administration of King Fahad was understandably anxious about allowing a massive infidel presence inside the country that guarded Islam's holiest sites. His doubts evaporated into the desert air when he was shown US spy satellite photographs of Iraqi forces massing along Kuwait's southern border. The Saudis needed help – if that meant using infidels, so be it. Thus began Operation Desert Shield.

The ending of the Cold War had freed the United Nations to do what it had been created to do. When faced with a serious and violent breach of the UN Charter, the Security Council was empowered to raise forces to fight under the UN banner. However, as the permanent Council members had a veto over the military option, it had been used only once. In 1950, an American-led UN force had gone to the aid of South Korea when it had been invaded by the Communist North. At the time pro-Western Taiwan represented China, and the Soviet Union was boycotting the Security Council and therefore unable to use its veto. Thereafter, UN military action had been limited to observing and peace-keeping.

In the autumn of 1990, East-West relations were better than they had been for almost half a century. The members of the Security Council unanimously agreed resolutions condemning the Iraqi invasion, calling for immediate withdrawal, and placing an economic embargo on Iraq. On 29 November, a further resolution gave Iraq until 15 January to withdraw or face armed intervention in the name of the UN.

The build-up of forces in the Gulf was the largest military operation of its kind since the Second World War. Munitions, money, troops and ships poured in from all over the world. The bulk – 500,000 of the 800,000 soldiers, for instance – was provided by the US. Japan, limited by its pacifist constitution, provided $10 billion. Ironically, in the light of future events, even the Mujahedin of Afghanistan managed a contingent of 300. One of the few hiccups stemmed from France's refusal, for commercial reasons, to provide the coalition with details of the weapons systems it had sold to Iraq.

If Hussein had planned to invade Saudi Arabia, he should have moved straight away. The longer he left it, the more difficult his task became. By Christmas it was all but impossible. Ranged against him were thousands of the most modern combat aircraft, helicopters, tanks and guns. In the Gulf steamed dozens of warships ranging from vast aircraft carriers to minesweepers and submarines able to launch the latest ship-to-shore missiles.

Despite the massive arsenal at their fingertips, the American officers in overall command of the operation were anxious. The last war the US had fought – against the Vietcong – had vividly demonstrated that technology alone could not guarantee victory. What if the Iraqi armed forces rallied behind their leader as steadfastly as the North Vietnamese had done behind Ho Chi Minh? With the exception of one or two Arab contingents, the coalition soldiers were fighting for an abstract principle. It mattered little to them personally who ruled Kuwait. It is unlikely that their morale would have held up in a protracted and bloody war. Nor would the public back in the USA have remained steadfastly behind the war if large numbers of their sons and daughters had been brought home in body bags. A swift and comparatively painless victory was a military and a political necessity.

Iraq's armed forces were considerable in size and battle-hardened after their recent war with Iran. Numerically the army was the fourth largest in the world. It was backed by 6,000 assorted battle tanks, 200 armed helicopters and thousands of anti-aircraft devices. The air force was the sixth largest in the world, boasting some of the latest Russian Mig-29s and French Mirage F1s.

Perhaps more alarming was Iraq's array of unconventional weapons. It did not yet have a nuclear bomb, but it did possess thousands of tons of mustard gas, quantities of the nerve agents Sarin and Tabun, and some biological weapons like botulinum and anthrax. Moreover, on elusive mobile launchers it had 800 Scud missiles capable of delivering a lethal dose into any neighbouring state. In the event, Hussein did not use his Weapons of Mass Destruction, perhaps because he feared that the coalition would respond with WMDs of their own. It is fairly certain that some coalition members did indeed have a range of such weapons at the ready.

Operation Desert Storm

Softening up

As the UN deadline of 15 January approached, national and international diplomats tried in vain to find a way out. Despite the overwhelming force ranged against him, and numerous UN resolutions demanding his withdrawal, Hussein refused to budge. He seems to have hoped that unwavering resistance to what he called 'imperialist bullying' would endear him to his people and perhaps bring some fellow Arabs to his side. In truth, he had no option. Had he called his forces home, the failure and humiliation would almost certainly have provoked rebellion. Even if he had survived that, he would still have been no nearer sorting out his economic difficulties. It had to be war.

The First Gulf War began on 17 January 1991. It was a war the like of which had never been seen before: more precise, more controlled, more technological, and less randomly destructive than any previously fought. It featured 'stealth' bombers, 'cruise' missiles and 'smart' bombs for the first time. Guided by satellite, laser and radio, bombs and missiles could pinpoint targets as small as a window. The enduring image of the new warfare was provided by a CNN reporter sitting in a hotel room in Baghdad. Looking out of the window, he watched a 5.5 m (18 foot) Tomahawk cruise missile fly down the street, turn right at the traffic lights and proceed on its programmed path towards its target. It might well have been launched from a B-52 bomber that had made the 22,500 km (14,000 mile) round trip from Louisiana.

Determined to make the recapture of Kuwait as straightforward as possible, over a period of five weeks the coalition systematically destroyed the enemy's command and control structure, his air force and airfields, his anti-aircraft defences, his communications, his oil refineries, and his navy. Once they were out of the way, the attack turned to the ground forces. Outgunned and isolated, the Iraqi troops lost all stomach for a fight long before one began. Even the famed Republican Guard cracked under the onslaught.

Soldiers whose previous experience of war had been mowing down waves of lightly armed Iranians found themselves targeted with terrifying accuracy by aircraft that had complete mastery of the skies. Iraq's armed forces might have been large but they were equipped with a hotchpotch of weapons that were at least a generation behind those of the coalition. In everyday household terms, the technological difference between the two sides was like that between a vinyl record and a CD.

Of course there were civilian casualties – part of what US litotes-speak termed 'collateral damage'. By the end of the war, some 2,500 Iraqi non-combatants had died (315 when an air-raid shelter was mistaken for a command bunker) and a further 6,000 injured. The numbers were dreadfully high, but comparatively less than in any previous bombing campaign of that scale. The number killed was half that in the village of Halabja when it was gas-attacked by Hussein's forces one afternoon in 1988 (see page 138).

A degree of mystery surrounds the Iraqi Scud missiles. It seems that for some reason only around 200 were ever fired. Half were directed at Saudi Arabia, where one hit a US army barracks. Three went for Bahrain, and some 40 were targeted at Israel. Two Israelis were killed, about 200 wounded and many buildings damaged. Hard-line Israeli leaders, including Ariel Sharon, demanded that their government persist with its current policy and retaliate immediately with great force. This is precisely what Hussein wanted. Had Israel gone to war with Iraq, Arab members of the coalition would have found themselves fighting alongside an impossible ally. This might well have pulled the coalition apart. As it was, the White House put immense pressure on the government of Prime Minister Shamir not to retaliate, and it did not. Coalition attempts to seek and destroy the Scuds' mobile launchers appear to have been a complete failure.

Desert Sabre

In overall command of the coalition's land operation – Desert Sabre – was the huge figure of General H. Norman Schwarzkopf. As impressive in intelligence as in bulk, this deceptively sophisticated and sensitive soldier skilfully handled the tricky relations with his partners. The success of his battle plan coupled with a formidable appearance and sometimes brusque manner led to the media dubbing him 'Stormin' Norman'.

Officially, Schwarzkopf's land war lasted 100 hours. One force of mainly US and Arab troops moved on Kuwait City. Advancing behind armoured helicopters that blasted every moving Iraqi target they could find, they swiftly liberated the capital. The battered Iraqis put up scant resistance. There were even rumours of commanders cutting their men's Achilles tendons to prevent them running way.

Meanwhile, a huge force of coalition armour drove into Iraq to the west of Kuwait. Their target was Iraq's armoured reserves, particularly the Republican Guard. When the Guard tried to fight a rearguard action before Basra they were pounded into submission.

Thousands were killed as they tried to escape, many thousands more surrendered. The road north from Basra – the 'Highway of Death' – became a ribbon of fire and smoke as coalition aircraft and helicopters made every effort to destroy as much enemy material as possible before the war ended. US pilots described the one-sided killing as a 'turkey shoot'. It is estimated that Iraq lost 80 per cent of its tanks and 90 per cent of its artillery.

There was a moment when, with the Iraqis in full retreat and the coalition forces hot on their heels, President Bush was tempted to allow his forces to press on to Baghdad and try to topple Saddam Hussein. President Eisenhower had faced a similar decision during the Korean War, when General MacArthur had wanted to carry the war into China. As Eisenhower had cautiously declined the escalation, so did George Bush. George Bush Jr took over where his father had left off 12 years later, and finished the anti-Hussein mission for him (see Chapter 14).

Repercussions and revolts

Losses

The most obvious consequence of the First Gulf War was the liberation of Kuwait. The al-Sabah family returned and over the next decade or so took steps to make their government more accountable to the people (see Chapter 14). Individuals and companies set about rebuilding and repairing the devastated buildings and infrastructure.

For a long time, Kuwait was at the heart of an environmental disaster. The retreating Iraqis had set fire to 700 oil wells and opened the taps so that the largest oil slick in history slid out over the northern waters of the Gulf. The price of the horrific water and air pollution may never be accurately ascertained.

The loss of human life could be more precisely worked out. Two thousand Kuwaitis had been killed and many more injured. A large number (around 600) had simply disappeared. The coalition had lost 246 lives, 147 of them American and 24 British (some from so-called 'friendly-fire'). A number of coalition troops reported suffering from a mysterious 'Gulf War Syndrome', a malaise they said they had contracted either from the injections they had been given or from an unknown enemy biological agent.

Iraqi military losses are less easily computed. Some estimates say 100,000 lives were lost. A more accurate figure is perhaps 20,000, with a further 60,000 wounded. Long after the war there were repeated complaints of the harmful effects on civilians of the depleted uranium used to harden the coalition's armour-piercing shells.

Hussein survives

Remarkably, Saddam Hussein survived. That he did so was partly due to a mistake by General Schwarzkopf, partly to the reluctance of the US to intervene in the internal affairs of Iraq, and partly to the dictator's sheer bloody mindedness. Schwarzkopf's error occurred during the cease-fire talks he held with Iraqi generals. He stipulated a list of weapons they were no longer to hold, including military aircraft. Since most of the bridges across the Tigris and Euphrates were down, replied the Iraqis, might they retain their helicopters to ferry essential supplies? Without thinking through the implications of the request, Schwarzkopf said that they might keep their helicopters.

Shortly afterwards, encouraged by US exhortations to overthrow the Butcher of Baghdad, the Shia of southern Iraq rose in revolt. Two days later the Kurds in the north rose up. In both north and south Hussein's forces – mainly surviving units of the Republican Guard – quashed the rebels with horrific force. Helicopter gunships played a significant part in the massacres. The Americans and British failed even to provide the dissidents with arms. In Basra captured insurgents were made to swallow petrol before being set alight. Perhaps 20,000 Shia were slaughtered. Entire Kurdish villages were razed and over a million men, women and children fled for their lives into Iran and Turkey.

In March 1991 the coalition delineated an autonomous safe area for the Iraqi Kurds. To defend it they declared a no-fly zone over wide swathes of the countryside. The following year a similar no-fly zone was declared in the south. For many thousands these measures were far too late.

Before we hasten to criticize the US and Britain too strongly, it is worth remembering that the United Nations' Charter specifically disallows intervention in the internal affairs of sovereign states. Technically speaking, once Kuwait had been liberated, there was no legal basis for taking action within Iraq. The leaders of the coalition knew well that the more they interfered in a Muslim Arab state, the more they would invoke Muslim and Arab hostility. In short, they were damned whatever they did.

The terms of the cease-fire were enshrined in a UN Security Council resolution (687). This also demanded the elimination of Iraq's WMDs. To verify that this happened a special UN commission was set up (UNSCOM) to work with the International Atomic Energy Authority. The weapons inspectors' sorry story is dealt with in Chapter 13.

The UN and the superpower

The Gulf War marked a massive restoration of the fortunes of the United Nations. Having been hamstrung for decades by East-West rivalry, it was now able to play an important role in guiding the affairs of nations. The Gulf operation was followed by a host of observer, protective and enforcing missions in countries such as Bosnia, Somalia, Angola, and East Timor. It is worth pointing out that since none of these places boasted vast oil reserves, superpower support for UN action was not always unstinting.

By the middle of 1991 it was clear that a world dominated by two rival superpowers had given way to one of a single superpower. The Gulf War marked America's emergence as the pre-eminent global power in military as well as economic and political terms.

The war also marked the beginning of a new phase of US involvement in the Middle East. Hitherto, apart from sending peace-keeping forces into Lebanon and the ill-fated rescue mission in Iran (see pages 106–7 and 129–30), it had been content to pull strings rather then intervene directly. From now on it was firmly and physically allied with the conservative, oil-producing Gulf states. It had fought for them and beside them. Their enemies were now America's enemies. The road to the terrorist attack of 11 September 2001 began almost exactly ten years earlier on the barren shores of the Gulf.

More immediately, closer US involvement in the Middle East meant hope for Israelis and Palestinians. Taking advantage of its new global authority and the 'peace dividend' brought by the ending of the Cold War, the White House was determined to make a concerted effort at settling once and for all the problems between Israel and the Palestinians.

12

the 1990s: searching for settlement

This chapter will cover:
- moves made after the First Gulf War to settle the Arab-Israeli conflict
- the Oslo Accords and the reactions to them
- the difficult progress of the peace process during the mid-1990s
- how the peace process finally broke down and a Second Intifada errupted.

Instability, religion and power

As the twentieth century drew to a close, the Middle East was entering a new and more dangerously unstable phase in its history. The basic ingredients of this instability had long been present: inequality, tyranny, oil, water, race, conflicting faiths, unsure frontiers and outside interference. By the 1990s these factors overlapped and intertwined in complex patterns that were hard to distinguish, let alone unravel.

Saudi Arabia proved a classic example. The controller of the world's largest oil reserves was fabulously wealthy, yet over its borders to the south and north dwelt some of the poorest people in the region. It was the defender of Islam's holiest sites, but needed the military umbrella of the Christian West to maintain that defence. The staunch ally of many liberal democracies, its own regime was one of the most illiberal and dictatorial on earth. Moreover, although the Saudi royal family professed adherence to the puritanical Wahabite sect, fundamentalists of both Sunni and Shia persuasion condemned it as corrupt and impure.

The principal factor responsible for raising the political temperature within the region was religion, specifically fundamentalist Islam. Before the Iranian Revolution of 1979, most inhabitants of the Middle East felt impotent in the face of Western military and economic power. Governments that wished to succeed invariably aligned themselves with a Western power, Communist or democratic-capitalist. After the poor showing of the Muslim Brotherhood in the early struggles with Israel, there seemed no other way of getting on. The Iranians demonstrated this to be a false assumption: Islam could provide a home-grown source of inspiration, a rallying point against outsiders, a reason for pride in one's own culture. Furthermore, it gave power. It enabled the Iranians to defy the mighty United States, an example that spread rapidly among the dispossessed and dissatisfied.

With this in mind, the moment the Gulf War ended in 1991, the US administration turned its attention to Israel. The new post-Cold War world order was very much in their favour. Russia would almost certainly co-operate in a peace initiative. The PLO was impoverished and isolated. Israel, still dependent upon US aid, was no longer needed as an anti-Communist bastion in the Middle East. In fact, given the US's new alliance with the Gulf States, Israel was becoming something of a liability. At last, the White House believed, there was a chance of extinguishing a long-burning fire before it did any further damage.

The Declaration of Principles

Towards Madrid

As soon as the First Gulf War ended, US President George Bush Sr announced an initiative to extend the peace of the Gulf across the entire Middle East. Secretary of State Baker, who had been dashing backwards and forwards in a frenzy of preparatory diplomacy, put forward a nine-point plan as the basis for an international conference. Ambitiously, he sought to usher in the new and widespread peace by ending the conflicts between Israel and the Palestinians, Syrians and Jordanians. As far as Palestinians were concerned, Baker suggested a form of interim self-rule that envisaged full independence at some future date. Arafat proudly rejected the proposal.

The Palestinian leader's reponse was merely a gesture of independence. The war had considerably reduced his influence. The PLO was in serious financial difficulties – staff were leaving and its bureaucracy becoming even less efficient than normal. Among the international community the Palestinians' reputation had been harmed by their joyful reaction to the Iraqi missile attacks on Israel, while the Israelis' refusal to react to Hussein's unprovoked aggression had won them sympathy and respect (see page 152). Consequently, Arafat was in no position to denounce the US–Soviet talks. Such folly would have been political suicide. Moreover, he was obliged to accept the PLO attending with the Jordanian delegation rather than with that from the occupied territories. The people of the West Bank and Gaza, expecting a negotiating team representing the Palestinian nation, were bitterly disappointed.

Israeli Prime Minister Yitzak Shamir was equally sceptical about the whole process. His foot-dragging so angered President Bush that he was refused US loan guarantees of £10 billion for Israeli housing projects. At a time when Israel was striving to assimilate around 250,000 Russian Jews, the move was no mere empty gesture. Shamir would attend the conference.

The Madrid talks

A series of conferences was held in Madrid, Spain, to find a comprehensive peace acceptable to all parties. Separate working groups dealt with issues such as water and the environment. Not surprisingly, the talks soon ran into difficulties. Prime Minister Shamir was happy to stall as a way of avoiding concessions:

treating the talks as a minor distraction, he actually returned home after barely 24 hours in the Spanish capital. He would not dream of agreeing anything without cast-iron guarantees of Israel's security. Israeli settlements in the occupied territories were essential to this security and they continued to expand throughout the period of negotiation. No act could have been better designed to persuade the Palestinians of Israel's half-hearted approach.

At the same time, the Palestinians were beset with internal frictions. The PLO, for instance, would not grant real negotiating power to compatriots attached to the Jordanian delegation. Arafat insisted on trying to control matters from long range, appointing dozens of useless coffee-sipping sycophants to the PLO delegation and not supporting his most able politicians. He was unhappy, too, with the US idea of some vague semi-autonomy for his people. He had not striven all his life to become head of a pseudo-Palestine, he complained.

A few months later, Arafat's position was strengthened by an accident. In April 1992 his plane crashed in the Tunisian desert and for 13 hours, until located by US satellite, he was believed to have been killed. Premature obituaries appeared, some flattering, others less so. His reappearance – seemingly risen from the dead – added considerably to his influence among Palestinians. To many of his supporters, though not to himself, his immortality had been confirmed. Worried by this, the Israelis were soon putting out stories that he really had died in the crash and the man calling himself Yasser Arafat was in fact an agent of Mossad, the Israeli Secret Service. It was not explained how they had found an Arafat look-alike, unless by plastic surgery.

The flagging peace talks had by now been moved to Washington DC. The change of venue made no difference. In an effort to get the Palestinians to walk away from the negotiating table and so bring the whole process to an end, the Israelis deported activists from the occupied territories. The move provoked a fresh wave of Intifada violence. By the summer of 1992 it looked as if the whole Madrid-Washington process would collapse. It was saved by a change of leadership and an inspired Norwegian initiative.

Yitzhak Rabin

In June 1992, the Israeli electorate placed Yitzhak Rabin at the head of a Labour-led coalition. Rabin also took over the defence ministry and made it responsible for the peace talks. He gave the foreign ministry to Shimon Peres. Rabin's negotiating freedom was hampered by his coalition's reliance on the support of the Shas religious party.

The new prime minister had campaigned on the ticket of peace. Soon after taking office, he announced a freeze on all new Israeli settlements on the West Bank and in the Gaza Strip. Arafat nodded in approval and President Bush re-activated his government's housing loan guarantees. (Actually, Rabin's offer was not as generous as it sounded: all planned new settlements went ahead and during his administration the settler population rose from 100,000 to 135,000.) The Knesset also relaxed the law on talking to members of the PLO, making it legal for individuals to hold discussions with the organization. So far, so good.

Oslo

Entirely unofficially and without the full knowledge of the US, secret and mostly informal talks began in the Norwegian capital of Oslo. On one side was a Palestinian delegation led by Abu Ala, head of the PLO's economic department, on the other an Israeli delegation led by the academic Yair Hirschfeld. The two parties talked over possibilities. It soon became clear that there was some common ground between them. The Israelis had no desire to remain in the Gaza Strip, for example, while the Palestinians wanted them out. There was an obvious solution here.

Gradually, step by step, a series of principles was hammered out amid the Oslo snows. When these ideas were shown to the world, they were heralded as a breakthrough. In some ways they were, as we shall see. But behind them lurked one inescapable fact: the Palestinians held precious few trump cards and negotiated from a position of extreme weakness. Their only power was the ability to make a nuisance of themselves and to evoke popular sympathy. Arafat knew this. Painfully aware since his desert experience of his own mortality, he wanted settlement at any price. He had changed. Even a pseudo-Palestine would now suffice, as long as he was its leader. If the talks failed, the destitute PLO would almost certainly break up.

Elsewhere the Washington talks finally collapsed in December 1992 when Israel deported 415 Palestinian militants. Nine months later, the fruits of the Oslo talks were on display in their place.

The US, now headed by the Democrat President Bill Clinton, came in on the 'Declaration of Principles on Palestinian Self-Rule' (better known as the Oslo Accords) late in the day, but in time to ensure that no side could back out and that the agreement was given maximum recognition. The Accords were signed in the White House on 13 September 1993. Afterwards, with Bill Clinton towering over them like a political godfather, the diminutive Yasser Arafat and Yitzhak Rabin shook hands before the world's media. The reluctance of the latter to extend the hand of friendship was obvious to all.

The Accords were mostly about what would happen in the future. For the present the key feature was recognition. The PLO recognized Israel's right to exist, denounced terrorism and promised to revise its charter to eliminate references to destroying Israel. In return, the Israelis recognized the PLO as the sole representative of the Palestinian people. The gain for Israel was great, as also it was for Arafat and his creaking organization. For the Palestinian people at large, however, there was nothing in the immediate principles at all.

The Accords talked of much more to happen over the next five years. There would be interim, limited self-government for Palestinians. Starting in Gaza and the city of Jericho, Palestinian rule would involve only non-strategic matters such as sanitation and education. Then elections would be held for a Palestinian president and council. After that the area of self-rule, and perhaps its scope, would be expanded. Talks on the permanent status of the Palestinians were to begin within three years and a solution agreed within five. In the short term Palestinian leaders would gain some control over their people but the land would remain Israel's. A Palestinian police force, when assembled, would help to keep Israel secure from extremist threats.

Again, as in the principles of the Accords, there was almost nothing specific in their more detailed proposals that would be of much benefit to ordinary Palestinians. They knew this too – the PLO executive committee had approved the agreement by only one vote, and even then the ballot had been of questionable veracity. The Israelis had their right to exist recognized, an end to the Intifada, and they kept all the territory they wanted. The Palestinians had only promises. No specific frontiers had been mentioned, nor had the question of refugees. There was to be no exchange of prisoners. Israeli settlements in the occupied territories could continue apace. Most significant of all, no mention whatsoever was made of a Palestinian nation.

The Palestinians of the occupied territories remained a stateless people. Many of them saw the whole Oslo business as a charade and a betrayal. Israel, they were now certain, would never let them have a country of their own. This attitude hardened in many minds over the years to come, making further progress towards peace very difficult.

Struggling for peace

Many hoped that the Oslo Accords would be the start of a long but ultimately successful peace process. Sadly, it was not to be. Almost 50 years of hatred, mistrust and bloodshed could not so easily be set aside. There was some progress, to be sure, but for each two steps forward there was at least one-and-a-half backward. By the end of the century, the divisions between Palestinians and Israelis remained almost as bitter as they had been at the beginning. Indeed, the more time went by, the more difficult bridging the divide between them appeared to be.

Onward from Oslo

The majority of Israelis welcomed the Oslo Accords as ushering in a new era of stability and security. The plan to pull out of the overcrowded and unpleasant Gaza Strip, in particular, was widely popular. Likud and the right, however, insisted on denouncing the agreement as a betrayal of a sacred trust. They argued that Rabin had given in to the barbaric violence of the Intifada and the bombs of militant Islamists.

As if to prove wrong those who accused him of weakness, Rabin maintained the traditional Israeli policy of reacting to violence with extreme force. A fortnight after the Washington ceremony there were disturbances in the Gaza Strip. Israeli security forces rumbled in, demolishing 17 houses; 16 suspects were arrested and two summarily executed. The new era of peace and co-operation had not got off to an auspicious start.

Hamas resumed its bombings. When asked to do something about them, Arafat said he wished to incorporate Hamas members within the peaceful PLO, not fight them openly. The Israelis were unimpressed. Hamas leaders were identified by Israeli agents, singled out and killed by a variety of means. Some were blown up, others shot or poisoned.

One incident above all from this period exemplified the depth of blind and irrational hatred that divided the extremists on both sides. On 25 February 1994, a 35-year-old doctor named Baruch Goldstein donned Israeli army uniform and crept in to the Ibrahimi Mosque in Hebron. It was the time of dawn prayers. Originally from New York, Goldstein had moved to Israel for religious reasons: he belonged to the extreme Kahane Chai movement that believed 'Greater Israel' should be cleansed of all Arabs. He chose to start his spring cleaning at the Ibrahimi Mosque, a religious building shared by Jews and Muslims. It contained the tombs of such ancient Jewish luminaries as Abraham and Jacob.

Goldstein was carrying an M16 automatic rifle. Carefully and deliberately he began to fire on the worshippers. Israeli guards stationed nearby either did not hear what was going on or chose to ignore it. Before Goldstein was stopped, 21 Palestinian worshippers lay dead and a further 300 had been wounded. The assassin was killed by enraged survivors.

This wicked act of bigotry almost brought the peace process to a complete halt. The volatile population of the occupied territories burned Yasser Arafat in effigy for keeping it going. He knew that he had no option: if the process stopped, the Islamists would take control and his career would be over.

Following bombings near Afula and in Tel Aviv that killed 14 Israelis and wounded more than 80, in May Arafat and Rabin signed a follow-up agreement to the Oslo Accords. Dealing largely with Jericho and the Gaza Strip, the paper took the peace process a bit further. The withdrawal of Israeli forces from certain areas was arranged in detail and plans for a Palestinian police force were established. Two months later Arafat returned to the occupied territories for the first time in 27 years. Hundreds of thousands of supporters set aside their recent misgivings and turned out to greet him. It was not so much the man they were lauding as the hope of freedom and nationhood that he seemed to symbolize.

Oslo Two

The next year, Arafat, Rabin and Peres (all recently awarded the Nobel Peace Prize) ratified the Oslo Two agreement that moved the peace process on another step. Palestinian elections were planned, arrangements made for the release of some Palestinian prisoners, and a phased Israeli withdrawal from certain zones in the West Bank was detailed. This would leave the area divided into three types of zone: those under Palestinian civilian rule (no more than 20 per cent), those that still had an Israeli military presence, and those that remained wholly Israeli. The new road network would enable the Israeli military to move swiftly between zones should the need arise.

The Knesset passed Oslo Two by one vote. Israeli disillusionment with the peace process was growing. With many on the far right of the Israeli political and religious spectrum still labelling Rabin a traitor for betraying the Jewish homeland and giving in to violence, the scene was set for another act of Israeli extremism. On 4 November 1995, seeking to rekindle support for his cause, the Israeli prime minister attended a peace rally in Tel Aviv. As he was leaving, the Jewish religious fanatic Yigal Amir shot him dead. The world mourned the death of the second Middle East statesman assassinated for seeking peace.

A broader peace

The original American peace plan, put forward by President Bush Sr and Secretary of State Baker, had looked for a comprehensive settlement to include Jordan and Syria. On and off talks with both countries had been conducted since the end of the First Gulf War. Although 20,000 Syrian troops had fought in the US-led coalition, it was Jordan that joined the peace process.

Jordan

King Hussein of Jordan had long been torn between a personal regard for the West and the fiercely pro-Palestinian feelings of his people. During the Gulf War, for instance, he had been obliged to repress his personal instincts and offer tacit support to Saddam Hussein (see page 161). Israel's accord with the PLO, therefore, finally gave him an opportunity to do what he had hoped to be able to do for a long time: end the state of belligerence between his kingdom and Israel.

Prime Minister Rabin and King Hussein, who got on well together, held a series of secret meetings in the early part of 1994. A peace treaty was announced in Washington DC in July and formally signed at the Wadi Araba border post in the Arava Desert at the end of October. President Clinton was witness to both actions, and US backing underpinned the whole process.

The first comprehensive peace treaty between Israel and an Arab neighbour since Camp David brought benefits to both parties.

Jordan was released of $700 million of debt to the US and $92 to Britain. It also received generous aid, including military hardware. The following year, seeking to mollify the Palestinians, Hussein signed accords with the PLO in which he pledged support for their drive for independent statehood. This enabled the Jordanian king to act as a broker between Israel and the Palestinians, something he did with patience and skill before his death from cancer in 1999. He was succeeded by his son, the 37-year-old Abdullah. Although the new king pledged himself to follow his father's policies of moderation and mediation, he found this middle road extremely difficult to negotiate (see Chapter 14).

Israel's motive for peace with Jordan was largely strategic. The treaty removed the threat of a three-pronged Arab attack from Syria, Iraq and Jordan. It also opened the way for other nations to recognize Israel. Within a few months diplomatic relations had been established with a number of countries, including Morocco and Tunisia. The Arab boycott of Israel was lifted, freeing major international companies to trade there.

Syria

Talks with Syria did not go so well. They were dogged by two problems. First, Syria's president Assad insisted that any lasting peace had to be based upon a return to the pre-1967 war frontiers. As this would mean Syria having a boundary on the Sea of Galilee, Israel's principal water supply, the position was unacceptable to Israel's negotiators.

Secondly, Syria continued to shelter the Hezbollah guerrillas. Frequent clashes between the group and Israeli security forces soured peace talks. In 1994, for example, Israeli planes bombed a Hezbollah camp within Syria, killing 40. The following month Hezbollah bombed a Jewish community centre in Buenos Aires. Almost 100 civilians were slain.

Vain attempts to reach a Syrian-Israeli understanding continued through the 1990s. Assad died of cancer in 2000 and was replaced by his son, Bashar Assad (see Chapter 14). The change of regime had no immediate impact on Syrian-Israeli relations.

The peace process crumbles

Rabin's assassination brought Shimon Peres back to the Israeli premiership as a wave of pro-peace, anti-fundamentalist sentiment swept over the country. Troop withdrawals from the occupied territories continued so that by early 1996 most Palestinians were under some form of self-rule. Thus far, though, the arrangement was only temporary and there was still no sign of a Palestinian state.

Violence returns

In accordance with the Oslo agreements, elections for the Palestinian Legislative Council and a Palestinian president were held in January 1996. Yasser Arafat won the presidency with an overwhelming 88 per cent of the votes cast. His Fatah party won control of the Legislative Council by winning 60 of its 88 seats. Abu Ala, the Oslo negotiator, was chosen as speaker.

At this point the peace process all but came to a halt. The Israeli security forces were being as ruthless as ever. In January their agents killed Yahya Ayyash, a Palestinian militant known as the 'engineer' for his bomb-making skills. Hamas and Islamic Jihad, both of whom remained pledged to destroy the state of Israel, responded with a prolonged campaign of terror that left over 50 Israelis dead. The Israelis countered with their customary harshness, sealing off Palestinian communities, conducting brutal searches and arresting suspects. In the north, Hezbollah stepped up its campaign across the Syrian border.

Despite support from President Clinton, who attended an international conference on terrorism in Egypt and promised Peres massive aid in his fight against Islamic fundamentalists, the Labour prime minister was defeated at the polls in May 1996. The elections were the first in which the prime minister was chosen separately from the Knesset. The victor by one per cent was Benjamin Netanyahu, a 46-year-old Likud hard-liner.

Benjamin Netanyahu

Netanyahu, recently Israel's ambassador at the UN, had campaigned on the slogan 'Peace with security'. Primary emphasis was on the latter. A member of an élite special operations unit in his youth, he had confronted terrorists face-to-face. He had also fought in the 1973 war and lost a brother in the successful Israeli commando raid on Entebbe that had freed a hi-jacked airliner and its passengers (see page 111). Although not born when Israel had been founded, he had been imbued with the fighting siege mentality of his older right-wing compatriots. If the Palestinians picked up so much as a whiff of Israeli weakness, he believed, the cause of the promised land would be lost.

In the September following Netanyahu's elections, his tough security policy produced a massive flare-up in Palestinian violence. The prime minister personally authorized the opening of an ancient tunnel near the northern end of Jerusalem's Western wall. The 2,000-year-old passage passed near the al-Aqsa Mosque and led into Muslim-controlled East Jerusalem. Although of great archaeological interest, its physical position made it of even greater religious significance.

Muslim worshippers saw the opening of the tunnel as a direct threat to the mosque. Crowds gathered, stones were thrown, shooting started. The mayhem saw Israeli soldiers and Palestinian police, who only days previously had been on patrol together, firing at each other. By the time order had been restored, 15 soldiers and 60 Palestinians had been killed. The future of the peace process hung in the balance.

Breakdown

Netanyahu had never approved of the Oslo Accords. Nevertheless, for practical reasons he did not want the peace process to fall apart completely. He was under pressure from President Clinton, and he feared the economic dislocation that prolonged violence inevitably brought. At the start of 1997, he signed an agreement by which the Israelis left the city of Hebron. This completed the hand-over to Palestinian authorities of the key West Bank towns named in the Accords.

The outbreak of goodwill did not last. Netanyahu had once said that 'Jewish sovereignty and Jewish power are the only deterrents and the only guarantees against the slaughter of the Jews'. He had little difficulty, therefore, in submitting to right-wing pressure to allow more settlements on land captured in 1967, and not to agree further withdrawal from the West Bank. As a consequence, a new Jewish settlement was announced at Har Homa (Jabal Abu Ghneim) in East Jerusalem. This was followed by a decision to hand over to Palestinian local government only another nine per cent of West Bank instead of the 30 per cent expected from the wording of previous agreements.

The details of what followed are all too painfully familiar. A fresh wave of Islamist bombings provoked the usual reprisals. Arafat released Hamas members he had previously detained and refused further co-operation with Israel over security. Outsiders, particularly the Americans, tried in vain to bring Israeli and Palestinian leaders together. Positions on each side became more entrenched, with the Israeli prime minister actually declaring that his country would always remain in possession of the entire West Bank. The troubles led to a deterioration in Israel's relations with countries within the Middle East and further afield. There was fighting on the borders with Lebanon and Syria, and a tragic shooting of seven Israeli schoolgirls by a Jordanian border guard.

Wye River

In 1998, relying heavily on his country's economic clout and position as the world's only superpower, President Clinton finally forced Netanyahu and Arafat to attend talks. They met at Wye Plantation, Maryland. King Hussein, in the US for cancer treatment, turned up to assist the president in his taxing task. The 27 hours of tough negotiating produced a deal known as the Wye River Memorandum.

Confirmed and signed later in Washington, the Memorandum was intended to pick up the peace process where it had broken off a year-and-a-half before. The old Oslo promises were restored, guaranteeing a safe passage from the West Bank to Gaza, for example, and establishing mutual anti-terrorist measures. Clinton's new thinking included linking staged Israeli withdrawal to specific Palestinian moves against Hamas and Islamic Jihad. This anti-terrorist activity would be monitored by the CIA. The agreement envisaged a phased Israeli withdrawal from the West Bank that would eventually leave the Palestinian Authority (still not a state) in control of about 40 per cent of the land there.

Moderates everywhere warmly welcomed the agreement. The Palestinian Authority accepted it and, as the Memorandum stipulated, took steps to curb Palestinian extremists. It also deleted clauses in the Palestinian National Charter that called for Israel's destruction.

The bulk of Israelis welcomed the Memorandum, too. It was agreed by the cabinet and the Knesset. By the end of the year, though, to keep the support of the right, Netanyahu was backtracking fast. He imposed new conditions for further Israeli withdrawal, to all intents and purposes rejecting the agreements he had made earlier in the year. Confused and annoyed, the Knesset voted to dissolve itself and hold new elections. Netanyahu's premiership was over.

The Second Intifada

The Israeli elections of 1999 produced a more fractured Knesset than ever before, reflecting the deep divisions within Israeli society. The premiership went to Labour's Ehud Barak, the most decorated soldier in his country's history. Yet the old warrior with an MSc from Stanford, California, was no blinkered warlord. He had played a key role in negotiating the treaty with Jordan (see pages 177–8) and had campaigned with a One Israel coalition on a promise to bring peace to the Middle East. He was certainly not the first and would not be the last to find that such a promise was much easier to make than to keep.

Talks re-open

True to his manifesto, Barak held talks with Yasser Arafat. The latter, finding it difficult to control the increasingly popular extremists within the Palestinian movement, set the bar high. Undaunted, Barak agreed to find a binding peace deal by September 2000 and to withdraw from more of the West Bank.

At the same time, Barak re-opened talks with Syria and withdrew all Israeli forces from Southern Lebanon. President Clinton was eager to find a permanent solution to the Israel-Palestinian problem before his term of office came to an end. In the summer of 2000, he made one last effort. Using a tactic that had succeeded in the past, he invited Israeli and Palestinian negotiating teams, each headed by their elected leader, to Camp David. For 15 days electric golf buggies buzzed negotiators and mediators between the complex of luxurious cabins. This time it was the Israelis who were prepared to give and the Palestinians who dug in their heels. Arafat was terrified of offering his people an agreement that might seem like a climbdown. The Islamists, gaining in power every month, were waiting to denounce him.

Clinton cajoled and shouted. At one point he actually yelled at Arafat for refusing even to look at a map on which the Israelis had drawn proposed new boundaries. On more than one occasion both sides threatened to leave. The central sticking point – the issue known to Palestinians as 'bones in the throat' – was the ownership of holy places.

'The problem is,' commented Secretary of State Madeleine Albright in despair, 'they both want the same thing.' On the issue of East Jerusalem neither side dared give way because of the reaction back home, although Barak had suggested that Israel might find a way of sharing the precious sites with Muslims. In the end, Clinton reconciled himself to the fact that on this issue even his legendary charm had failed. Barak returned home in sombre mood. His Palestinian counterpart was welcomed back in the occupied territories as a conquering hero: Arafat had proved his strength by daring to say 'no' to the Israelis and the Americans.

Enter Sharon

At this point, with the peace process stalling again, one of Israel's most controversial and experienced politicians took steps to see that it finally crashed. In September 2000, Ariel Sharon visited East Jerusalem's al-Aqsa Mosque. A visit to this controversial site by the man widely believed to have been responsible for the Sabra and Shatilla massacres and other attrocities was bound to provoke hostility, and it did.

The day after Sharon's visit, a Friday, the leaders of the Muslim community incited anger among their flock. After prayers, stones were thrown at Israeli soldiers. The military responded with tear gas, then with rubber bullets. When the rioting continued, a commanding officer over-reacted: Israeli snipers appeared, firing down on the crowd in an attempt to pick off the ringleaders. Many Palestinians were killed.

The next day armed Palestinian paramilitaries went into action. The wave of Palestinian rage rose, fuelled by the image of an innocent 12-year-old boy cowering beside his father while a gunfight raged around them. Suddenly the boy fell forward, dead. He had been shot several times by Israeli soldiers supposedly targeting the gunmen behind him. The pictures were shown on television in every country in the world. The Second or al-Aqsa Intifada began shortly afterwards.

Barak, the man who had based his reputation on being able to bring peace, had failed. A joint plea for a cease-fire from himself and Arafat was ignored. As the violence escalated, Sharon's criticism of the Labour prime minister became more vitriolic.

With the peace process in tatters, Ehud Barak resigned in December 2000. The following February Ariel Sharon was elected prime minister of Israel. If the outlook for the region was bleak, terrifying events in New York would soon make it bleaker still.

The prospects for the new century were ominous indeed.

13

regime change

This chapter will cover:
- the state of the Middle East at the start of the new millennium
- the events of 11 September 2001 and their immediate impact
- War on Terror and the US-led coalition's invasion of Iraq
- the troubled occupation of Iraq to mid-2006.

The Middle East in 2001

During the 55 years between the ending of the Second World War and the start of the new millennium, the Middle East had been swept by a series of traumatic and far-reaching changes. These may be outlined under the followings headings: oil wealth, the withdrawal of the old colonial powers, the foundation and growth of the state of Israel, and the emergence of militant Islam. Together these developments ensured that the Middle East had moved to the very centre of global politics: analysed, argued over, bargained for, feared, wooed. By 2001 the region mattered more to the rest of the world than perhaps ever before.

Oil

The key to the Middle East's new importance was oil. The region's output had been significant in 1945 – enough so for President Roosevelt to have had a personal meeting with King Abdul Aziz of Saudi Arabia – but it still accounted for considerably less than ten per cent of the 2.5 billion barrels the world needed annually. Fifty years later global consumption had risen to some 24 billion barrels a year, around half of which came from the Middle East and its immediate neighbours.

By the early twenty-first century, oil from the Middle East was powering almost 50 per cent of global transport. This gave the region's producers – OPEC – the theoretical power to bring the world to a halt. And the position was set to strengthen in the future. Middle Eastern reserves were being used up less quickly than those in other oil-producing regions: it was estimated that by 2020 they would account for 83 per cent of the world's entire stock of crude oil. Stocks of natural gas were similarly impressive.

Oil revenues funded spectacular economic growth in the areas fortunate enough to possess 'black gold'. Around the Gulf new cities soared into the cloudless skies; highways laced across once impenetrable desert; families whose ancestors had dwelt in tents now lived in air-conditioned villas equipped with every convenience modern technology could provide.

Growing pains

The region's dramatic economic advance brought as many problems as benefits. The painful contrast between a country like Kuwait, where the annual national income per person averaged around $18,000 at the turn of the century, and Yemen, where the equivalent figure was less than $600, made the rhetoric of Arab and Islamic unity sound somewhat hollow. Nor did wealth protect the region from outside intervention, as the Gulf War of 1990–1 and the 2003 invasion and occupation of Iraq showed (see Chapters 09 and 13). Indeed, the richer the oil-producing states became, the more precious their reserves, the closer grew superpower attention.

To some extent the increase in wealth was offset by astonishing demographic growth. The annual rate rose to almost three per cent, lifting the region's population from just over 100 million in 1945 to more than triple that 55 years later. The increase was accompanied by massive migration into the towns, where more than half the population of the Middle East now lived. Perhaps the most spectacular development was that of Riyadh, which grew from an oasis settlement of traditional mud brick dwellings to an ultra-modern capital of broad highways and skyscrapers housing some 4.7 million citizens. At the other extreme was Cairo. The 16.5 million inhabitants of the 'mother of the world' dwelt in a chaotic and almost ungovernable metropolis that sprawled over 214 sq. km. (83 sq. miles).

Social challenge

At the same time, two developments were rapidly transforming the traditional Middle Eastern social scene. One was education. Huge numbers of schools were constructed and staffed, and the wealthier states developed university systems of their own so that those seeking higher education no longer needed to travel abroad. Of particular significance was the rapid expansion of education for girls and young women. The region's overall illiteracy rate fell from around 75 per cent to less than 40 per cent.

The second force for social change was the media, particularly television and the internet. Part of TV's impact came from its ability to portray in simple images the lifestyles of other cultures, especially American, and thereby feed aspirational dreams. The development of satellite TV – less easily controlled than traditional broadcasts – not only brought CNN and the BBC into millions of Middle Eastern homes, but also allowed the region's own viewpoints and priorities to impact on the rest of the world. The success of the Arabic TV station Aljazeera, operating out of Qatar, was one of the more remarkable media stories of the new century. So great was its influence that in 2005 it was reported that President Bush had considered launching an air strike against it. The rapid spread of the internet also facilitated the swift dissemination of a wide variety of information both into and out of the Middle East.

Wealth, a new status and widespread links to the outside world forced the peoples of the region to reflect upon their identity. They wanted much that the capitalist Western world had to offer – its conveniences, luxuries and freedoms – yet they were afraid that in accepting such imports they would lose their distinctive character. The result was a sort of social schizophrenia in which individuals and indeed whole societies were torn between past and present, puritanism and consumerism, hatred and love of the US. Traditions of dress and social arrangement, especially the subjugation of women, were often clung to with an irrational intensity. The Turkish model of the modern secular state, pioneered by Mustafa Kamal Ataturk and attempted by Saddam Hussein in Iraq, was elsewhere rejected in favour of a tense and sometimes conflicting blend of traditional Islam and consumerism – the black robe covering the mini-skirt.

New nationalism

The second major post-war development was the withdrawal of the Western mandate powers – Britain and France. This bequeathed the difficult task of consolidating into true nation states the countries into which the Middle East had been divided during the first half of the twentieth century. Egypt, Syria and Iran, each with distinctive cultures, traditions and histories, accepted Western-style nationalism relatively readily. Elsewhere central governments often struggled to create a sense of unity powerful enough to overcome the traditional allegiances of tribe and clan.

Saudi Arabia, Oman and Jordan did better than most, consolidating around their effective royal families. Elsewhere, especially in Iraq, Yemen and Israel-Palestine, nation-building proved a painful process. At the end of the twentieth century several of the region's frontiers were still in dispute, notably those around Iraq and Israel-Palestine. Moreover, many of its citizens, especially in rural areas, placed local, religious or blood loyalties above those to the state. This was particularly so in Iraq.

Israel

The third major development in the Middle East since 1945 was closely coupled to the second: the creation and expansion of the state of Israel. As we have already seen, the emergence of Israel had a number of conflicting consequences. Regionally, it fostered a sense of Arab solidarity as Israel's neighbours sought – some more wholeheartedly than others – to destroy the parvenu nation. Then, when it was clear to most that Israel could not be eliminated, enmity arose between Arab governments as first Egypt then other states came to an accord with the enemy.

The presence of Israel also led directly to the emergence of a Palestinian nation. This had not existed, in a modern sense, before 1948. Gradually, however, prompted and guided by Yasser Arafat, the displaced Palestinian people came to think of themselves in the same terms as the Jews had done before the creation of Israel – as a people seeking to establish themselves as a nation within their traditional homelands. Thus, ending the so-called 'Jewish problem' had led to its replacement by the 'Palestinian problem', which remained far from solution in 2001.

Moreover, the presence of the state of Israel had further increased the certainty of superpower involvement in the Middle East. This was already guaranteed because of the region's oil reserves. It intensified during the Cold War because of the tendency of the communist and capitalist blocs to take opposite sides in any conflict, and because of the influence of the Jewish vote in the USA. Also significant were the West's feelings of guilt at the Nazi Holocaust and an inclination to support a state that elected its leaders democratically against unelected dictators and monarchs. By 2001, with the Cold War ended, it was arguable that the most powerful figure in Israeli politics was the president of the USA.

Militant Islam

Finally, the twentieth century left its successor a daunting and wholly unexpected legacy. As late as 1975, commentators were describing their century as one of 'secular creeds': communism, capitalism, democracy, fascism, nationalism and so forth. Then, quite suddenly, beginning with events in Iran at the time of its revolution in 1979, Islam re-emerged as a major socio-political force throughout the Middle East and beyond.

It was significant that the new movement took much of its inspiration from Shia Iran. Here the power of the imam (priest) was traditionally greater than in other Islamic cultures, making it easier for religious leaders to assume a political role. Also significant was the approval in some radical Shia circles of dying for one's faith, no matter how hopeless the circumstances in worldly terms. Hence the recruitment of young men and women to serve as soldier or suicide-bomber 'martyrs'. Equally important was the later development of militant Sunni fundamentalism in the form of Al-Qaeda, instinctively hostile to the Shia.

The importance of these new religious movements would be hard to overestimate. Together they gave focus and purpose to those in the Middle East who had long harboured misgivings about the apparently all-conquering Western morality. Islamists' 'victories' against seemingly overwhelming odds, measured in deaths and destruction, restored a sense of racial and religious pride. Here, at last, was a movement around which the downtrodden and exploited of the earth could gather. As it was based in the impenetrable human heart, against radical Islam neither air-strikes nor tanks could prevail. Where communism had failed, its adherants claimed, it would triumph and usher in a new world order.

This then was the Middle East at the start of the new millennium: an explosive cocktail of economic power, socio-cultural tensions, conflicting nationalisms, and radical religion. Whatever the future held, it would certainly be neither calm nor predictable.

War on terror

On 11 September 2001, the Middle East came to New York when Islamic militants hi-jacked four aircraft on domestic flights from east-coast airports and turned them into gigantic flying bombs. At about 8.45 a.m. the first plane smashed into the North Tower of the World Trade Center, New York. It struck about two-thirds of the way up the building, killing all aboard and hundreds either at work in the Tower or on their way there. About 15 minutes later, a second plane buried itself within the South Tower. Like the first, it started a raging fire and caused extensive structural damage and loss of life.

Seventy-five minutes after impact, the north tower collapsed to the ground in a billowing cloud of suffocating dust and smoke.

The second tower came down some 30 minutes later. The number killed and injured was swollen by the presence within each structure of numerous fire-fighters. Before the Towers crashed to the ground, many of those trapped on the upper floors had flung themselves out of the buildings. All fell to their death.

Meanwhile, the hi-jackers had launched a third plane into the south-west side of the Pentagon, the headquarters of the US Department of Defense. A fierce fire broke out immediately. Mobile phone calls informed passengers on board the fourth hijacked aircraft what was happening elsewhere and, to prevent further catastrophe, they turned on their captors. The details of what happened remain obscure, but the plane plummeted into the Pennsylvania countryside killing all on board. Some say it had been en route for the White House.

The final death toll was almost 3,000. Some 2,750 had perished in the World Trade Center, 184 in the Pentagon and a further 40 in the Pennsylvania debacle. It was the most devastating terrorist strike the world had ever seen and by far the worst in US history. Many Americans likened it to the Japanese attack on Pearl Harbor which had brought their country into the Second World War.

Al-Qaeda

The link between the attacks of 11 September and the Middle East was a 44-year-old Saudi Islamist named Osama Bin Laden. Thirteen years earlier Bin Laden had set up Al-Qaeda, meaning 'the Base', and all those responsible for the 11 September attacks were connected to this movement. Initially the US described Al-Qaeda as an organization, like a business or a warband, with a specific structure, leadership and aims. Later commentators saw it as something less concrete: an idea, a set of ideals shared between people who would do anything to see them implemented. To Madeleine Albright, a former US ambassador to the United Nations, it was like 'an ideological virus'.

As a young man Bin Laden had assisted the Afghans in their fight against the invading Soviet army. In 1988, as the Soviets withdrew, he established Al-Qaeda to pursue holy war (jihad) elsewhere. Shortly after his return to Saudi Arabia, brimming with Wahabite (an extreme Sunni sect) zeal, he was horrified when the Saudi government, uniting with the US to drive

Saddam Hussein from Kuwait, invited infidel soldiers onto Arabia's holy soil. Bin Laden was already disillusioned with what he saw as the immoral corruption of the godless West, and in 1991 he moved to Sudan where he set up terrorist training camps. His aim, it seems, was to halt the advance of the West and return to the days of the Caliphate (a single government for the entire Muslim world, see page 8).

Islamic terrorist attacks were nothing new. In 1988, Libyan-backed assassins had killed all 259 passengers and crew by blowing up their Pan Am jet airliner over Lockerbie, Scotland. Al-Qaeda brought a new level of intensity to the killing. It was linked to a first attempt to destroy New York's World Trade Center (1993), to the deaths of 18 US servicemen in Somalia the same year, to further US military deaths in Saudi Arabia in 1996, and to the loss of over 220 lives when the US embassies in Dar es Salaam (Tanzania) and Nairobi (Kenya) were bombed simultaneously. Responding to these outrages and to Bin Laden's assertion that it was the religious duty of all Muslims to kill Americans, President Clinton launched missile strikes against targets in Afghanistan, where Bin Laden was once again in hiding. The UN imposed sanctions on the Afghan Taliban regime and demanded that they surrender their notorious guest. Refusal led to further sanctions. In October 2000, less than a year before the second, successful attack on the World Trade Centre, Al-Qaeda-inspired suicide bombers rammed *USS Cole* in Aden, Yemen, killing 17 American sailors.

America goes to war

During the 1990s the US's principal concerns in the Middle East had been ensuring an uninterrupted supply of oil, maintaining the state of Israel (ideally at peace with its neighbours), curbing the spread of militant Islam, and trying to prevent the spread of Weapons of Mass Destruction (WMDs) throughout the region, principally from Iraq. The 11 September attacks forced the last two concerns to the top of the list and galvanized the US administration into taking immediate action.

Within three days of the Twin Towers attacks, Congress had voted $40 billion to fund America's response and Attorney-General John Ashcroft had pointed the finger of blame at Al-Qaeda. By October the US government was blaming Al-Qaeda directly and specifically. Shortly afterwards the US and Britain launched heavy air strikes against the Taliban regime in

Afghanistan. Support in the form of money, material and personnel was also given to Afghan groups (the Northern Alliance) eager to remove the killjoy fundamentalist regime. By the end of the year, spied on by satellite, blasted from the air, and harassed at every turn on the ground, the Taliban had been overthrown. However, neither its leader, Mullah Omar, nor Bin Laden had been taken.

On 29 January 2002, President George Bush Jr delivered his annual State of the Union Address. 'Our nation is at war,' he declared, a 'war on terror'. Amid the patriotic hyperbole that followed, he announced that the US faced an 'axis of evil'. North Korea, Iran and Iraq were singled out as being within this axis. Four months later, Cuba, Libya and Syria were added to the list. Three of the six (Iran, Iraq and Syria) were in the Middle East. A fourth, Libya, came within a broader definition of the region.

The Middle East was now directly in the firing line of the world's only superpower. Furthermore, President Bush had named specific groups – Hamas, Hezbollah and Islamic Jihad – as belonging to a 'terrorist underworld'. As all three were dedicated to Israel's elimination, the Israel-Palestine confrontation lay near the heart of the US's war on terror; nor was there much doubt whose side the Bush administration was on.

Investigations, action and arrests

The United States pursued its war on terror with customary energy. The CIA, expanded and boosted in powers and funds, began investigating 50,000 leads from the 11 September attacks. A Department of Homeland Security was set up. For a while the US had world-wide backing, too, with governments of every persuasion sending the American people their sincere condolences and offers of support. A detachment of US troops went to Yemen to support government forces attacking an Al-Qaeda stronghold there. Later, US missiles were launched against the group believed to have been responsible for the bomb attack on the *USS Cole* (see page 192). The UN, almost unanimous in its condemnation of 11 September, approved this action and established a Counter Terrorism Committee of the Security Council.

Investigations revealed that the attacks on the US, planned since 1996, had been organized in Germany and funded with Gulf money. Periodic states of high alert, as at London's Heathrow airport in 2003, may have prevented further terrorist attacks.

Around the globe the bank accounts of those suspected of having links with Al-Qaeda were frozen and suspects arrested, countries as far apart as Indonesia and Spain joining in the sweep. Notable arrests included Khalid Sheikh Mohammed, a senior figure in Al-Qaeda, and Ali al-Ghamdi, the mastermind behind Saudi bombings. Several of those apprehended early on, however, were later released when no specific evidence against them could be found. The US military was less scrupulous: the hundreds of prisoners taken during the Afghan conflict were held without trial in harsh conditions at Camp X-Ray on the US base of Guantanamo Bay, Cuba.

'Axis of evil'

Arrests of genuine terrorists and suspects were all very well, but they did not make convincing television viewing nor did they appear to be putting the Al-Qaeda movement out of action. At the end of 2001 a British citizen professing allegiance to Bin Laden was arrested after trying to blow up a Miami-bound flight with explosives hidden in his shoes. The next year Al-Qaeda was believed to have been behind bomb outrages in Tunisia, Bali (Indonesia), Yemen and Mombassa (Kenya). A US citizen was also arrested for planning to detonate a 'dirty bomb', and Muslim rebels from the Russian province of Chechnya killed over 100 hostages in a Moscow theatre.

Despite huge efforts to track him down, Osama Bin Laden remained at large. He and other Al-Qaeda leaders even appeared on video-tape, urging their supporters to continue their jihad. The tapes, often shown through Aljazeera TV, referred to the West's anti-terrorist action as an anti-Muslim 'crusade' and its participants as 'the infidel'. To some young, insecure and disaffected Muslims such vocabulary was inspirational. Bin Laden became their hero, ensuring that Al-Qaeda was never short of recruits.

By the time the first anniversary of 11 September came round, the Bush administration was clearly frustrated by the elusive nature of the enemy they were pursuing. After Yemen and Afghanistan, opportunities for overt shows of strength had dried up. Even with satellite surveillance and laser-guided weapons, it was proving difficult to bomb a 'mentality'. Aware that the public wanted action showing that the war on terrorism was being won, the US government re-focussed on the 'axis of evil'.

The six countries of the axis did not appear equally dangerous. Following the collapse of the Soviet Union, communist Cuba was hardly a serious threat. At the time the US believed North Korea could be dissuaded by non-military pressure from developing nuclear weapons. Of the four Muslim states – Syria, Libya, Iran and Iraq – for the moment the first two were discounted: traditionally Syria had been wary of Muslim extremism, and Libya's President Gaddafi hated Bin Laden and was probably afraid of him.

Iran, the birthplace of modern militant Islam, had done most to promote international terrorism. To US annoyance, the Iranian government refused to hand over Al-Qaeda suspects it claimed to have arrested. However, any possible attack on Iran would face the double danger of inhospitable terrain and a guarantee of suicidally ferocious Shia resistance. Moreover, Prime Minister Khatami's elected government appeared to be trying to moderate his country's fundamentalism. No, US advisors concluded, Iran was not a suitable target for direct US intervention. Right next door lay a much more realistic alternative: Iraq.

Invasion of Iraq

Saddam Hussein's Iraq was in a sorry state. A UN oil-for-food programme had limited the country's income and not all the money intended for food and medicine was spent on such necessities. The programme's organizer resigned in 1998. The UN responded the next year by abolishing limits on Iraqi oil exports, although a range of imports was still officially forbidden. The United Nations Children's Fund (UNICEF) estimated Iraq's child poverty to have doubled during the 1990s.

Meanwhile, Hussein played a game of cat and mouse with the UNSCOM inspectors charged with seeking and destroying his stock of illegal weapons. For seven years the team struggled to overcome resistance, obfuscation and obstruction until, in 1998, denied access to the country's numerous 'presidential palaces', it gave up and withdrew. Britain and the US responded with Operation Desert Fox, a bombing campaign to 'degrade' Hussein's WMD capacity. How many he still had by this stage was uncertain (see page 200). Hussein then rejected a second UN weapons inspection service, Unmovic, prompting fresh Anglo-US air strikes in early 2001. These drew a hostile international reaction. Previously, British and American forces had also destroyed Iraqi anti-aircraft systems that locked onto planes patrolling the northern and southern no-fly zones. Further targets had been hit after a failed Iraqi assassination attempt on former president George Bush Sr, and another strike had been made when Iraqi forces had joined in the fighting between Kurdish factions in northern Iraq.

Within the country, Hussein maintained his iron rule. Although the dictatorial prime-minister-cum-president had never been popular, his position was probably strengthened rather than weakened by the USAF and RAF attacks. They enabled him to justify his crushingly tight security and allowed him to demand patriotic support to combat aggression by the 'imperialists'. Backing came most readily from the Sunni minority. Iraqi Shia, whose spiritual leader was assassinated in 1999, went along with the diktats of Baghdad largely because they had little option: memories of the bloodletting that had followed their unsuccessful 1991 rebellion were still raw.

WMDs

Britain and the US had never really stopped being at war with Iraq since 1991. As they regretted not having finished off Hussein then, tackling him in 2003 was to some extent finishing old business. Of course there were other motives for attacking Iraq, spoken and unspoken. President George Bush Jr, keen to avenge Hussein's attempted assassination of his father, had not been impressed when the Iraqi dictator offered no condolences for the events of 11 September 2001. He may also have been persuaded that control over the Iraqi oil fields would be a priceless asset and that a show of overwhelming military might would overawe other real and potential opponents around the world, though neither of these motives could be even whispered abroad. There were also serious difficulties trying to establish whether the Iraqi regime had any links at all with Al-Qaeda. Hussein might have relished the sight of the collapsing Twin Towers, but he was no admirer of the brand of fanaticism that had brought it about.

The only card left for President Bush and his faithful British ally, Labour Prime Minister Tony Blair, was Iraq's supposed retention of weapons of mass destruction. Both men claimed this as sufficient reason for 'regime change' in Iraq – the removal of President Hussein being essential for lasting global peace and security. Most of the rest of the world disagreed. They argued on two grounds: one, that Hussein's possession of WMDs was not proven and, two, that pre-emptive action against another state because of what it might do was illegal in international law, especially without UN approval. The forceful removal of the Taliban had been expressly sanctioned by the UN Security Council. None of its resolutions specifically permitted military action against Iraq should it retain its WMDs.

By 2002 the US and Britain seemed prepared to defy international opinion and take unilateral action against Iraq. At this point, Saddam Hussein, who had refused to accept UN weapons inspectors for the past four years, agreed to let them return. Delighted, the Security Council passed Resolution 1414 that said he would face 'serious consequences' if he did not co-operate with their work. In December, Hussein produced a monster 12,000-page document detailing the status of his weapons programme. A couple of months later, to the further embarrassment of Bush and Blair, leading weapons' inspector Hans Blix announced that Iraq was co-operating with the UN team's work. Announcing that he had not been 'watching the breaking of toothpicks' (BBC News, 16 January 2003), he cited as evidence the destruction of 40 Iraqi missiles. More significantly, he also said that he had found no evidence of any remaining WMDs.

The Security Council was divided. On one side stood the US and Britain, declaring that Hussein still had WMDs and was merely playing for time. Eager for legality to dampen domestic opposition, the British government pressed for a new resolution stating clearly that the 'serious consequences' of Resolution 1414 meant war. The opponents of immediate war were headed by France, which had serious economic interests in Iraq. They argued that there were many regimes as wickedly oppressive as Hussein's and international law prohibited outside interference in Iraq until it was shown still to possess and be ready to use WMDs.

In all probability the Bush administration had set its heart on an invasion of Iraq many months before. The troops, missiles, ships and aircraft were all in position, and the battle plans had been drawn up. The business with the Security Council had been largely at the request of Britain, seeking a fig leaf of legal respectability for an inevitable campaign. That is not to say Prime Minister Blair lied about Iraq's possession of WMDs – he almost certainly believed they were there, as probably did President Bush. In the end, though, the presence of WMDs was just the most politically acceptable of a multitude of reasons for a war that most of the rest of the world believed to be contrary to international law.

The Iraq War

The Iraq War, alternatively known as the Second Gulf War, was a strange affair. In some ways it went just as everyone had prophesied; in others it proved surprising and, to the invading coalition, even slightly embarrassing.

The most predictable aspect of the war was its outcome. The Coalition (basically the US and Britain with largely moral support from around 30 other goverments) launched their attack on Iraq on 20 March 2003. Baghdad fell in mid-April and on 1 May President Bush, upright and proud on the deck of *USS Abraham Lincoln*, declared that the Coalition had won their victory and the campaign was over.

Also predictable was the precision of the Anglo-American bomb and missile assault that destroyed Iraq's command and control structure far more swiftly and effectively than in the 1991 war. Whereas around ten per cent of the weapons used in the First Gulf War had been 'smart', in 2003 the figure was nearer 80 per cent. The US unleashed a new 'shock and awe' tactic based upon overwhelming firepower and 9.5-ton MOAB bombs that wielded the destructive power of a small nuclear device. With grim humour, US service personnel called them the 'Mother Of All Bombs'.

The enormous onslaught from the air was backed up by armoured brigades tearing at great speed through the desert towards Baghdad. US tanks, equipped with the latest sighting equipment, destroyed their Iraqi counterparts even before they came into view. The land forces launched their assault mainly from Kuwait. The Coalition used other bases around the Gulf, although no Arab government openly declared its support of the invasion. Countries as diverse as Albania, Australia, Denmark, Japan, Spain, and Uzbekistan provided further military backing.

Unwelcome liberators

What most observers had not predicted was the extent of Iraqi resistance. After the experience of 1991, Hussein's commanders knew that there was little point in tackling the Coalition head on – direct confrontation meant inevitable defeat and obliteration. Instead, specially trained Iraqi units, some known as 'Saddam Brigades', let the enemy roar by before emerging to attack them unawares from the flank and rear.

This happened first in the Gulf port of Umm Qasr. Here, fighting to the last, a mere 50 Iraqi soldiers held at bay the entire might of the US for six whole days. Whatever one's point of view, it was a feat of remarkable, even heroic resistance. Similar bravery was encountered elsewhere as the Coalition pressed on towards the capital. The consequence of these rearguard actions – and of debilitating sand storms – was that a campaign optimistically predicted to be over in a fortnight dragged on for six painful weeks.

The attitude of ordinary Iraqis also took the Coalition by surprise. The invaders had come, they said, as liberators. Their politicians had led them to expect streets lined with cheering crowds, as had met the Allies advancing across Europe in 1944–5. In Iraq there were few crowds and even less cheering. There was some celebration and pulling down of grotesque statues when it was clear that the feared Hussein really had been toppled, but the most common reaction to the Anglo-American soldiers was one of stolid, even sullen, indifference.

Those who knew Iraq well had predicted this. Had the Coalition forgotten that they had been blasting the country with their bombs and starving its people with their sanctions for the past 12 years? Did they not realize that Muslims, Sunni and Shia, do not readily see an 'infidel' as a saviour? Were they blind to the massive destruction, loss of life and injury that even smart weapons had inflicted? Surely they realized that Hussein's propaganda, however laughable to Western eyes and ears, had been cleverly preparing Iraqis to reject the seemingly arrogant and overfed invader? Finally, had they forgotten how cruelly the US had let down the Iraqis when they had risen up against Saddam Hussein in 1991? For all these quite predictable reasons, the reception afforded the Coalition was at best luke warm.

There were other unexpected features of the war. One was the hurried way it had started. It went off with a bang, literally, when the US hastily targeted Dawra Farm, a base that intelligence reports said was being used by Hussein and his closest associates. If they were there, they escaped the onslaught. Had the attack succeeded, the whole campaign might have taken a very different course; but it did not, and the failure of intelligence or ordnance, or both, proved to be the first of several such heavy-handed blunders.

Two other unexpected aspects of the campaign are worth mentioning. One was the enormous opposition that it aroused around the world. In dozens of cities, from London to Sydney, millions of men, women and children turned out in the streets to protest against a war that they believed to be illegal bullying by an over-confident superpower and its ex-imperialist lapdog. The other aspect was the time it took to find and capture Saddam Hussein. Uday and Qusay, detested sons of the sometime president, were killed in a shoot-out with US troops in July. By this time most of the other leading members of the regime had been either killed or captured. But the ex-dictator himself, with an enormous bounty in dollars on his head, remained at large until December. It was not because they feared the 66-year-old fugitive that people risked their lives to shelter him. They were motivated by something else the Coalition had underestimated – clan and tribal loyalty. Grey-haired, bearded and gaunt, the 'Butcher of Baghdad' was eventually found hiding in a crude spider-hole beneath a farmhouse south of his home town of Tikrit.

Victory but little peace

With the capture of Saddam Hussein at the end of 2003, the US-led coalition had fulfilled one of its three main aims in invading Iraq: removing a despicable dictator. Over the months that followed, as mass graves and other evidence of his regime's cruelty came to light, the achievement appeared wholly laudable. Almost two years later, in October 2005, the ex-dictator and seven others, all closely associated with the Hussein regime, were put on public trial in a heavily-guarded Baghdad courtroom.

The specific charge was killing 148 Shia in the village of Dujail in 1982. Through censored TV coverage, the Iraqi people saw a side of Hussein that he had previously avoided showing to the media. He refused to accept the validity of the court, interrupting, ranting, swearing, throwing himself about, boycotting, pleading illness, going on hunger strike and generally making life as difficult as possible for everyone around him. During the year-long trial, three of the defence lawyers were killed by anti-Baathist elements. At one stage, believing that he was going to be found guilty and therefore condemned to death, the incorrigible ex-president demanded to be shot rather than hanged.

Back in early 2003, however, the elimination of Iraq's weapons of mass destruction, not its dictator, had been the Coalition's avowed primary aim. Where had the WMDs now got to? The truth is, they were nowhere to be found because, as the UN inspectors had rightly surmised before the occupation, they did not exist. Nor had they existed since the early 1990s when they were destroyed in response to international pressure. Their non-existence was formally declared in October 2004. President Bush and Prime Minister Blair gradually came around to admitting their error in public. 'Much of the intelligence turned out to be wrong,' declared the US president in December 2005, while still justifying the invasion on the less specific grounds that 'Saddam was a threat, and the American people and the world is better off because he is no longer in power' (BBC, 14 December 2005). It was, of course, too late to point out, as UN Secretary General Kofi Annan had done in 2004, that such woolly justification for war was unacceptable in international law.

The Coalition's third avowed aim was to establish Iraq as a beacon of democracy in the Middle East. It was not long, however, before democracy was proving almost as elusive as the infamous WMDs. The problems were fourfold.

First, democracy can operate only if there is a general consensus among the governed that they will accept their government and its laws. In post-war Iraq, such a consensus was hard to find. The newly created state was marked by deep and overlapping ethnic, political and religious divisions. Since its creation by the British in 1921, it had been dominated by the Sunni minority that comprised around 20 per cent of the population. The majority Shia group (perhaps 60 per cent of the population with their own holy places, such as Najaf and Karbala) saw the ousting of Hussein as an opportunity for settling old scores and asserting their authority. Fellow Shia in Iran were quite prepared to offer support. The large Kurdish population in the north, itself riven with hostile factions but all eager for independence, made the situation more complex.

Second, true democracy was something Iraqis had never experienced before. Its necessary traditions of freedom of expression, toleration and the rule of law could not simply be transplanted from Washington DC to Baghdad and expected to root and flower overnight. They needed time, and time was something the Coalition was short of. Third, many Iraqis felt that a form of government was being imposed on them from without. They were allowed to vote whether to accept it or not, but resented the fact that it had taken a foreign power – and an 'infidel' one at that – to bring this situation about. The implicit humiliation to the Arab world and Islam was clear. Fourth, the more fundamentalist Muslims did not share the West's love of popular democracy and free-market economics. Both, they said, permitted licence, not liberty, and paved the way to selfishness and sin by pandering to people's baser instincts.

Securing the country

The occupation force initially numbered around 170,000 troops. The great bulk, some 150,000, were American, with the British contingent of 8,000 being the second largest. These two undertook most of the active peacekeeping. Other forces included 3,600 South Koreans, 1,700 Poles and 400 Australians. The Spanish contribution was withdrawn in 2004, while the Italians gave conflicting signals about their commitment. The UN, which was eager to help with the reconstruction of Iraq after the invasion, withdrew when its Baghdad headquarters were destroyed by a bomb in August 2003. More than a year later it still had only 59 staff in the country.

The British were for the most part based in the Shia south, around the regional capital of Basra. To begin with, drawing on years of peace-keeping experience in Northern Ireland and elsewhere, they had some success in being accepted by the local population and took relatively few casualties. By the end of 2005 they had lost less than 100 soldiers. Elsewhere, the Americans had a much tougher time. Not only did they handle the major confrontations, but their heavy handed tactics – relying on armour and air-power rather than on-the-street policing – sometimes made them appear aloof and bullying. Both the American and British scored spectacular own goals when revelations came to light of serious mistreatment of Iraqi prisoners and detainees. The US Marines were heavily criticised for the unnecessary killing of civilians while sweeping houses for insurgents, and the British forces' 'good boy scout' image was shattered when a video appeared showing them beating up Iraqi civilians. Although the alleged offenders were duly questioned and dealt with, the damage done to the Coalition's image was incalculable. Its mission, after all, had been to liberate Iraqis from such inhumane behaviour.

Unsure what to call their multifarious opponents, in the end the occupying forces settled on the catch-all term 'insurgents'. Some were the remnants of Hussein's old Baath Party, others appeared to be simply disaffected and unemployed youths protesting against an unwelcome foreigners. More difficult to handle were those inspired by a heady mix of religion and nationalism. Foremost among these was the Mehdi Army of the fiery and unpredictable young Shia cleric, Moqtada Sadr. Formed in the summer of 2003, the Army grew in numbers and strength until in the summer of 2004 it was able to take control of the centre of Najaf, from where it was ousted only with great difficulty.

Not surprisingly, the situation in Iraq was ripe for intervention by the country's neighbours. The extent of direct Syrian and Iranian involvement was uncertain, although the British were sure that armour-piercing weapons used against them must have been provided by Iran, and US Secretary of State Condoleezza Rice (appointed November 2004) made clear that she believed the Syrian regime was backing at least some of the Iraqi insurgents. By mid-2004, an estimated 1,000 Al-Qaeda supporters had infiltrated across Iraq's notoriously leaky boarders. Siding with the Sunni, they targeted Shia and Westerners alike.

The insurgency

At first the insurgents employed sniper fire, roadside bombs, car bombs, mortar attacks – whatever weapon or tactic might prove the most effective – to strike at Coalition forces. Occasionally, as when they besieged and eventually captured the Sunni city of Falluja in the spring of 2004, the US military engaged in large-scale action with sizable numbers of their opponents. They hit Falluja again later in the same year. By 2004 insurgent suicide bombers had made their appearance, and attacks were being made on fellow Iraqis as well as the forces of occupation. In February, for example, the offices of the main Kurdish groupings were devastated by suicide bombings, and the following month 140 died when Sunni suicide bombers blew themselves up during a Shia religious festival.

This was what the Coalition leaders feared most – insurgents seeking not only to drive out the occupying forces but also to foment religious discord that would destroy the new system of government that the US and its Iraqi allies were busy setting up.

This was made plain by the number of attacks on oil pipelines and Iraqi security forces' recruitment and training centres: in September 2004, for instance, a bomb killed 47 and injured many times that number when it detonated near Baghdad's central police station. The previous month hundreds had been trampled to death when rumours of an imminent suicide attack caused a stampede among Shia festival-goers.

To the surprise of the Coalition and many outside observers, over time the scale of the insurgency mounted rather than diminished. April 2005 saw 67 separate attacks and by August civilian and military casualties were running at an average of 60 a day – three times what they had been a year previously. When in September 2005 Al Qaeda's shadowy leader in Iraq, Abu Musab al-Zarqawi, demanded extermination of all Shia as bedfellows of the Western 'crusaders', several commentators began talking of imminent civil war.

As well as the alarming death toll (see page 206), the invasion and occupation had other painful costs. By early 2006, US taxpayers were forking out some $4.7 billion each month for operations in Iraq. By the end of August that year, the total figure stood at an astounding $311,088,969,000. By then, over 50 per cent of Americans believed their country should never have gone into Iraq in the first place and about two-thirds of them felt President Bush had handled the situation badly.

If Americans were disenchanted, the Iraqis were close to despair. Three years after the invasion, unemployment in Iraq stood at around 50 per cent and inflation was running at a savings-destroying 70 per cent. The economy, potentially one of the most buoyant in the world at a time of soaring oil prices, was at best stagnant. When in 2004 the World Bank estimated that Iraq needed $36 billion over the next 36 months to recover from the effects of the war, a fair proportion of the money had already been pledged. By early 2006, however, very little had actually been paid because of the deteriorating security situation. Education and health services had collapsed in many areas, corruption, smuggling and other malpractices were widespread, and life expectancy had fallen to 57 for men and 60 for women. Not surprisingly, the figure of around 70 per cent of Iraqis who viewed the future with optimism in 2004 had fallen to 50 per cent a year later and less than 40 per cent a year after that.

Terror ongoing

Although Prime Minister Blair made strong statements to the contrary, it was clear to most observers that the Coalition's action in Iraq fuelled Muslim extremism elsewhere. By 2004, Al-Qaeda was estimated to have 18,000 operatives at large in 60 countries. No country that supported the US-led invasion of Iraq was safe. In May 2003 bomb attacks rocked the Saudi Arabian capital, Riyadh. Four days later 45 died when Western and Jewish targets were hit in Casablanca, Morocco. In December it was the turn of Turkey, where two synagogues, the British consulate and a British bank were blown up.

The year 2004 saw further shooting in Riyadh and an horrific bomb attack on the Madrid rail network that left 191 commuters dead and more than 1,800 injured. When the Spanish government, which had initially failed to recognize the work of Al-Qaeda, was voted out of office and replaced by one pledged to withdraw Spanish troops from Iraq, Bin Laden achieved his first electoral success.

The following year London became the terrorists' target. On 7 July four suicide bombers blew up underground trains and a bus, killing dozens and injuring many hundreds. A similar plot two weeks later was foiled by the authorities. When, towards the end of the year, Al-Qaeda bombs smashed two hotels in Amman, Jordan, the 56 dead included several Palestinians. Westerners were again severely inconvenienced when, in the summer of 2006, security forces in Britain and the US claimed to have uncovered a sophisticated plot to down some dozen passenger aircraft using liquid explosives smuggled aboard in hand luggage. Ironically, it appeared that rather than making the world safer by removing Saddam Hussein, as the US had predicted, the military action had served only to inspire Muslim fanatics even more.

Constructing democracy

Despite mounting unrest within Iraq and terrorism elsewhere, the Coalition pressed ahead with its plans to establish a genuinely democratic system of government for the country it had taken over. The idea was for a provisional government to assume power at the end of June 2004, for elections to a provisional assembly six months later, and for this assembly to agree a constitution to be put to the people. The arrangement was accepted by the UN Security Council in June 2004 (the US being happy to involve the UN when it was deemed useful) and on 30 June 2004 a Provisional Authority under the leadership of long-term exile Ayad Allawi took over nominal rule of the country. This formally ended the occupation. The Authority could, in theory, ask all foreign troops to leave, but since it was dependent upon their presence until Iraq's own security forces were recruited and trained, this remained a purely academic option.

Amid a considerable increase in insurgent activity, January 2005 saw elections to a Transitional National Assembly. The great majority of Sunnis (98 per cent in some areas) refused to vote, somewhat weakening the Assembly's legitimacy. Undaunted, it elected a Kurdish president and two deputies, one Shia and the other Sunni. These in turn chose an interim prime minister, the Shia Ibrahim Jaafari. A Constitutional Committee then drew up a constitution which, after much wrangling, was put to the popular vote on 15 October. Although rejected in two Sunni provinces, the terms of the referendum were carefully worded to stop this being a veto on the creation of an Islamic federal democracy.

The last step on the path to democracy was taken in December 2005, when amid tight security nation-wide elections – described by Al-Qaeda as a 'satanic plot' – were held for the country's first 275-seat National Assembly. The turnout was over 70 per cent, with most Sunnis who had boycotted previous elections deciding to join in the process. Chosen for four years, the Assembly comprised 230 seats allocated according to the population of each of Iraq's 18 provinces. The remaining 45 seats were distributed among parties whose support was spread over more than one province. Remarkably for an Islamic nation, one third of each party's candidates had to be women.

Project finished?

The elections left the Shia-led United Iraqi Alliance (UIA) with 128 seats in parliament. This was sufficient to give it a majority but not an overall one, and therefore required the formation of a coalition administration around the UIA. Coalitions, though, mean compromise and this was not a word that featured prominently in the Iraqi political vocabulary. One answer – to outsiders at least – was to include the 25 secular supporters of Ayad Allawi. Many Shia saw the ex-prime minister as a puppet of the US and refused to work with either him or his party. Agreement with the more extreme or neo-Baathist Sunnis was well-nigh impossible and most of the 58 elected Kurds made virtual independence the price of their support. Days of argument slipped into weeks and then months. Finally, the re-elected Kurdish president, Jalal Talabani, put forward a Shia compromise candidate, Jawad al-Maliki, and he was accepted as prime minister.

Meanwhile, the blood-letting continued. By August 2006, the bare facts were bad enough. In 41 months since the coalition invasion, recorded deaths totalled: 42,358 Iraqi civilians; 5,182 Iraqi security forces (excluding war casualties); 2,596 US military; 115 UK military; 115 other military; 77 non-Iraqi journalists. These terrible figures concealed as much as they revealed. Most worrying was the increase in sectarian attacks since Abu Musab al-Zarqawi's outburst (see page 203) and the bombing of the Shia shrine in Samarra in February 2006. At the risk of over-simplifying, the violence took the form of Shia extremists (Iran-backed) v Sunni; Sunni extremists (al-Qaeda-backed) v Shia; all extremists (including Sunni followers of the old regime) v the new non-sectarian government; Kurdish extremists v Arabs; and all insurgent groups taking pot shots at coalition forces when the opportunity arose. In other words, by the summer of 2006, Iraq was perilously close to anarchy.

The killings were carried out by single rifle shots, mortar attacks, roadside pipe bombs, suicide bombs attached to individuals, and huge car bombs. As the attackers became more sophisticated, the incidence of multiple fatalities rose. Estimates of the number of insurgents varied widely. The US put the figure at around 20,000 and growing, while the Iraqis themselves estimated double that number and another 160,000 supporters. Some ten per cent of insurgents were said to be foreign nationals. These included the Jordanian-born Abu Musab al-Zarqawi. A prime target for the Coalition, he was eventually killed in an air-strike in June 2006. Small successes such as this enabled optimistic Coalition leaders to prophesy that, by 2007–8, Iraq would be stable and secure enough to manage its own security. There would then be no need for anything but a token Coalition presence.

Others took a more pessimistic view. In March 2006, Zalmay Khalilzad, the US ambassador in Baghdad, admitted that the toppling of Saddam Hussein had opened a 'Pandora's Box'. Five months later, a senior official in the Iraqi government said off the record that he believed 'Iraq as a political project is finished'. (Reuters)

14

a region divided

This chapter will cover:
- the Middle East's reaction to the 9/11 attacks on New York
- the way Egypt, Jordan and Lebanon struggled to manage their various domestic difficulties
- attempts by the states of the Gulf and Arabian peninsular to find a suitable strategy for the conflicting demands of the twenty-first century
- how Syria and Iran remained largely outside the community of nations.

Reaction to terror

Along with almost all other world leaders, the Middle East's premiers were virtually unanimous in their condemnation of the terrorist attacks which had accounted for almost 3,000 lives in New York and Washington DC on 11 September 2001. The most predictable reaction came from Israel, itself subject to terror attacks for many years. In some Israeli circles there was even a sense of macabre relief as it was hoped the outrage would strengthen Israeli-US links still further. This may have been at the back of Prime Minister Ariel Sharon's mind when he declared that 9/11 would be 'a turning point in the war against international terror' (www.september11news.com).

Not to be upstaged, a genuinely shocked Yasser Arafat expressed his horror at what had been done, condemning it utterly. The more militant Hamas, on the other hand, simply distanced itself from the attacks by saying that it had no interest in action outside 'Palestine'. The governments of Egypt, Jordan, Saudi Arabia, Yemen and other states in the region (except Iraq – see page 196) all made public declarations of support for the American people. Many expressed themselves in Islamic terms, reminding the world that Muslims were prohibited from harming the weak and defenceless.

The three Muslim states that President Bush would later say were within his 'axis of evil' (see page 194) – Libya, Iran, Syria – all joined the general chorus of disapproval of Al-Qaeda's action. There was, however, a hint of reserve in some of what they said. For example, President Khatami of Iran spoke of the 'international duty to try to undermine terrorism' (www.september11news.com). Although 'undermine' may not be a perfect translation of his words, it does make clear his reluctance to speak of a 'war' against terror, as Sharon had done. The problem, Khatami implied, was not simply a matter of evil people behaving wickedly but of a deeper, socio-political malaise that, like poverty and disease, needed to be tackled from the roots upwards.

Balancing act

Around the Middle East popular reaction to the attacks was mixed. This helps explain the reservations in some official statements. It was widely mooted in the press, for instance, that the whole business had been a conspiracy planned by 'the Jews', perhaps even with American help, to make the rest of the world hate Arabs and Muslims. Many dismissed this as nonsense, of course, but it shows the extent of public paranoia throughout the region.

While the majority shared the rest of the world's revulsion at the mass slaughter, a minority with extremist views welcomed it as a blow against the arch enemy of Islam. Furthermore, even in the hearts of those who decried what had been done, there was a sneaking admiration at the way Bin Laden and his tiny movement had managed to inflict such massive damage and injury on so powerful an enemy – a modern-day version of the David and Goliath story.

Such mixed reaction only added to the considerable difficulties already faced by most Middle Eastern governments trying to balance the need for modernization with the efforts by spiritual leaders to maintain Islamic values and traditions. They also had to find strategies for handling the mounting pressure from ordinary citizens for a greater say in government. Steering a safe course between the rocks of autocracy and democracy, secularism and Islam, modernization and tradition, independence and friendship with the US was no easy task. The way the region's governments sought to cope with this challenge during the early years of the twenty-first century is the subject of what follows.

Egypt, Jordan and Lebanon

Egypt

After the trials and tribulations of the Nasser and Sadat years, Egypt's history under the astute President Mubarak was comparatively calm. His continuation in office, making him the longest-serving head of state in the Arab world, was confirmed by a series of referendums. In 2005, when he was re-elected for a fifth term, for the first time opposition candidates were permitted to stand. However, as religious parties were not permitted by the Egyptian constitution, the main opposition grouping – the Muslim Brotherhood – was unable to field a candidate. Later in the year, during the parliamentary elections, the Brotherhood got around the ban by standing as independents and won 20 per cent of the seats. Even so, Mubarak's National Democratic Party maintained its grip on power.

Opposition groups complained bitterly that the presidential and parliamentary elections had been neither free nor fair. Having survived six assassination attempts, the most dangerous taking place when he attended a meeting of the Organization of African Unity in Addis Ababa, Mubarak was not going to give up his position easily. Nevertheless, the political climate in Egypt remained more open than in many Middle Eastern states. The media, in particular, were given a fairly free rein and Cairo reinforced its position as the cultural heart of the Arab world. Most censorship was self-imposed, although those who criticized the status quo too harshly were liable to be prosecuted under a variety of laws, including that imposed when a state of emergency was declared after Sadat's assassination.

The Egyptian economy proved as sluggish as it had been under Sadat. This meant that Mubarak's friendship with the West, particularly the US, was partly determined by his country's reliance upon billion-dollar aid packages. In an attempt to disrupt the tourist industry and foster political unrest, in 1997 Islamic terrorists shot dead 58 tourists before the Nile temple of the Pharaoh Hatshepsut. The number of foreign visitors fell dramatically and it was some while before tourism began to pick up again. Starting in 2004, further terrorist strikes set it back again. In July 2005, the Red Sea resort of Sharm al-Sheikh was targeted, leaving almost 90 dead, and the following April over 200 were killed at Dahab on the Gulf of Aqaba.

The position in Egypt in mid-2006, therefore, was uncertain. No public plans had been declared for what to do on the president's incapacity or death. Some hesitant political reforms had been instigated but nowhere near far-reaching enough to satisfy the regime's critics. And all the while Islamic fundamentalist groups, especially the Muslim Brotherhood, were gaining support among the country's impoverished masses.

Jordan

Life was no easier for Jordan's King Abdullah II than it had been for his father, Hussein. Without oil, short of water, and home to a large population of Palestinian refugees, the country inherited by the 39-year-old monarch had few natural advantages. British- and US-educated Abdullah, a collector of antique weapons and a car-racing enthusiast, maintained his father's balance of friendship with the West and support for the Palestinian cause. His position was well reflected by his family circumstances: his mother (Toni) was British-born while he himself was married to a Palestinian.

Abdullah also promised social and political reform, set out within a grand-sounding National Agenda, to bring his state more into line with the world of the twenty-first century. Implementing these reforms proved more difficult. A succession of prime ministers came and went, appointed then dismissed by the king, but little actually happened. The key engine of change – the king himself – apparently vacillated when it came to reducing his own power. Significantly, in the parliamentary elections of 2003, two-thirds of the seats were won by royalist candidates standing as independents and, when change was made, such as the appointment of three women as ministers in 2003, it was done by the king himself.

Pressure for reform came not only from the US, the country's principal benefactor, but from opposition within Jordan itself. The year 2002 saw serious riots in the southern town of Maan and the shooting of an American diplomat in Amman. The US-led invasion of Iraq, condemned by the general public throughout the Arab world, made Jordan's position as a key American ally even more tricky.

The Jordanian embassy in Baghdad was bombed in 2003, in the summer of 2005 missiles were launched from Aqaba at a US warship, and three months later Al-Qaeda suicide bombers blew apart two luxury Amman hotels. The explosions killed 56 people, mostly Arabs, including guests attending a wedding. Abu Musab al-Zarqawi's Jordanian nationality (see pages 203, 206) was an obvious embarrassment to King Abdullah. So too was Israel's massive, US-backed attack on Hezbollah in the summer of 2006, which he felt it expedient to condemn openly.

Lebanon

To the north-west, Lebanon entered the new millennium with a degree of reserved optimism that the ghastly troubles of the previous 25 years were finally over. Following a US-brokered deal that halted all but light and sporadic Hezbollah attacks, Israel withdrew from its 'security zone' in the south in 2000; the divisive Syrian peace-keepers left Beirut the following year but maintained their positions in the east of the country.

In the easier atmosphere and under the second premiership (2000–4) of Sunni billionaire Rafiq Hariri, the country made considerable economic and political headway. Although the prime minister's tycoon-style handling of the economy was not to everyone's taste, his commitment to religious and political toleration was recognized everywhere. So was his charitable generosity: some thousands of students were said to have been educated at his personal expense.

All was not sweetness and light, however. There were rows with Israel over shared water supplies from a tributary of the Jordan, and periodic bomb blasts reminded everyone of past horrors. A major crisis erupted in the autumn of 2004. It began with a French-backed UN Security Council resolution that all foreign troops – i.e. Syrian – leave Lebanon. This raised the political temperature within Lebanon itself, where parliament voted to extend the term of office of the Christian, pro-Syrian president, Emile Lahoud. Prime Minister Hariri, who had initially opposed the extension, then resigned.

On St Valentine's Day 2005 a massive explosion rocked Beirut. Said to have been made by the equivalent of 1,000 kg (2,200 lbs) of TNT, the blast left Rafiq Hariri and some 20 of his supporters and bodyguards dead and fuelled a so-called nationalist 'Cedar Revolution'. Anti-Syrian politicians and media openly blamed Assad for the assassination and demanded that he withdraw his troops and stop meddling in Lebanese affairs. Pro-Syrians turned out in their thousands in the streets of Beirut to display neighbourly solidarity. Despite this, the Syrian dictator bowed to UN and French pressure and took his forces from Lebanon.

Elections in the summer of 2005 produced an anti-Syrian government. It was headed by the son of the assassinated Rafiq Hariri and for the first time included Hezbollah ministers, who had opposed the Cedar Revolution. The Assad regime, not noted for its grace in defeat, took revenge for the international humiliation by picking off prominent Lebanese opponents in a series of car bomb attacks. Local and international investigators came to the conclusion that evidence linking Syria to the Hariri assassination was incontrovertible.

During 2006, Lebanon took a long, tragic stride backwards. A major factor was the rising power of Hezbollah, the Shia party whose militant wing called themselves the Islamic Resistance. The whole organisation was condemned as terrorist by the US but backed by Iran as a way of furthering the Shia cause and as a vehicle for attacking Israel. The Syrians also supported Hezbollah in order to maintain their influence in Lebanon.

There were signs of a newly militant Islam within the country when, at the beginning of the year, Denmark's Beirut embassy was torched because a Danish newspaper had printed cartoons poking fun at the Prophet Mohammed.

Things became vastly more serious in July when, in response to the kidnapping of two Israeli soldiers by Hezbollah's Islamic Resistance, the IDF blockaded Lebanon and launched massive retaliatory strikes intended to set the country back 20 years (see page 241). Islamic Resistance retaliated with surprising vigour, launching thousands of rockets into northern Israel that killed some 43 civilians. Lebanese casualties were far higher: about 1,100 civilians killed, many more injured and almost a million forced from their homes. Days of continuous air strikes smashed roads, bridges, power stations and other vital structures. A ceasefire brokered by the UN in mid-August pledged a large force of international peacekeepers in the south of the country.

The summer war and blockade were disastrous for Lebanon. The tourist industry, 15 per cent of the country's economy and rising by 50 per cent in the first half of 2006, was utterly destroyed. Although much aid was promised from abroad, including the US, it was nowhere near enough to rebuild the shattered infrastructure. More worrying was the way the war had polarised opinion about Hezbollah. Some Lebanese saw it as a doughty organisation fighting against the odds to further the cause of the Palestinians and Islam in general, while others condemned it for drawing Lebanon into a costly struggle that it neither needed nor wanted. Such sectarian division had lain at the heart of the previous century's terrible civil war (see Chapter 7).

Rumblings around the Gulf

Nowhere were the difficult decisions facing the people and governments of the Middle East at the dawn of the new millennium more apparent than in the states of the Arabian peninsular. Where did they belong in the catalogue of nations? Many had the wealth of the developed countries but the political institutions of the Developing World. Equally tricky was the clash between their material development and their socio-religious heritage. Sensitivity, skill and no little good fortune were needed if they were successfully to overcome these challenges.

Saudi Arabia

The Saud family's personal possession of the bulk of the Arabian peninsular had long been an international anomaly and the situation became even more incongruous as the twenty-first century developed. Those members of the enormously rich and profligate royal family who were sensitive to the situation faced the constant difficulty of carrying their less politically aware relatives with them. As a consequence, the regime found itself under more and more pressure from two directions.

On the surface the less threatening opposition came from Western-orientated Saudis who wanted to open up the government of their homeland and remove some of its more oppressive laws, notably those placing extraordinary restrictions on women. There was also hostility towards the corruption and conspicuous improvidence of the royal family, personified in the character of the chain-smoking King Fahad.

Open protest was rare, but in 2003 a strongly supported reform petition appeared and a public demonstration took place in the capital, Riyadh. It was swiftly broken up by police. Although the demonstrators, mainly from the middle and intellectual classes, posed little or no physical threat to the regime, the Sauds needed the support of the articulate classes to keep the bulk of their subjects on side and to help in the fight with religious extremism. Consequently, setting aside its reactionary instincts, the government instituted some minor political reforms. These included the establishment of a Consultative Council permitted to suggest legislation, and limited municipal elections (2005). Just how lukewarm these measures were is born out by the fact that women were not permitted to vote and elections had to be organized without the benefit of political parties, which were banned. Some believed that rather than dampening down opposition, such feeble measures only encouraged it.

The royal family's lifestyle attracted criticism from religious groups as well as liberals. This was temporarily diverted when the wheel-chair-bound Fahad eventually died in 2005 and was replaced by his more austere brother Abdullah. The new king, who had effectively ruled the country since his brother suffered a stroke some ten years before, promised to root out corruption and continue the programme of moderate reform. Needless to say, this was not enough for Al-Qaeda and its followers. They wanted nothing less than the destruction of the House of Saud and for Arabia to become an Islamic republic governed by Sharia law.

Fundamentalists had been targeting foreigners on Saudi soil since the mid-1990s. These attacks continued into the new millennium, when Saudis themselves were also hit. Among the more memorable actions to hit the headlines were the arrest and torture of British nationals accused of terrorist attacks on their own people, massive suicide bombings in 2003 and 2004, and the beheading of an American hostage, an event that was filmed and later broadcast. 2006 saw a failed attack on an oil installation and gunfights with Al-Qaeda. Amid the mounting unrest and bloodshed, the government could at least take some comfort from the fact that as the world's oil supplies began to run down, the value and importance of Saudi Arabia's reserves increased almost daily.

Kuwait and the Gulf States

Of all the Gulf states, Kuwait was the one most subjected to Western influence. This came willy-nilly from the presence of thousands of foreign troops and other military personnel on its soil, first in the War of Liberation (1990–1) and then in the US-led Coalition's invasion and occupation of Iraq (2003 onwards). Partly as a result of this and partly because of the small, oil-rich state's tradition of comparative toleration, it avoided some of the tribulations of its neighbours. It was the first Arab Gulf state to set up an elected parliament and in 2005 it gave women full political rights. Even so, no women candidates were elected in the June 2006 vote.

The 2003 elections had revealed a dangerous division between Islamists and those loyal to the ruling house of Sabah. In 2006, the situation became more complicated when various reformers (the Orange Movement) banded together after the elections to oppose the ruling Sabah family. The young activist Monirah Al Eidan summed up the situation as 'a bit chaotic' because the opposition groups mistrusted each other as much as they did the government (www.aljazeera.net). The age of the Sabah clique was another destabilizing factor. They were all in their 70s and when the emir, Sheikh Jaber, died in early 2006, his successor lasted only a few days before being obliged to step down on grounds of ill-health. His job then passed to Sheikh al-Ahmad. Outside the political process there always loomed the grim shadow of Al Qaeda-style fundamentalists intent on bringing the entire system down.

The Bahrain archipelago, a firm ally of America and base of its fifth Fleet, became a constitutional monarchy in 2002. Although the Sunni Al-Khalifah family retained much power, the country continued to develop along liberal lines. It built up a flourishing tourist trade, allowed considerable freedom to the media and granted female emancipation. Nevertheless, tensions remained between the Shia majority and the Al-Khalifahs, and between Westernizers and Islamists.

Staggeringly high revenues from oil and gas, freedom of the press and TV, and a burgeoning democracy made twenty-first-century Qatar a miniature haven of luxury for its fortunate inhabitants. Guided by the Al Thani family, it stuck closely to its alliance with the US and therefore attracted some Islamic fundamentalist violence. By and large, though, it remained one of the most settled and harmonious states in the region. Its tolerant attitude made it an obvious home for Aljazeera, the leading Arab news agency. The six states of the nearby United Arab Emirates, guided for many years by their president, Sheikh Zayed of Abu Dhabi, rivalled Qatar in wealth and toleration. Paradoxically, though, the UAE was slow to introduce democracy. Only after Zayed's death in 2004 did his replacement, his son Khalifa, announce plans for a Federal National Council elected on a limited franchise. He also vigorously pursued a policy of economic liberalisation.

Yemen and Oman

The recently united republic of Yemen, blessed with far less mineral wealth than its Arabian neighbours, struggled into the twenty-first century under the leadership of President Ali Abdallah Saleh. Nominally elected in 1999 (the chief opposition group was not permitted to field a candidate), he maintained power through personal loyalty and the support of the powerful, US-backed army. The principal opposition came from religious dissidents in the north and Al-Qaeda operatives and sympathizers in the south. The former were tempted by a truce in mid-2005, while the president expelled many of the latter when expressing solidarity with America over the 9/11 attacks.

Unlike Yemen, in the twenty-first century Oman began developing a busy tourist trade. This was an indication of Sultan Ali Abdallah Saleh's success in bringing law, order and a modern infrastructure to his small but strategically important country. Like some other Arab states, Oman had an elected Consultative Council. It was chosen on a full adult franchise but all real political power remained in the hands of the sultan. He maintained his inheritance's traditionally strong links with

Britain (which was believed to have used Oman as a base for operations in Afghanistan) and cultivated close relations with the US. Understandably, therefore, he willingly joined the anti-fundamentalist campaign, arresting dozens of suspects in 2005.

The outsiders

American power and influence in the Middle East increased sharply after the Al-Qaeda attacks of 9/11. Although the mass of the population remained at best sceptical of the aims of the Bush administration, their governments by and large toed the Washington line. By 2004, with two apparent exceptions, the prime ministers, kings and presidents from Aden to Beirut, Cairo to Baghdad had decided that their best interests were served working alongside the US rather than against it. The exceptions were the fundamentalist Islamic regime in Iran and the Baath party regime in Syria.

Bashar Assad

The death in 1994 of Basil Assad, eldest and most favoured son of Syria's iron president Hafiz Assad, catapulted his shy younger brother Bashar into the limelight. The lean, slightly bewildered-looking 35-year-old was summoned from London, where he had been training as an ophthalmologist, and quietly groomed as his father's heir. Apart from heading the Syrian Computer Society, Bashar had almost no previous political or administrative training. Six years later, following Hafiz's death, he was elected unopposed as his country's president.

The new leader had already expressed support for reform and his accession heralded a brief liberal spring. Hundreds of political prisoners were released, press censorship was relaxed and open discussion of political matters tolerated. The withdrawal of Syrian troops from Beirut and the visit to Damascus by Pope John Paul II in May 2001 appeared to symbolize Syria's coming in from the cold. The thaw did not last. By September, outspoken MPs were being detained and free speech curbed. The re-emergence of the militant Muslim Brotherhood, a group that had attempted to assassinate Bashar's father, may have had something to do with the disappointing about turn. A visit from British Prime Minister Tony Blair later in the year failed to produce an agreement over a common policy towards terrorism.

Some commentators suggested that the crackdown was instigated less by the president himself than by an oligarchy of elderly Baathists. This group, including the vice president and minister of defence, were said to be the real power within Syria. True or not, President Assad had to recognize that for the time being he needed the same three pillars of support that had underpinned his father's rule: the army, the Baath party and the small but influential Alawite Shia sect to which the Assad family belonged. Critics suggested that Bashar was not made of the same tough material as his father. Unable or unwilling to exert his authority, he relied heavily on his highly intelligent sister, the pharmacist Dr Buishra Assad – the 'brain of Syrian politics' (www.aljazeera.net) – and her husband, General Assef Shawqat, head of military intelligence.

Troubled times

Bashar Assad's presidency was soon in trouble. The sluggish economy was not helped by disproportionate military expenditure and the government's failure to dismantle the old Soviet-style state control. By 2006, despite exploitation of its oil and gas reserves, Syria's income per capita was barely one quarter that of neighbouring Lebanon. Disappointed by the government's failure to institute meaningful political or economic reform, Syrian goodwill towards its new president quietly evaporated into the dusty air.

Meanwhile, despite Bashar's professed willingness to improve relations with Israel, tension with the Jewish state remained high. Ongoing peace talks made little headway and Hezbollah's spasmodic cross-border forays attracted sharp Israeli reprisals. In 2003 Israeli jets even attacked Palestinian targets close to Damascus. Potentially far more damaging was the US's inclusion of Syria within its so-called 'axis of evil' (see page 194). This was followed in 2003 by warnings that Syria would face serious consequences if it failed to curb extremist groups said to be operating from within its borders. At one stage Washington even suggested that Assad had sheltered Saddam Hussein's stocks of Weapons of Mass Destruction. When this was shown to be ridiculous, the Syrian leader was warned not to develop WMDs of his own.

American anger with Syria increased after the invasion of Iraq, which Assad openly criticized. He was accused of allowing anti-Coalition insurgents to pass freely across his country's borders into Iraq and then to flee back there when pursued by their adversaries. President Bush's neo-conservative backers stated openly that they wanted Assad and his regime removed. More moderate advisors, backed by Britain and France, warned that the fall of Assad might well spark civil war. There were other, more sinister undercurrents flowing, too. By the end of 2005, well-founded rumours suggested that the US administration had found a use for Assad's brutal regime after all: torturing information from terrorist suspects who could not be so treated within US jurisdiction. Evidence was mounting of the secret, 'extraordinary rendition' of such suspects to Syria in US military aircraft.

Assassination and investigation

In early 2005, following the assassination of the former Lebanese prime minister Rafik Hariri (see page 213), Syria's external crisis deepened sharply. Lebanese public opinion swung away from Syria and international pressure obliged Assad to bring his peacekeeping forces home. A UN commission investigating the Hariri murder found that there had been definite Syrian involvement and criticised the Baath regime for trying to mislead it. Meanwhile, inside sources said members of the Assad family were implicated in the murder. In October the story took a fresh twist when Syrian media suddenly announced that Ghazi Kanaan, the Interior Minister who had for years managed Syrian affairs in Lebanon, had committed suicide. Rumours abounded.

In an effort to reduce its international isolation, the Assad regime improved relations with Turkey and talked of reconciliation with Israel. To boost its standing at home, officials at a Baath Party Congress spoke of further reforms being imminent. These conciliatory gestures were undermined somewhat when Egypt, Saudi Arabia and other powerful Arab states offered to mediate between Assad and his adversaries. Nor was the regime helped by the threat of UN sanctions and a demand from US Secretary of State Condoleezza Rice that it make 'a strategic decision to fundamentally change its behaviour' (BBC 21/12/05). US-backed Syrian exiles, some of them ex-members of the Baath Party, did their best to stir up resistance within their homeland.

By early 2006, Assad's position was extremely dangerous. He had two choices: either submit to growing external pressure, irrevocably weakening his own position, or refuse to cooperate with his accusers in the hope that something would occur to divert attention elsewhere. The Hezbollah War in Lebanon (see page 214) provided just the diversion he needed. The conflict raised Assad's prestige in the Arab world because he openly supported Hezbollah against Israel. It also made him an important power broker. This was made clear when, during a visit from UN Secretary General Kofi Annan in September 2006, he promised to increase security along his borders with Lebanon and to stop the flow of arms to Hezbollah.

Iran relaxes

Iran was in a state of flux at the beginning of the new millennium. With over half of the country's 69 million inhabitants under the age of 25, discontent with the rule of the conservative old men who had overthrown the shah and led the country during the immensely costly war with Iraq was all but inevitable (see page 136). Ayatollah Khamenei, who in 1989 had replaced the trail-blazing Ayatollah Khomeini as the supreme authority in Iran, was almost as rigid in outlook as his predecessor had been.

In the 1990s, technological developments, such as satellite television and the internet, gave the country's young population almost uncontrollable access to a more liberal world. This fuelled the tension between them and the strict Islamic revolutionaries. The man who sought to bridge this gap was the moderate cleric, sometime newspaper editor and minister of culture, Mohammed Khatami. Elected president by an overwhelming majority in 1997, he relaxed censorship and encouraged a more liberal interpretation of Islamic law. The new mood was captured in the massive pro-democracy protests at Tehran University in 1999. The anti-liberal establishment responded with thousands of arrests.

The Iranian constitution reserved supreme authority to Shia religious leaders, but it did embrace a considerable degree of popular participation. In 2000, the people's will made itself felt in a way that dismayed conservatives: Khatami supporters and liberals won 170 of the 290 seats in the Majlis (assembly), leaving the hard-liners with a mere 44 seats. The liberal swing was maintained with Khatami's re-election the following year.

Lest it be thought that Iran was returning to the pro-Western days of the shah, it is necessary to remember that it continued to fund Islamic extremist groups like Hezbollah. Furthermore, whatever Khatami and his young supporters might have wanted, the final say in all matters still rested with elderly and conservative clerics supported by the judiciary. These occupied the so-called Assembly of Experts, charged with appointing the country's Supreme Leader (Ayatollah Ali Khamenei), and the Guardian Council. Able to veto legislation and bar candidates from standing for election, this body of six theologians had effective control of Iran's development. By labelling them 'anti-Islamic', it vetoed liberal reforms on many occasions.

Nuclear power

The difficulties faced by Iran's moderates at home were matched by hostility abroad. Broadly speaking, this had two sources. The first stemmed from the country's nuclear power programme, the second from its association with fundamentalist terrorism.

Iran began to build its first nuclear reactor in 2002. Even before this, rumours were circulating about the country's plans to produce uranium suitable for use in a nuclear weapon. Alarmed, the International Atomic Energy Authority (IATA) sent an inspection team to Iran to see what was going on. Although not given all the access it wanted, the inspectors realized that Iran had not been open about its nuclear activities. This led to a meeting with three European foreign ministers in 2003 at which the Iranians agreed to stop producing enriched uranium. At the end of 2003 they signed a protocol to this effect.

Barely two months later Iran was again accused of dabbling in nuclear bomb technology, which it had bought from Pakistan. IATA and the US once more insisted that Iran cease such activities. Further negotiations were held with the trio of Europeans and a provisional halt to experimentation was agreed. A year later, the EU, still mistrustful of Iran's intentions, threatened trade and economic sanctions if it ignored IATA and resumed its weapons programme. At this point the government of Iran changed and the whole issue assumed a much greater importance.

About turn

President Bush's condemnation of Iran as part of his 'axis of evil' had caused outrage among Iranians of every class and persuasion. The moderates felt particularly depressed; in their struggle to liberalize the country they needed American support, not hostility. Massive anti-clerical protests in the summer of 2003 confirmed Khatami's popularity among the urban young and middle classes, although by now events in neighbouring

Iraq were beginning to prize open an alarming gap between them and their potential American allies.

The extent to which Iran interfered, officially or unofficially, in the affairs of Iraq after the Coalition's 2003 invasion was unclear. Certainly the establishment was eager to assist fellow Shia in their efforts to throw off years of Sunni domination. Although direct help was difficult to prove, the US was convinced that many insurgents entered Iraq from Iran with the connivance of – or at least behind the conveniently turned backs of – police and border officials. As already noted (on pages 202–3), the British were sure that insurgents in the south of Iraq could have obtained their sophisticated weaponry only from Iran.

The worsening relations between the West and Iran played into the hands of Shia conservatives. The presence of Western troops just across the border, killing Muslims in the name of liberal democracy, set back the moderate cause too. Moreover, Khatami's support in the countryside and among the poor had also been wearing thin because his much vaunted reform programme had failed to provide the promised jobs and wages. As a result, in February 2004, greatly assisted by the Council of Guardians' disqualification of thousands of candidates before the voting took place, reactionary candidates recaptured the Majlis. The next year, to the surprise of almost everyone, Tehran's ultra-conservative mayor, Mahmoud Ahmadinejad triumphed in a reduced turnout at the presidential elections.

From the moment he assumed office, the inexperienced Ahmadinejad started making enemies. By planning increased state control of industry, he alienated the business community and so weakened Iran's economy. Those to suffer most were the poor and needy who had brought him to office. Many clerics were suspicious of his mystical religious beliefs that talked of the second coming of the tenth century Imam Mahdi. The world community was horrified to hear him announce that his country had an 'inalienable right' to develop nuclear energy as it saw fit. Equally scary was his denial of the holocaust and insistence that Israel be 'wiped off the face of the map.' (www.news.bbc.co.uk)

During 2006, Ahmadinejad's ongoing wild rhetoric and radical actions brought serious confrontation with the international community still closer. In February, the UN's International Atomic Energy Agency (IATA) reported Iran's nuclear programme to the Security Council because it was unsure that the uranium enrichment was for peaceful purposes only. US scientists opined that the manufacture of uranium metal could have only one purpose – the preparation of a nuclear weapon. In April, the Iranians announced that their plant at Natanz had successfully enriched uranium – for peaceful purposes.

Faced with mounting international criticism, President Ahmadinejad showed no signs of backing down. The atomic energy issue was rallying nationalist support behind him, weakening his domestic opponents. Besides, he pointed out, there was no need for anyone to worry about Iran misusing its nuclear fuel programme because Supreme Leader Ayatollah Khamenei had issued a fatwa (religious condemnation) against nuclear weapons. That said, when the Russians offered to help Iran process its nuclear fuel, Ahmadinejad's response was no more than equivocal.

After much discussion, in July 2006 the UN Security Council gave Iran until the end of August to suspend its nuclear activities. The deadline came and went, leaving the Security Council in a difficult position. If it came down harshly on Iran, the country would probably unite in defiance behind its maverick president and so further strengthen his hand. Inaction, on the other hand, might put nuclear weapons into the hands of fanatics who were known to embrace death, including suicide, for what they saw as a righteous cause. Would extremists of this persuasion view nuclear holocaust in quite the same way as the rest of the world?

15

forward?

This chapter will cover:
- efforts to reach a settlement amid ongoing violence
- death of Yasser Arafat and incapacity of Ariel Sharon
- electoral success of Hamas and Kadima
- Israel-Hezbollah War of 2006

New century, old problems

By the start of the new millennium the population of Israel had risen to over 6 million, approximately double the number of Palestinians living within what were known as the Emerging Palestinian Autonomous Areas (2.4 million in the West Bank and 1.2 million in the Gaza Strip). Israel also retained possession of East Jerusalem and the Golan Heights. Jerusalem was Israel's official capital, although few states recognized it as such. Successful peace negotiations meant that Syria was the only Arab state technically still at war with Israel.

The peace process between Palestinians and Israelis that had started with the Oslo Accords and continued with the Wye River Memorandum (see pages 181–2) was stalled. Quite how little the Israelis had been prepared to give way is borne out by crude figures. Of the 5,900 sq km (22,500 sq miles) of the West Bank, only 342 sq km (130 sq miles) were under the direct rule of President Yasser Arafat and the Palestinian Authority. A further 2,189 sq km (845 sq miles) were under joint Israeli-Palestinian administration. The rest (well over half) remained in the hands of Israelis, of whom scarcely 200,000 lived there. Within the Gaza Strip, territory which the Israelis had no great desire to hang on to, the picture was different. Of the enclave's 363 sq km (140 sq miles), 236 sq km (100 sq miles) were administered by the Palestinian Authority. The Strip's Israeli population was a mere 7,000.

The Israeli prime minister, 72-year-old Ariel Sharon, had been elected in February 2001 on the slogan 'security and true peace.' With only 19 of his own right-wing Likud party in the Knesset (the Israeli parliament), he had been obliged to form a coalition government that included members of the Labour Party. For example, Sharon's old Labour rival, Shimon Peres, took the position of foreign minister in this 'Government of National Unity'.

The violence continues

Sharon's political record, besmirched with tales of provocation, corruption and deliberate slaughter, was hardly one to inspire hopes of a compromise, and few were surprised at the dismay with which the Palestinians greeted the hard-liner's election. Hamas, the uncompromising Palestinian group formed in 1990 to oppose the Oslo Accords (see pages 173–5), launched into the first of what it said would be ten suicide bombings by Islamic 'martyrs'. True to its word, an attack on Israeli civilians in the seaside town on Nelanya was followed by further bloody bombings across the country. Hamas received vocal and, many believed, financial and military backing from Shia Iran.

The Israelis responded to the Hamas onslaught with 'targeted killings' of those believed to be urging and planning the suicide missions. It also isolated Palestinian communities thought to have had links with the killers. As part of these operations, Yasser Arafat was confined to his West Bank HQ in Ramallah. Reprisals sparked more suicide attacks, and so the cycle of killing continued in the new millennium much as it had in the old. A well-meaning attempt by ex-US senator George Mitchell to find a peace plan came to nothing. On 1 June 2001, a particularly bloody suicide bombing, blowing up 20 young Israelis at a Tel Aviv disco, served only to cement prejudices. Sharon refused to enter into talks as long as the terrorist strikes continued; even then, he insisted, discussions would be only about an agenda for future, more meaningful talks. The Palestinians would not end their attacks until they knew where negotiations might lead.

In short, therefore, on the eve of the 11 September attacks on New York, the so-called 'Palestinian question' appeared as far from solution as ever. Despite the best efforts of well-intentioned intermediaries, the Second Intifada still raged and Prime Minister Ariel Sharon was adamant in his refusal to surrender territory acquired by Israel. Both sides continued to perpetrate acts of unspeakable violence against each other.

The effect of 9/11 on this situation was two-fold. Initially it simply reinforced US support for the Israelis, whom it now viewed unequivocally, if rather illogically, as fellow victims of Islamic terrorism. In the longer term, it led the US and other Western governments to realize that a comprehensive Middle East peace settlement – essential if global terrorism were to be undermined – had to rest on a solution to the long-standing Israeli-Palestinian conflict. From that realization sprouted small shoots of hope.

A route to peace?

Any possible Israeli-Palestinian peace settlement had inevitably to involve the ageing but still irascible and unpredictable Palestinian president, Yasser Arafat. Successive Israeli administrations had never trusted the man; the Americans, on the other hand, had been prepared to work with him as the only person with sufficient authority to bring the Palestinians to the negotiating table. However, by the time of the 11 September terrorist attacks, US faith in Arafat was wearing thin. They were coming to realize two things. First, that his support in the West Bank and Gaza depended primarily upon his ability to follow popular sentiment rather than create it. The way he had attached himself to the Intifadas, for instance, was a good example of this political pragmatism. Second, Arafat's strength was also his weakness: his refusal ever to take a step back, to even contemplate a modicum of surrender, made him an impossible peace negotiator. Old and set in his ways, he personified both Palestinian determination and Palestinian obduracy.

Arafat and Hamas

After 9/11, which he openly condemned unequivocally, Arafat declared a ceasefire against Israel. By the end of the year this had collapsed under the weight of the Intifada. Many suspected that Arafat had condoned or even supported the ongoing violence in order to prevent his authority being undermined by the increasingly well-backed Hamas, Hezbollah and Islamic Jihad. His closing of Hamas and Islamic Jihad offices was seen in this light, as a move against rivals rather than against terrorism in general. Just when the US had declared war on terror, he was treading a dangerous path. Ignoring the warnings, at the start of 2002 Arafat duly stepped on a rather obvious political landmine.

In January, the Israeli authorities seized a Palestinian-owned ship stuffed with arms from Iran. Despite Arafat's hot denials, it was soon ascertained beyond reasonable doubt that he had links with Tehran and had agreed the illegal shipment. The weapons seemed destined for the Al-Aqsa Martyrs Brigades, an extremist offshoot of his Fatah organization. Two months later, during which IDF tanks had penned Arafat within his Ramallah headquarters, documents seized there appeared to confirm his links with the Brigades. Sharon declared the Palestinian president to be 'an enemy of Israel' and 'irrelevant' to the peace process. President Bush was equally dismissive, saying the Arafat era had ended and urging the Palestinians to elect a new leader not 'compromised by terror.'

figure 8 the west bank 2005–6

The trouble was, Arafat was the Palestinians' chosen leader. Those who rejected him appeared to be also rejecting the entire Palestinian nation. To make compromise more difficult, the Intifada and Israel's measures to counteract it had caused massive economic hardship in Palestinian areas. Unemployment was estimated to be around 50 per cent of the workforce and GNP had more than halved since 1999. For this suffering the Palestinians blamed Israel, of course. At the same time, the hardship increased Palestinian affection for Hamas, whose political wing provided money and other assistance for essential medical, educational and social services. One man's terrorist was not only another man's freedom fighter, he was also his generous benefactor.

The Roadmap

There was near universal recognition that the 11 September attacks on the US were not just an American problem. Terror, specifically Islamic fundamentalist terror, was a global phenomenon that needed global solutions. To this end, in 2002 an international quadrilateral alliance of the UN, the US, the European Union and Russia (the Quartet) came together to find a peaceful resolution to the problems of Israel-Palestine. If this stubborn primary cancer were cured, the argument ran, the chances of secondary growths elsewhere would be considerably reduced.

Three factors were stalling the peace process begun by the Oslo Accords: Israel's refusal to negotiate while its people were under attack, Palestinian unwillingness to enter talks that did not have as their ultimate goal the creation of an independent Palestinian state, and sovereignty over the holy sites in Jerusalem. To guide both parties out of this impasse, the peace-seeking Quartet planned what it called the 'Roadmap to peace'. The idea behind this document, published in 2003, was to present concrete and time-specific steps towards an agreed goal: a two-state solution to the Israel-Palestine conflict. Hesitatingly, the Israeli and Palestinian leadership agreed that the Roadmap had possibilities.

After the Arafat arms scandal early in the year, the situation remained dire throughout 2002. Two examples among many are sufficient to illustrate what was going on. In March, a Hamas suicide bomber slew 30 elderly Jews as they were enjoying a Passover feast at the seaside. Israel retaliated with a massive land operation code-named Operation Defensive

Shield. In July, one of its F16 aircraft dropped a one-ton bomb on the apartment of Hamas's military leader, blowing him and 16 civilians to smithereens. Nine of the dead were children. That summer, as part of a second huge incursion into Palestinian areas – Operation Determined Path – the IDF reoccupied most of the West Bank. The US was eager to be seen to support counter-terror measures everywhere and did not object. Understandably, throughout all this slaughter the Roadmap remained in the diplomatic glove box.

Two steps forward ...

The following year, with the invasion of Iraq out of the way, the Bush administration turned its attention to the Roadmap once more. The Intifada was wrecking Israel's economy as much as the Palestinians', making it even more dependent upon US aid. When, at the end of April, US pressure persuaded the Palestinian parliament to choose the moderate Mahmoud Abbas (also known as Abu Mazen) as prime minister, Washington once again blew the dust off its negotiating clipboards. Here, at last, was someone with whom both the US and the Israelis believed they could do business. Shortly after Abbas's election, Sharon said he accepted the Roadmap, and his government then supported the decision. The Israeli prime minister even admitted that it was not right for Israel to be ruling over 1.3 million Palestinians. As spring turned to summer, things were definitely looking up.

In June, President Bush, Prime Minister Sharon and Prime Minister Abbas attended a peace conference in Aqaba, hosted by King Abdullah II of Jordan. Tentative agreements were made about implementing the Quartet's proposal to establish an independent Palestinian state within three years. Of course, a good deal of negotiating remained to be done, especially over Jerusalem, Palestinian terrorist groups and Israel's construction of a 'security fence' (see overleaf) along its eastern border. Nonetheless, at the end of the month, Fatah, Hamas and Islamic Jihad announced a cease-fire, and Israel pulled its troops out of Gaza. It was almost too good to be true.

... and two back

It was too good to be true. On 19 August an Arab suicide bomber blew up himself and 22 civilians on a Jerusalem bus. Over 130 passengers and passers-by were injured. The Israeli cabinet suspended peace talks and launched an all-out war against the terrorists who threatened their country's security. Hamas and other similar-minded groups responded with further suicide bombings. Deeply depressed and unable to work with the inconsistent and unsupportive Arafat, Prime Minister Abbas resigned. He was replaced by the extrovert banker Ahmed Qurei (Abu Ala).

The Israeli defence forces planned to castrate the militant Islamic opposition with surgical strikes at their leadership. With such men out of the way, they argued, the bodies of the top-led organizations would shrivel away. This was essential, Israeli politicians argued, to prevent extremists taking power after Israel handed back territory to Palestinian control. March 2004 saw one of the most controversial of these assassinations when helicopter gunships shot down the founder and spiritual leader of Hamas as he was leaving a Gaza mosque. Sheikh Yassin was not only a cleric, but also a wheel-chair-bound paraplegic. His killing was met with horrified disbelief throughout the world, and the UN Security Council drew up a resolution condemning the action. Unwilling to be seen as soft on terror, the US vetoed it. A Hamas spokesman warned Prime Minister Sharon that the murder had 'opened the Gates of Hell'.

Gaza and the security fence

Undaunted by such threats, the following month Israeli missiles targeted the car of Abdel Aziz al-Rantissi, the head of Hamas in Gaza. Al-Rantissi and two others were slain. While condoning acts that his opponents vilified as 'state terrorism', Sharon offered what appeared to be a startling concession: while retaining most settlements in the West Bank, Israel would leave the Gaza Strip completely. President Bush endorsed the plan and his fellow Roadmap cartographers came in behind him. At home, Sharon's plan split the country in two. His own party, Likud, for whom talk of surrendering Israeli-held territory was virtually blasphemy, rejected it. The prime minister's principal right-wing opponent, ex-prime minister Benjamin Netanyahu, dismissed the proposed Gaza pull-out as 'a prize for terror.'

When the dust settled, Sharon was left at the head of a minority government whose compromise peace appeared to have the backing of the majority of Israelis. This was the result not just of the peace proposal but of the success of an equally controversial policy: the construction of a massive concrete and barbed wire barrier between Israeli- and Palestinian-occupied land in the West Bank. Wishing to avoid parallels with the Iron Curtain that had divided Europe during the Cold War, the Israeli government referred to the partition as a 'security fence'. It insisted that the barricade was designed solely to keep out terrorists.

The fence's construction was all the more controversial because its 700 km (435 mile) route did not follow the old pre-1967 war border (known as the 'Green Line') but snaked into the West Bank to embrace recent Jewish settlements there. In several places it became an impassable barrier between Palestinian communities that had lived alongside each other for centuries. The International Court of Justice, giving its verdict in July 2004, condemned the fence unreservedly and ordered that it be dismantled. Israel ignored the ruling but did re-route sections of the fence closer to the Green Line. Controversial or not, the barrier cut dramatically the number of suicide attacks inside Israel. Not to be outdone, the Palestinians responded by firing homemade Qassam rockets over it.

The end of Arafat

Amid all the bombs, blood and bitter words, many within the Middle East and beyond despaired of a solution to the region's longest standing conflict ever being found. The latest proposal, the Quartet's two-state solution, was unacceptable to hard-liners on both sides. As Likud's rejection of Sharon's proposed withdrawal from Gaza demonstrated, right-wing Jewish groups promised never voluntarily to surrender part of their 'Promised Land' to the Palestinians. Sharon himself – now their arch apostate – had received a number of credible death threats from Jewish extremists. Simultaneously, though, and with US backing, he was giving the go-ahead to an enormous expansion of Jewish settlements in the West Bank. Most controversial was a huge housing programme, with all its attendant infrastructure, in East Jerusalem.

On the other side, the Palestinians were hardly more united. Rifts were widening between Arafat's mainstream Fatah, the Al-Aqsa Martyrs Brigade, Hezbollah and Hamas. Islamic fundamentalists remained wedded to the principle never to give up their holy war until the infidel state of Israel had been obliterated. Like so many previous peace plans, therefore, by the autumn of 2004 the much-vaunted Roadmap was looking more like a piece of wishful thinking than a realistic route to peace.

Armistice day, 2004

By the fall of 2004 the 75-year-old Yasser Arafat was not a well man. For two-and-a-half years the Israeli military had kept him cooped up in his Ramallah headquarters, unable to do much more than peer out of the window at the land he had dreamed of governing. In October he complained of stomach pains. Local doctors were mystified and diagnosed gallstones. The discomfort continued. On 29 October he was flown to Paris in a coma for emergency medical treatment.

The French doctors fared no better than their Arab counterparts. On 9 November Arafat had a stroke and two days later, amid wild rumour and counter-rumour, the darling of the Palestinian movement died of multiple organ failure. The date was poignantly significant: 11 November is widely observed worldwide as Armistice Day, the day the fighting stopped at the end of the Great War.

For security reasons the funeral was held in Cairo, where heads of state and other dignitaries assembled from around the world. King Abdullah of Jordan was there, as was Syria's President Assad. The United Kingdom sent its foreign secretary, while the United States was represented by envoy William Burns. No one attended from the state of Israel. After the funeral the body was flown back to Ramallah for burial. The original request, internment in the al-Aqsa mosque, Jerusalem, had been vetoed by Ariel Sharon.

Arafat's senior colleagues planned a dignified burial to impress the world's watching media. Instead, the ceremony was hijacked by mobs of young enthusiasts who broke into their ex-leader's compound and fomented scenes of hysterical chaos. Wailing crowds surged back and forth, guns cracked into the autumn air. The faces of bewildered onlookers twisted between sorrow and horror. Somehow, amid the pandemonium the coffin of the old warrior was lowered into its marble tomb, the grave was filled with holy soil and the crowds eventually melted away. In a macabre sort of manner, it had been an appropriate farewell: governance had never been Arafat's strong suit.

Flawed hero

For better or for worse, Yasser Arafat had been the enduring dominant figure in Middle Eastern politics for decades. The majority of Palestinians had adored him and a 40-day period of mourning was declared after his death. They admired his physical bravery, his doggedness, his determination and perseverance. More than any other single figure, he had created the Palestinian nation and given it credence. His was the face of Palestine and, whatever one thought of it, it could not be ignored. For the leader of so small a group of scattered peoples, it was no small achievement.

That said, Arafat's aggressive attitude may have brought his people as much hardship as respect. He was blamed for refusing to accept reasonable compromise, especially when offered to him by President Clinton in 2000. Not without justification, he had gained a reputation as a man who could not or would not keep his word. Most serious of all, he had allowed personal ambition to get in the way of the best interests of those he represented. He was also a poor administrator, a weakness made more damaging by his refusal to recognize it.

The Israelis greeted the passing of Arafat with relieved delight – no one, in their eyes, had been more responsible than he for years of criminal slaughter. The United States, too, viewed his death with relief. For several years they had stopped seeing him as someone capable of bringing peace to the region, but they still feared his ability to raise great passions among his people. Now he was gone, the way ahead looked a little more predictable. In the rest of the world his death evoked mixed emotions. Few questioned his dogged single-mindedness but many questioned the tactics with which he had pursued his ends. He may have been responsible for introducing the Palestinians to the world, but he had been heavily responsible for introducing modern political terrorism, too.

Mahmoud Abbas

As many predicted, ex-prime minister Mahmoud Abbas was elected to replace Arafat as President of the Palestinian Authority. The West were pleased with the choice, the Palestinians less so. The rifts within their ranks, open during the old leader's lifetime, now widened still further. Not long after Arafat's funeral, for instance, several Fatah supporters in Gaza were shot dead during vicious in-fighting. The Strip's local elections in 2005 saw Hamas make notable advances at Fatah's expense. In more widespread mid-year elections Fatah recovered somewhat, gaining 55 per cent of the vote. Nevertheless, with the support of 35 per cent of the electorate, Hamas had cemented its position as a very real opposition and even a possible alternative ruling party. Not that it really wanted to take over the Palestinian Authority. It saw that organization as merely an insulting, American-concocted compromise designed to divert the Palestinians from their true goal – the destruction of Israel and the establishment of a Palestinian state in all lands west of the Jordan River.

In such circumstances, Abbas' task was not an enviable one. He wished to negotiate a compromise with Israel that would establish a universally recognized and viable Palestinian state. Any settlement he reached he then had to sell to all his people, fundamentalists as well as moderates. At the same time, he had to try to reform the chaotic Fatah party whose administration of the Palestinian areas was at best inept and at worst criminally corrupt. And he had to do this without alienating his core supporters among the old guard Fatah, many of whom benefited from the malgovernance he wanted to root out.

The first major test of Abbas' popularity came in the 2006 elections to the Palestinian Legislative Council, postponed since mid-2005. The weeks preceding the vote were marked by escalating violence and lawlessness as the many factions and parties pursued their own agendas. As they had been doing intermittently for some time, Hezbollah sent rockets from southern Lebanon into northern Israel. The Israelis responded with sporadic artillery fire.

The Al-Aqsa Martyrs, the militant wing of Fatah, and Islamic Jihad launched their rocket attacks on Israel from within Gaza. This broke the ceasefire that had been in place since the beginning of the year. Their aim was to prove to the Israeli administration that the Strip was incapable of managing its own security. This would provoke an Israeli response, they hoped, that would bring about the cancellation of the elections, the collapse of the Palestinian Authority and the end of compromise with Israel. A Hamas spokesman in Syria announced that his members were also ending their ceasefire. Their purpose, it seemed, was the same as that of the other Palestinian militants. To make matters even more complicated, the Israeli government said that Fatah – as a 'terrorist' group – could not legally field election candidates.

Mainstream Fatah, the principal Palestinian party and the only one dedicated to the peace process, continued to have problems of its own. One of these was the personality of its new president, Mahmoud Abbas. He was widely thought to have been the principal architect of the Oslo Accords, a pragmatist who had achieved much out of the glare of the media spotlight. However, his quiet manner came over as rather uninspiring after the fiery, inspiring rantings of Arafat. In the political culture of the Middle East, where rhetoric, hyperbole and flamboyance could carry great weight, an uncharismatic academic was not an obvious candidate to lead his people out of decades of humiliation and poverty.

One of Abbas's most potent Fatah opponents was Marwan Barghouti, the reputed founder of the Al-Aqsa Brigades. A dynamic leader of popular protest in the Arafat mould, simultaneously he had rejected the Oslo peace process while openly criticizing the corruption and human rights abuses of Fatah. He also made public statements condemning the killing of innocent Israeli citizens. In 2002, though, he was arrested by the Israelis, tried and sentenced to five life sentences for murder. This immediately gave him martyr status among ordinary Palestinians. With only weeks to go before the 2006 elections, his followers split from the mainstream Fatah and formed Al-Mustaqbal – 'The Future'. Desperate negotiations healed the rift and enabled the party to present a united front to the electorate. It was, though, little more than papering over the cracks.

Sharon, Hamas and Hezbollah

When 73-year-old Ariel Sharon was elected prime minister of Israel in 2001, he came to the post with a reputation for unflinching devotion to his country's security, at almost any price. To many the single adjective that best summed up the man was 'ruthless'. Nicknamed 'the bulldozer', he had fought with the Haganah, first against the British then against the Arabs. In the 1950s he had taken part in retaliatory military operations that had led to the deaths of many unprotected Arabs. After the 1967 war, in which he served with much skill as a brigadier general, he enhanced his hard-line reputation with harsh rule over territories occupied by the Israeli army. These actions were capped in 1982 when, as defence minister, he unilaterally ordered the IDF to advance as far as Beirut in order to flush out the PLO from Lebanon. This led directly to the mass slaughter of refugees in camps supposedly under Israeli protection (see page 106).

Removed from office after an inquiry found him indirectly responsible for the killings in Lebanon, Sharon soon bounced back. In the 1990s he masterminded a widespread expansion of Jewish settlements in Gaza and the West Bank, while his visit to Jerusalem's al-Aqsa mosque in 2000 sparked the second Intifada. It is hardly surprising, therefore, that 'the bulldozer' was far and away the Arabs' most hated Israeli – to many Palestinians his election was virtually a declaration of war. Then, to the surprise of almost everybody, in the early years of the new century Sharon's hard-line attitude began to soften.

Several reasons were put forward for the change. The simplest was that as he neared the end of his life the grossly overweight Sharon was eager to leave an enduring and positive legacy. Rather than be remembered simply as a hard man, he dreamed – as many others had done – of going down in history as the statesman who had finally ended decades of Israeli-Palestinian conflict.

Sharon was also aware of the mounting toll of the Intifada. By September 2005 it had cost more than 4,000 lives, of which almost 700 were Israeli civilians. The Israeli economy had made poor progress: unemployment was over ten per cent and one-third of the population lived in poverty. Although they can hardly have played much upon Sharon's mind, the statistics from the Palestinian areas were far more depressing: the Intifada, for example, had cost over 3,000 Palestinian lives. Since repression had failed to quell the damaging uprising, Sharon had little choice but to try another tactic.

A third factor in Sharon's change of heart was pressure from Washington. The Israeli economy had always been propped up by US aid. It was estimated that by 2005 this had amounted to a staggering $1.6 trillion since 1973. Israel was the recipient of America's biggest aid hand-out – around $3 billion a year in the twenty-first century when loan guarantees and 'military assistance' were included. This gave the Bush administration – eager to settle the 'Palestinian Question' as part of its war on terror – huge influence in Israeli politics. It was surely no coincidence that at the end of 2005, as Sharon was pressing ahead with the peace plan, the US Congress announced a massive $600 million aid package for Israel to fund 'joint defence projects'.

Imposed settlement

While Arafat was still alive, Sharon and his American backers seem to have come to the conclusion that a negotiated settlement between Israel and the Palestinians was impossible. This position did not seem to change after Arafat's death, either. Although talks between the two sides took place, the Israeli prime minister did not believe Abbas had enough Palestinian support to make him worth bargaining with. Instead, Sharon opted for an imposed settlement.

The basis of the plan was simple. Secure within defensible frontiers, Israel would hand back to the Palestinians what it did not need. Clearly, Sharon did not want the Palestinians who had left in 1967. The countless thousands of Palestinians still stuck in refugee camps, therefore, were to remain where they were – an 'Arab problem' in the eyes of the Israeli's hard-nosed premier. Nevertheless, the imposed settlement was not all one-way. In the spring of 2005, the 8,500 Israeli settlers in the 21 fortified settlements in the Gaza Strip – some of which Sharon had helped establish – left or were forcibly evicted by the Israeli army. The move was vociferously opposed by the Israeli far right but backed by two-thirds of the population overall. Israel retained control over Gaza's borders, coastline and airspace. It also threatened to re-enter Gaza if security forces there proved incapable of preventing attacks on Israel.

An equally controversial part of the Sharon plan involved consolidating existing Israeli settlements on the West Bank (apart from four outlying ones that had been abandoned at the same time as the Gaza handover) and expanding into the land between them. The security fence (see page 231) was routed to enclose most Israeli-occupied land within the West Bank. This aspect of the proposed settlement, conducted with a minimum of publicity, actually meant more Israelis entering the occupied territories (14,000) than had been pulled out from Gaza. The policy produced the greatest tension around East Jerusalem, where new settlements like that at Maale Adumim threatened to cut off the Palestinian quarters from the rest of the West Bank.

Roadmap shelved

By the end of 2005 a number of commentators believed that the frenetic Israeli settlement to the east of the Green Line was a precursor to Sharon handing back what remained of the West Bank to the Palestinians as the basis of their new state. By then, the argument ran, the newly expanded Israel would be safe behind its security fence and there would be little that the Palestinians would be able to do about it. They would have lost most of Jerusalem and, in all likelihood, easy access to that part of it they retained, as well as the West Bank's best farm land and access to its most plentiful water supplies.

All this ran counter to the Roadmap, which had planned for a return of the Palestinian refugees, a two-state compromise based on the pre-1967 borders, and shared ownership of Jerusalem. By going along with Sharon's proposed eastward expansion, President Bush was in effect tearing up the Quartet's peace plan without, as far as is known, consulting with the other three members. Britain's Tony Blair greeted the *fait accompli* with limp praise. Hamas continued to express fierce opposition to all that Sharon was doing, describing the newly independent Gaza as nothing but a 'huge prison', while Mahmoud Abbas seemed impotent to influence events one way or the other.

In late 2005 Sharon made his last and most surprising move. He left Likud, the party he had helped found, and established the Kadima (Forward) Party. He was soon joined by the veteran Labour leader and former prime minister Shimon Peres, and other front-rank Israeli politicians. Shortly afterwards he suffered the first of two strokes that left him totally incapacitated.

Hamas

If the sudden disappearance of Ariel Sharon from the political scene sent shockwaves round the Middle East, they were mere ripples compared with the tsunami-like breakers that crashed over the region at the next development. The January elections to the Palestinian parliament gave a clear majority (74 seats out of 132) to the Sunni party Hamas. Two months later, a Hamas cabinet was in place with Ismail Haniya as Palestinian Prime Minister. Israel responded to the Hamas revolution by imposing financial sanctions on the Palestinian Authority.

The Palestinians had elected Hamas representatives because they perceived their party to be honest and efficient compared with Fatah. Nevertheless, in the eyes of several states, including the US, Israel, the EU and Arab states such as Jordan, Hamas was still a terrorist organisation. It remained dedicated to the elimination of Israel. Using suicide bombings, its militant section, the Izzedine al-Qassam Brigades, had recently been responsible for the deaths of more Israelis than any other group. These attacks continued after the election, prompting strong Israeli responses. Facilities of the Palestinian Authority were bombed and many Hamas officials, including one third of the cabinet members, were arrested. Their people also suffered badly from the cancellation of crucial overseas aid and Israeli tax rebates.

Meanwhile, there had been changes in Israel too. The 2006 Knesset elections had left Kadima leader Ehud Olmert, Sharon's replacement, as prime minister in the customary coalition administration. He pledged himself to continue the policies of his comatose mentor, aiming to abandon some West Bank settlements so that Israel had permanent, internationally-accepted borders by 2010. Hamas attacks had dented such optimistic targets almost before they had been set up. Shortly afterwards, Olmert found himself in even greater trouble.

The Lebanon War

In July 2006, the IDF moved into Gaza in an attempt to free a soldier captured earlier by Hamas fighters. Perhaps spurred by Israeli aggression, Hezbollah militants struck from southern Lebanon. They bombarded northern Israel with rockets and raided across the border to kill several Israeli soldiers. A retaliatory patrol from Israel led to further IDF losses and the capture of two of its soldiers. Olmert's cabinet met promptly and blamed the Lebanese administration for what had happened. The same day, it instigated an air and sea blockade of Lebanon and launched a massive (and almost certainly pre-arranged) attack on the country (see page 214).

The war, which lasted until mid-August, did not follow the pattern that IDF commanders had predicted. Despite almost continual pounding from Israeli artillery and aircraft, the scattered Hezbollah fighters continued to rain rockets down on targets inside Israel. When IDF ground forces entered southern Lebanon, advancing as far as the Litani River with heavy armour, they suffered numerous casualties at the hands of the enemy. In the end some 50 Israeli soldiers were killed and 1,250 injured. Even though the figures for Hezbollah casualties were perhaps ten times as great, it was not defeated. When the fighting stopped its jubilant supporters in Syria and Iran claimed victory. For the first time since 1947, they announced, the Israeli war machine had not had its bloody way.

To make matters still more difficult for the Israelis, international opinion condemned their 'over-reaction' to the Hezbollah threat. The destruction of so much of Lebanon's infrastructure was seen as bullying, particularly as the country's cabinet claimed, probably quite rightly, that it had no control over the elements of Hezbollah that had started the conflict. For the first time, Israel was suffering from the reverse of the David and Goliath syndrome that in previous wars had worked in its favour. In short, the costly conflict had failed to win an outright victory, alienated much world opinion and boosted the morale of Israel's enemies. Certainly, absolutely nothing had been done to bring peace in the region any nearer.

glossary

Al-Aqsa Martyrs Brigades Extremist offshoot of Fatah.

Arab One who speaks Arabic.

Arab League Organization of Arab states formed to promote cultural, economic and political co-operation.

Arab Legion British-trained (Trans)Jordanian army.

Ashkenazi Jews from Eastern Europe.

ayatollah Shia religious leader.

Caliphate Empire comprising the entire Muslim world.

DFLP Democratic Front for the Liberation of Palestine.

Druze Religious offshoot of Islam with separate leaders and emphases.

Fatah Yasser Arafat's Palestinian guerrilla organization that developed into the largest Palestinian political party.

Fedayeen Palestinian guerrillas.

Gaza Small strip of territory beside the Mediterranean Sea with Gaza City at its heart.

Greater Israel Israel extending across both banks of the River Jordan.

Green Line Ceasefire line in the 1967 Arab-Israeli war.

Gulf, the Persian or Arabian Gulf.

Haganah Jewish guerrilla organization of the pre-Israel era.

Hamas Palestinian organization fiercely opposed to Israel.

Hezbollah Iranian-backed organization fiercely opposed to Israel.

IDF Israeli Defence Force.

Intifada Palestinian uprising against Israel.

Irgun Jewish guerrilla (terrorist) organization of the pre-Israel era.

Islamic Jihad Anti-Israeli guerrilla (terrorist) organization.

Jihad Muslim holy war.

Knesset Israeli parliament.

Likud Israeli right-wing political party.

LNM Lebanese National Movement, largely Shia organization to help Lebanon's Muslim majority.

Maronite Lebanese Christian group.

NATO North Atlantic Treaty Organization.

Occupied territories Lands on the West Bank of the River Jordan, and around Jerusalem and Gaza City, conquered by Israel in 1967.

OPEC Organization of Petroleum Exporting Countries.

Ottoman Empire Former Turkish Empire.

Persia Iran.

PFLP Popular Front for the Liberation of Palestine.

Phalange Right-wing Lebanese Christian paramilitaries.

PLA Palestine Liberation Army.

PLO Palestine Liberation Organization.

PNA Palestine National Authority.

PNC Palestine National Council.

Roadmap Early twenty-first-century peace plan for Israel-Palestine.

Sephardi Oriental Jews.

shah Hereditary ruler of Iran/Persia.

sheikh Arab chief.

Shia Minority branch of Islam centred around Iran.

Sinai Largely desert peninsular between Israel and Egypt.

Sunni Majority branch of Islam.

Transjordan Original name for the state of Jordan.

UAE United Arab Emirates.

UAR United Arab Republic.

UEFA Union European Football Association.

West Bank Land on the west bank of the River Jordan captured by Israel in 1967.

WMDs Weapons of mass destruction.

Zionism Movement for the establishment and maintenance of a Jewish state.

taking it further

Objective history of the Middle East in recent years is rare, if not impossible: researchers are advised to consult as many sources as possible. Here are a few starting points:

Books

Aburish, S. K., (1999), *Arafat: From Defender to Dictator*, Bloomsbury, London

al-Rasheed, M., (2002), *A History of Saudi Arabia*, Cambridge University Press, Cambridge, UK

Cockburn, A. and P., (2002), *Saddam: an American Obsession*, Verso, London

Etherington, M. (2005), *Revolt on the Tigris*, Cornell UP

Fisk, R., (1990), *Pity the Nation: Lebanon at War*, Andre Deutsch, London

Franklin, D., (2003), *A Peace to End All Peace*, Orion, London

Keay, J., (2003), *Sowing the Wind: Seeds of Conflict in the Middle East*, John Murray, London

Keddie, N. R., (2003), *Modern Iran: Roots and Results of Revolution*, Yale University Press, New Haven, Connecticut

Laqueur, W. and Rubin, B. (eds), (2001), *The Israel-Arab Reader*, Penguin, London

Neff, D., (1988), *Warriors Against Israel*, Amana Books, Battleboro

Ross, D., (2004), *The Missing Peace*, Farrar, Straus & Giroux, New York

Shlaim, A., (2001), *The Iron Wall: Israel and the Arab World*, Penguin, London

Schulze, K. E., (1999), *The Arab–Israeli Conflict*, Longman, Harlow

Thomas, B., (1999), *How Israel Was Won*, Lexington Books, Oxford

Websites

Israeli government website:
http://www.israel.org/mfa

History in the news:
http://www.albany.edu/history/middle-east

Modern history sourcebook:
http://www.fordham.edu/halsall/mod/modsbook54.html

Arab Gateway:
http://www.addameer.org/september2000/front.html

BBC:
http://news.bbc.co.uk/1/hi/world/middle_east/default.stm

CNN:
http://search.cnn.com/cnn/search?source=cnn&invocationType
=search%2Ftop&sites=cnn&query=middle+east

Pars Times (Iran):
http://www.parstimes.com/Iran_history.html

Arab world:
http://www.arab.net

Al Jazeera:
www.aljazeera.com